PRAISE FOR
TERRORIZED

"Father Fred Thelen has written a fascinating description of the multifaceted journey of his life and priesthood... Relationships—in the family, across cultures, with brother priests and fellow missioners, with the legacy of a cousin-bishop, with Pachamama and the spirit-world as well as the farmland of home—all provide more than a background; they are the texture, the connecting fibers of the story, and what allows for the openness to mystery as Father Fred tries to piece it all together."

— Bishop John Stowe, Diocese of Lexington, Kentucky

"Coming face to face with terrorism, poverty, and corrupt systems, while also forming indelible relationships, the author shares the scars left by his missionary journey... At once deeply personal, there is as well a universal invitation to the readers to ponder the deepest questions of meaning, identity, and mission for themselves."

— Sister Barbara E. Reid, president, Catholic Theological Union

"When I first stepped into this beautifully written inspirational story, I was full of fear for the people of Peru and for our beloved Father Fred. By the grace of God, I prayed, I cried, and was rewarded with a powerful lesson in courage, faith, and love."

— Ana Garcia-Ashley, executive director of the Gamaliel Network

"Fred Thelen recalls the fear and suffering that stalked the lives of Peruvians during the Sendero years and the consequences in his own life of terror-related long-term trauma. He captures well the strength and beauty of the Aymara communities who welcomed Maryknoll missioners to the Peruvian altiplano and the deep respect of the missioners for Peruvian culture."

— Marie Dennis, senior director of Pax Christi International's Catholic Nonviolence Initiative

"Fred Thelen honestly, often humorously and with deep insight, recounts his journey into the Aymara cultural world and the violence that led to his post-traumatic stress and journey home to healing. Anyone who seeks insight into working within another culture and the journey of healing from trauma will find a gem in this well-written and personally revealing book."

— Sister Patricia Ryan, president of the Civil Association Derechos Humanos y Medio Ambiente in Puno, Peru

"Trauma, though not universal, is experienced by many, and those who seek to recover from trauma will find in Father Fred Thelen's well-written account of trauma, terror, and healing an accessible guide to what one can do to find a way forward . . . Moreover, because Thelen's story illustrates how foreign surroundings push one to grow in unexpected ways, it is good reading for anyone who has migrated from one country to another or is contemplating work in an intercultural setting."

— Robert A. Hurteau, director of the Center for Religion and Spirituality, Loyola Marymount University

TERRORIZED

TERRORIZED

A Memoir of Trauma, Healing, and Coming Home

FRED THELEN

Cover image by Fred Thelen
The cover photo is a Peruvian mask worn by the devil figure in the diablada dance of the struggle between good and evil.

Readers are encouraged to go to www.MissionPointPress.com to contact the author or to find information on how to buy this book in bulk at a discounted rate.

MISSION POINT PRESS

Published by Mission Point Press
2554 Chandler Rd.
Traverse City, MI 49696
(231) 421-9513
www.MissionPointPress.com

ISBN: 978-1-965278-00-0
Library of Congress Control Number: 2024916440

Printed in the United States of America

DEDICATION

To all who suffer from trauma and those who help heal the wounds through relationships of care, love, and support.

CONTENTS

Introduction vii

Chapter 1 Punched in the Face 1

Chapter 2 The Labyrinth. 8

Chapter 3 A Hot August Night 18

Chapter 4 A Pilgrim's Journey 23

Chapter 5 Walking on Holy Ground 33

Chapter 6 Evil. 43

Chapter 7 Loss, Loneliness, and Connection 54

Chapter 8 The Fist of Fear 60

Chapter 9 Fiesta. 70

Chapter 10 Deflated 76

Chapter 11 Moving On 82

Chapter 12 Fear Seeps Into the Pores of My Skin 87

Chapter 13 Death Strikes Like a Terrorist. 95

Chapter 14   Part of the Family 99

Chapter 15   A Mountaintop Experience 104

Chapter 16   Home for the Holidays. 111

Chapter 17   Burn Barrel 114

Chapter 18   Taking Leave 120

Chapter 19   Will I Make It Out Alive? 125

Chapter 20   Margarita Nightmare 129

Chapter 21   Admitting I Have PTS 135

Chapter 22   Home but Not at Home 144

Chapter 23   Unfinished Business 151

Chapter 24   Shattered and Scattered 163

Chapter 25   Depression 170

Chapter 26   Healing 176

Chapter 27   Love Your Enemy. 187

Chapter 28   Not a Helpless Victim 191

Chapter 29   Reshaping Shards of the Shattered Pot. 198

                Acknowledgments 213

INTRODUCTION

1

This is a memoir of working in the midst of an ancient culture in a time of civil war. More deeply, it is the story of trauma and finding my way home to a place of healing.

I arrived in Peru in June of 1989 after five months of intensive Spanish classes. So I knew a lot of Spanish and had some introductory knowledge of the Aymara culture of the people where I would be working. What I did not know was that a terrorist movement called the Shining Path was ramping up its operations and would hit its peak of power during my time in Peru. I barely knew the name of Abimael Guzmán, the cult-like head of the insurgency. I did not know that he had started as a philosophy professor in the poverty-stricken mountain province of Ayacucho where he held student discussions about injustice in Peruvian society and promoted a peasant rebellion. I did not know the history of how that discussion group became the Shining Path, the Communist Party of Peru, and grew into a guerrilla army that launched its operations in 1980, or how they expanded through rural areas and then into Lima, the capital city, by the time I arrived. Their strategy was to destroy the existing government and social structures and then build the new utopian society out of the ashes of the old. The Catholic Church, for which I was working, was to be the "dessert" in their banquet of destruction.

I couldn't have known at the time that the government response, largely in the hands of the military, would eventually account for nearly half of the thousands of deaths during the years of brutal violence. Or that by mid-1992 the terrorists would declare they had reached a "strategic equilibrium" of power in the country. That was the point at which I and my colleagues began to fear they could actually pull off a takeover of the country.

While there had been some news of a growing number of terrorist incidents while I was still in language school in neighboring Bolivia, the threat seemed remote enough that I could downplay it as I focused on my Spanish classes. But the day I arrived in June of 1989 in the southern highlands of Peru known as the Altiplano, I was thrown into the thick of it. That is where this story begins.

Some names have been changed for privacy concerns.

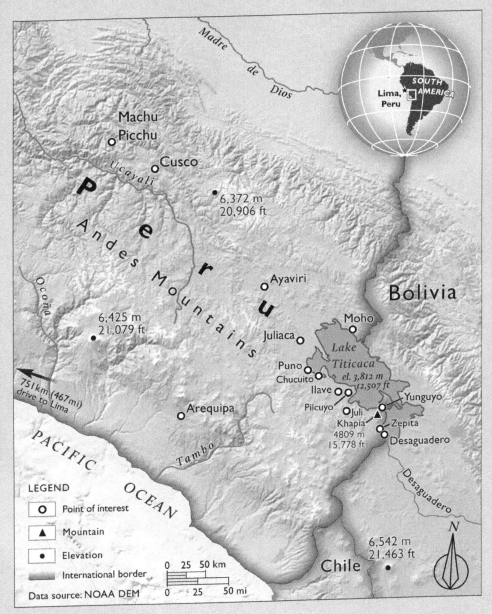

Map of southern Peru and the Lake Titicaca area where I served

Cartography by Tom M. Ruehli

PUNCHED IN THE FACE

Southern Peru
June 15, 1989

The road stretching north from Lake Titicaca across the Peruvian highlands is a sea of dust and potholes. The aging chartered bus slows to navigate each crater, then lurches forward with a roar of its diesel engine as the
passengers bounce and shift. The bus driver's face is taut, his eyes searching every hill and mountainside we pass, penetrating the folds of ponchos
draped over the herders of sheep and llamas, and peering into faces in
passing vehicles. His strong, brown hands grip the steering wheel as if it
were a life preserver. I have a direct view of the driver, front row, orchestra
right, as we head to the protest massing against the recent terrorist attack
on the Church's Rural Education Institute. I turn and peer out the window
from time to time wondering what, or who, might be around the next
bend. As I gaze through the glass, my cousin Alberto, who served in Peru
before his untimely death three years ago, slides into my thoughts clear as
a photograph, his white, short-trimmed hair, rugged face sturdy as a
woodblock sculpture, his eyes penetrating my veneer of courage through
black-frame glasses. I return his gaze silently saying to him, *Alberto, you
would have been on this bus, fearless and ready to lead the march. When I
was boarding the bus in the dark this morning like everyone else, your
brother priest Steve Judd spotted me and announced me like I was royalty,
"This is Padre Federico, Monsignor Alberto's cousin!" I wanted to disappear in the back of the bus, but he directed me to this front seat, making me
the guest of honor on this bus ride to terrorism. This should be your seat.*

The woman sitting next to me is clutching a well-worn blue nylon bag of provisions for the long day ahead. Our shoulders bump as they have off and on for the past two hours. Two tightly braided tresses of jet-black hair sway behind her. A traditional bowler hat, slightly tilted to one side, sits like a crown on her head. Multiple layers of colorful skirts speak of status in her Aymara culture of southern Peru. We fumble a few words in Spanish, until I realize her first language must be Aymara, not Spanish. Great, I spent five grueling months studying Spanish so I can be deaf and mute in her Aymara world where I'm supposed to work for the next four years.

By this time, the treeless, rolling pasturelands are awash in the morning light. Small herds of sheep, llamas, and alpacas dot the passing landscape. We are part of a caravan of buses traveling together for safety. Clouds of dust from the bus in front of us billow past the windows. The government has been promising for twenty years to pave this main route across the mountains. It can't come soon enough.

I have been sitting too long with my legs cramped against the metal partition between the front seat and the entrance steps, so I step into the aisle to stretch. I scan the crowd and see Pat Ryan, a Maryknoll Sister, in the third seat from the back. She might be able to tell me a little more about what lies ahead. I make my way to the rear steadying myself against the seats as the bus continues to heave like a ship in a storm at sea. In her jeans and alpaca wool sweater she appears casual, even calm. She looks up from her copy of *Sí*, a magazine of current events, and gives me a warm, slightly wry smile. "Well, hello Fred, how are you? I'm surprised to see you here."

"I'm doing ok, but I'm as surprised as you that I'm here. The bishop invited me at the last minute when I arrived in Juli yesterday to say hello after finishing language school. So here I am on Peru's finest transport." We share a smile at that. Then my grin fades, "Should we be worried about the terrorists?"

She settles the magazine on her lap and her eyebrows narrow. "Well, the bombing was quite a shock. The original plan was to celebrate their twenty-fifth anniversary, but now we are going in solidarity with them against the violence, and we expect a couple thousand people for the march. We don't anticipate any attacks, but there are no guarantees."

After getting the short version of what she knows about terrorist activity in the country, I return to my seat thinking, *this isn't exactly what I signed up for.* Mulling over what Pat shared with me takes me back to the student lounge at language school in Cochabamba, Bolivia. It was barely two weeks ago. I was reading an article in *Los Tiempos* reporting evidence of terrorist activity spilling over into Bolivia from the Peruvian side of Lake Titicaca where I would be working. *Sendero Luminoso*, the Shining Path, were the presumed terrorists. I didn't know it at the time, but Sr. Pat Ryan and her team at the *Vicaría*, the human rights office, were responsible for seeding the story into news outlets to alert people to the growing threat.

There had been talk of Sendero during the three months of orientation in New York last fall. Maryknoll leadership was concerned enough that they decided they would no longer send missionary families with children to Peru. While the prospect of working in a country with escalating violence felt worrisome, at that time there were few details and the reality was still a continent away. But when I read that article in *Los Tiempos*, it started to feel like a puma eyeing its prey from a distance. Even though the question, *"Should I go through with this?"* prowled around in my mind, reversing course was not in my character. One kept one's commitments. So the fear mostly got relegated to my emotional deep freezer.

Packing away fears and strong emotions consciously or unconsciously is a survival instinct that came out of my childhood experience. We had a huge white chest freezer in the basement of our farmhouse. Mom would freeze all kinds of summer produce there and periodically a whole side of beef would go in, divided into small packages that came back from the processor where we sent the cow. Some things would remain at the very bottom of the freezer for years until a new inventory would be taken and they would be pulled out to unthaw. My emotional life was like that freezer. As a child I learned, absorbed really, the lesson that in order to keep safe, emotions like fear, anger, and even love needed to be packed away as long as possible in the deep freezer of one's life.

I think of my father who most of the time was steady and controlled, a stalwart provider for the family and a man with the conviction of his Catholic faith. But every so often the volcano would erupt and spew forth molten anger the color of his red hair. He was wiry and a little shorter than most of his peers, but at such times he seemed to double in size. Like the time when I was six years old watching TV with my parents and three older brothers. I was sitting on the carpeted floor leaning against the white vinyl ottoman where Dad was sitting paging through the *Reader's Digest*. It was a happy scene until I said or did something that set him off. What, I don't remember. What was branded in my memory is how he began beating me with the *Reader's Digest* magazine. Maybe that's why I don't much like the *Reader's Digest*. I started wailing and curled up on the floor with my arms around my head to protect myself. Rage at the unfairness of it began smoldering. At other times it was the black leather belt stinging the flesh of mine or my brothers' behinds. Things get passed on. I've been told he had similar experiences with his father. A pool of molten anger is part of my family inheritance. The unspoken message I absorbed in childhood and adolescence was *emotions are dangerous* and it is safest to keep them locked away.

During my Peruvian sojourn, many fears were to get packed away along with traumas from my childhood. Eventually they would emerge like demons from the deep, each demanding its due. But at this juncture, in my determination to stay on course, I continued to tamp down the fears and wrap them in butcher paper to pack away like those packages of beef in our family deep freezer.

Fear seems to have a way of stalking me. Like what happened two days ago. After finishing language school in Cochabamba, I flew to La Paz. I spent a few days at the Maryknoll Center House at 12,500 feet, adjusting to the altitude. I was the only guest at the time. It was a bright, sunny day when I decided to explore the city. I was walking alone down El Prado, the main thoroughfare, and out of the blue I got sucker punched in the face. I never saw it coming. My glasses were broken in half at the nose bridge. I stood there holding the two halves, shocked and dazed, wondering what had just happened. A crazy person? Someone with anti-American hatred venting on the spur of the moment? Part of an organized movement? I'll never know. But it struck home the possibility of experiencing serious violence going forward.

For the first time I was really scared. I wanted to be comforted. But no one was there to hold or comfort me. The brother in charge of the house was unsympathetic. I felt alone, far from the family and friends I left behind in the US and a long way from the friends I had hung out with during our five months at language school. So I recorded the experience in my journal, my faithful companion, always eager to absorb the ink of my pen soaking into its pages. That helped to calm me and tamp down some of the fear. Early the next morning, I boarded the bus that took me to Juli, on the Peruvian side of Lake Titicaca, where I checked in with the bishop.

Our chartered bus for the solidarity march is nearing the area of the town of Ayaviri. I watch the bus driver getting more erratic in his movements the closer we get to the staging area. Was it a moment of destiny when I accepted the bishop's invitation yesterday to join him for this march? Obviously "join him" didn't mean riding together on the bus with Bishop Raimundo Reveredo Ruíz, my bishop while I'm here, who is so different from his predecessor, my cousin Alberto. *What do you think of him Alberto? I heard he is pretty conservative. He's living in the obispado, your old residence next to the cathedral. He showed me the bullet holes in the banister. They looked as fresh as the night they shot at you back in 1983. I could still feel the splinters feathering out around the edges where the bullets had exited while you stood at the top of the stairs. Was their aim that bad, or were they warning you to leave Peru because you were so outspoken in defense of the poor?*

Some say they were terrorists-in-training "practicing" for bigger things to come, or possibly government agents. No one seems to know for sure. What was sure was that those bullet holes were real and they hung there like a warning sign.

As we approach our drop-off point, the road is getting crowded with other buses and vehicles. The bus driver frequently has to stop, then jerks ahead and speeds up again when he can. His nerves are frazzled. When we arrive, he hurries us off the bus and gets out of there as fast as he can. I hope he will have enough nerve left to pick us up again for the return trip at the end of the day.

The staging area is a wide, flat pocket along the mountainous road outside of Ayaviri. It is heartening to see some three thousand people converging from across the region spanning Lake Titicaca to Cusco. Steve Judd, bullhorn in hand, announces we will march from the staging area to the Rural Education Institute for a rally, then on to the plaza in Ayaviri. People are unfurling an array of banners. Several Andean music groups are warming up, creating a cacophony of sound. It's a beautiful, sunny day, partly cloudy with fear.

Soon the signal is given and the march begins to wind along the mountain road. I am near the front where a twelve-foot-wide banner carried by a phalanx of marchers proclaims *Sí a la Paz, No a la Violencia*—Yes to Peace, No to the Violence. Three bishops walk with us behind the banner as drums sound a rhythm for our steps. There are smiles, laughter, and light chatter as we snake down the hillside. After an hour or so we arrive at the institute that sits on an open plain surrounded by hills and mountains.

The bombed-out building is deserted. It is a square structure of offices and meeting rooms built around an open courtyard. The windows are shattered. Equipment has been stolen or destroyed. Two large sections of the red-tiled roof were blown away, leaving only the remains of charred and broken rafters. The building stands exposed and vulnerable. The feeling is mutual. There is talk that the terrorists are very likely in the hills watching us. The fear in me wants to slip away and take cover. I tamp down the fear and take some pictures of the destruction with my Canon Sure Shot. It affords some emotional distance between me and the stark reality of what I see. I step back into the crowd as we stand for a program of speeches calling for respect for human rights and rejection of the violence. I squint in the bright sun and scan the hills and mountains around us wondering, *are they watching and listening?*

One of the music groups with *zampoñas, charangos*, drums, and guitars breaks the tension in an interlude, sending their notes dancing in the air. The director of the institute lifts a megaphone to his mouth and proclaims that this day is a celebration of the solidarity of the people that has not been shattered by the bombs. This gathering, he says, that originally was planned to celebrate the twenty-fifth anniversary of the institute's work promoting leadership, agricultural methods, and human rights, has grown into something much larger. I feel Alberto's spirit stirring in his words.

When the program at the institute concludes, we converge on Ayaviri and fill the central plaza. A large platform has been erected in front of the colonial cathedral for mass and a program to follow. In his homily, Msgr. Francisco d'Alteroche, Apostolic Administrator of the Ayaviri Prelature, boldly states, "As believers we proclaim loudly that life is stronger than death, love is stronger than hate, forgiveness is stronger than rancor." After the mass we hear speeches interspersed with music and folkloric dances. In the midst of it all, gratitude for the opportunity to be here comes welling up. Maybe this is what I signed up for.

We are invited to line up to receive the late afternoon lunch our hosts have prepared for us. It materializes before us like the multiplication of the loaves and fishes. When all have had their fill, the buses begin to arrive for the return trip. With all aboard, we head off. The bus driver becomes visibly calmer as we move away from Ayaviri. It is a bumpy and, by this time, sleepy ride back with the tensions of the day trailing behind us in the dust. As the light of the day slips away, I drift in and out of sleep, wondering what the future holds. Night falls on my second day in Peru.

2

THE LABYRINTH

Lima, Peru
June–August 1989

My early morning flight from Juliaca down to Lima is blessedly calm. I'm so glad I'll be staying in one place for a while at the Center House. During the past four nights in the Juli area, I slept in four different places. It was a great opportunity to talk to a lot of people. But enough is enough! I'm in need of time for resting, reading, and letter-writing that Lima will afford while getting the documents I need to work in Peru.

I marvel as the landscape outside my window transforms from mountain peaks and plains in the highlands to the barren sandy foothills of the desert coast. We circle over the blue waters of the Pacific Ocean and land at Jorge Chávez International Airport on the outskirts of Lima. I collect my bags and head through the large glass doors of the terminal to negotiate a price with one of the taxi drivers lined up at the curb. We head off on the winding, hour-long drive across the traffic-clogged city to the Maryknoll Center House. The tension in my neck and shoulders subsides when Manuel, the office manager, answers the doorbell and, in his ever-calm way, welcomes me saying, *"bienvenido padre,"* and lets me in.

He offers to carry one of my bags and we walk the hallway past his office to the foyer. Manuel shows me my room number posted on the bulletin board and, with a gentle *"con permiso,"* takes his leave and returns to his office. I carry my bags up the wooden staircase to my room on the second floor, then head down to the dining room to see if I can get a late-morning bite to eat. I pop into the kitchen to say hello to Maria, the Peruvian cook for the Center House. Her ample girth balances the shortness of her height as she stands to welcome me. A big smile splashes across her face, and in her inimitable way, she plants a sloppy kiss on my cheek. At her invitation I take a seat at the little kitchen table while two eggs sizzle in the fry pan with a sprinkle of salt on top. It feels a little like home.

Back home on the farm, my mother often fried eggs for us when we came in from the early morning chores. First, she heated up the black cast-iron skillet and cooked the usual four soupy eggs with toast and coffee for Dad the way he liked them. To a young boy, it looked like a plateful of snot and drool. Mom would ask me and my brothers, "Do you want your eggs fried, scrambled, or poached?" For her, the kitchen was not only the heart of the home, it was a place for variety and adventures in cooking. Like a treasure hunter, she would sit at the table and search recipe books and magazines for new ideas. She found a recipe for soft shell tacos at a time when our family had never even seen a tortilla. The smell and crackle of the rolled out dough deep frying in the skillet whetted our appetites as she boldly went where no farm mom had gone before. The warm and fluffy discs folded in half sat softly in our hands as we filled them with seasoned hamburger topped with shredded cheese and lettuce to the delight of all the senses. I remember homemade pizzas that I helped put the toppings on, and thick slices of bread hot out of the oven and dripping with butter. She was not one to physically embrace or caress us but she hugged us with her food.

When I finish eating Maria's fried eggs, I cut across the courtyard to the chapel to give thanks for my safe arrival. There are three rows of chairs in a semi-circle facing the simple freestanding wooden altar. The same Peruvian crucifix that I saw the first time I entered here hangs on the wall behind the altar. I sit down and close my eyes as the memories rush in. Four years ago I was sitting here as Alberto celebrated the morning mass. He was down from the *Altiplano*, the southern highlands, for the annual meeting of the Peruvian Bishops' Conference. He gave my friend Dick Preston and me a tour of downtown Lima, then took us into the Bishops' Conference building and the Office of Social Concerns that he headed. I think about what a special day it was, how it meant so much to me that he took the time. Well Alberto, the space behind the altar looks empty without you there.

Officially, I'm in Lima to pursue two practical matters at hand. I need a *carnet de identidad*, the official identification document that will give me permission to work in the country, and a driver's license. Unofficially, I am concentrating on all that is so new to learn about the people, their culture, and how to navigate my way around Peruvian society. Everything is so new. All the unfamiliar elements make me feel anxious and vulnerable. I don't have the level of control over my life here like I had back home where I knew how things operated. I feel an urgent need to get a better handle on how things work here.

I am still straining to understand and speak Spanish even after five months of intensive language study. I keep pushing myself to learn more vocabulary, looking up new words and writing down definitions in my 8½″ × 11″ spiral notebook. Working on vocabulary is one of the few things I have some direct control over. The Center House is a hub of activity. Missionaries and visitors are always coming and going for overnight stays, meetings, or just a day of respite. I learn a lot just talking to them over meals.

There is no break from hearing about the growing threat of Sendero and the growing turmoil in the country. I hear about a priest assassinated last Tuesday and a British tourist who was killed recently. They are infiltrating youth organizations, universities, teachers' unions, and on and on. I feel a certain holy urgency to read pertinent resources, continue refining my language skills, and talk with people in the know.

At this point in my sojourn there is a growing fear for my safety, a fear that would continue to escalate. Being dropped into Peru in a time of growing terrorism and government oppression was like being placed in a pressure cooker with all the raw ingredients of life that were being thrown at me. I couldn't help but wonder if I would be able to survive under the pressure.

I find my way to my ten o'clock meeting with Father Bill McCarthy, the Regional Superior of Maryknoll in Peru. He is a soft-spoken, gray-haired man, originally from my home state of Michigan. He taught history for years at the Maryknoll Seminary in the US. We slide easily into conversation and he recounts how, as a young man, he joined Maryknoll because he felt called to serve in the foreign missions. That was put on hold during his teaching. He smiles as he tells me how, finally now in his senior years, he was given this assignment to work in Peru. Then he calmly breaks the news to me that I should expect a long process with a lot of waiting between steps to get my documents. Teaching history all those years seems to have helped him take the long view of life. I on the other hand like efficiency and getting things done quickly. It is starting to sink in that this is not going to be an efficient process, or anything close to quick. Bill tells me that Manuel in the office will guide me through the paperwork and application processes.

Maryknoll, the Catholic missionary society founded in the US in 1911, has a policy against paying bribes. It is an attempt to take the moral high ground against corruption. Talking with other missionaries at the Center House, I get the idea that in the bureaucracy of Peru, bribes are considered something of an expected part of doing business if you want to move things along—like paying extra in the US to get your passport application expedited or using an express mail service. The difference in my experience in the United States of paying extra fees for service is that it was aboveboard, and I knew where, how, when, and who to pay. In Peru, as with so many things at this beginning stage of my time here, how the system works is largely a mystery to me, like standing at the entrance to a labyrinth I've never seen before. I would not know how to "expedite" the paperwork, even if I were allowed to do so. My impatience is wrestling with the prospect of standing in government office lines, filling out paperwork and waiting interminably for documents and forms to be processed. I hope taking the moral high ground doesn't lead me over an emotional cliff.

With all I'm trying to learn, the first week in Lima goes by quickly enough. The paperwork, though, is going slowly. The police are supposed to come to the house to verify I'm here. They haven't shown. I did get my TB test, x-ray, and blood test done ok. One step completed!

During this past week, workers arrived to install metal grates over all the windows on the first floor of the Center House. Fr. Bill McCarthy, or Bill as I have come to know him, is the one who ordered the installation. Several of us got into a discussion about it while we were sitting in the library waiting for lunch to begin. One person ventured that it was just Bill's way of responding to his growing fears of a terrorist attack. Another questioned whether it was an overreaction. Most just seemed to accept it. *It is just a practical safety measure,* I think to myself, trying to dismiss the image of prison bars they conjure up. But I can't deny how the fact that Bill saw a need for them peels away one more layer of the illusion of security and safety I so wish I could hold on to.

As the days of waiting for my documents drag on, I feel periodic waves of frustration at all this "wasted time." In my upbringing on our family farm, working long hours and working hard to get things done was a measure of one's worth. Sitting idly around was not.

I remember when Lester, my second oldest brother, tried to claim independence from the family work ethic. He was home one weekend after beginning his first year at Michigan State University. Most of us were at the kitchen table finishing breakfast on Saturday morning. Lester was still sleeping in when my grandpa Thelen, who lived a half mile up the road, arrived at the house. He owned and ran the farm before selling it to my mom and dad when he retired. Grandpa still showed up regularly to help with the farm work. He drove to our house in his Mercury Monterey with its flat reverse-slanted rear window that could be moved up and down with an electric switch. For the half-mile trip, he would get in, start the engine, put it in gear and drive just over the crest of the hill halfway to our farm, turn off the engine, put the gear shift in neutral and proceed to coast the rest of the way to save gas until he rolled to a stop under the big ash tree by our house, satisfied that he had saved the brakes from any extra wear and tear. Frugal and efficient. When he found out my brother Les was home and still sleeping upstairs at 8:00 a.m., he opened the maple-veneered door to the stairwell and called up to him, "Lester! Get up! It is time to get to work!" I don't remember if Les complied, but it was a firm reminder of the generational expectation that we pull together and work hard until the work was done. Of course work was never done, and along with that, a strong dose of perfectionism was part of the package passed down through our German-American heritage.

I remember the oft-repeated story of my great-grandfather Nick Bauer on my dad's side who had his hired hands put up a new fence along the field next to his fine brick house. When he inspected it after they finished, he found the main anchor post was a couple of inches off from where it was supposed to be. He made them do the whole project over again to get it right.

∽∼↩

As the documents process continues to drag on, I am increasingly anxious to fly back up to the Altiplano and get to work. I don't feel called to be a long-suffering foot soldier in this latest Maryknoll skirmish with corruption. The pragmatic, can-do culture I brought with me from the US is already colliding with the realities of Peru. I have a lot to learn.

One step in the process of getting approved for a driver's license is the test for "psychological soundness." Manuel told me to take a taxi to the address he gave me, and now I am with a group of some thirty applicants in a gymnasium. As we are waiting, I scan the crowd and everyone looks Peruvian except me. Finally, an official looking person enters the room and instructs us, "Line up side by side in three rows and leave two arm's length of space between each one of you." We shuffle into place and then he tells us, "Stretch your arms out full length from your sides and hold them parallel to the floor." After we accomplish this he says, "Now stand on one foot until I call time." I pass the test, but I am left feeling a little crazed by the seeming absurdity of considering this a test for psychological soundness. I may only have a BA in psychology, but it sure seems like any assessment of psychological health would be a bit more complicated than this. If they knew of my crescendoing incredulity threatening to spill over into anger, would they still judge me psychologically sound? And what psychologically sound person would come to work in Peru in the middle of a terrorist uprising anyway? I have been judged "sound" by this arbiter of sanity according to some local criteria I can't fathom. But good enough for now. I'll take it and move on to the next step. And there's always a next step.

While waiting between steps, I visit some of the places where Maryknoll missionaries are working in Lima. One couple I have gotten to know is Ginger and José Yantas. At breakfast today they invite me to go with them to their home in Pamplona Alta in one of the shantytowns of Lima commonly called *pueblos jóvenes* or "young towns." "It is all built on sand," they tell me, explaining how the Pacific coast of Peru is the driest desert in the world. The mountains sweeping up from the coast are barren. The only exceptions are places where a river cuts through the mountains to the coast, providing water for homes and irrigation. The desert hills and mountains of sand stand in envious contrast to the ocean waves rolling up against the shoreline. As we eat our scrambled eggs, toast, and orange juice, José and Ginger describe how over the years people have come down in waves from the poor and remote mountain communities, seeking a better life in the city. They begin by claiming squatter's rights to a patch of sand on the edge of the city and then put up makeshift walls of *estera*, woven reed mats, to form their first living space. Next, they buy one cement block or brick at a time from meager earnings to eventually build the first solid walls of a house. At some point the government begins building infrastructure for water, electricity, and eventually even some paved streets. Over the years, they tell me, Lima has expanded across the sand hills to hold a third of the country's population.

After breakfast, I cram myself into the back seat of José and Ginger's Volkswagen Bug. They tell me how they met and got married while working in the sprawling parish in *Ciudad de Dios*, "the City of God," one of the more established pueblos jóvenes. Ginger is a lay Maryknoll missionary from the US and José is Peruvian. We drive away from the relative luxury of the Maryknoll Center House in Miraflores to Ciudad de Dios in one of the southern rings of Lima. Signs of poverty become more and more evident the closer we get. In Ciudad de Dios, we soon leave the few paved streets and begin driving up through neighborhoods on hilly streets of pure sand. The wheels of the Bug are spinning a lot as we struggle through to the area of Pamplona Alta where their house is located. Dogs are barking and lots of children are running around, laughing and playing with makeshift toys. A soccer game is in progress on a field of leveled-out sand. Children approach us asking for money when we get out of the car. Ginger cautions me, "Don't give them anything or we will be swarmed."

My heart goes out to them. I grew up on our family farm at a time when Mom still darned holes in our socks and patched our pants multiple times to save money and help us get by. But we always had enough food and the basics of life. Life is clearly much more precarious in this place. Ginger lives here and I am still an outsider, so I accept her advice in spite of what my heart is telling me to do.

Days later, I am on my way to the church in Pamplona Alta with Maryknoll Father Tom "*Tomás*" Burns to help with confessions. It is part of the large group gathering this evening of the home-based groups of *Catequesis Familiar*, the family religious education program of the parish. Tom is tall and lanky with a full black beard and a distinctively Queens, New York, accent. He's been working here many years and tells me, "I decided to live with a family among the people I serve in solidarity with them and to have some of the warmth and support of family life." I wonder if something like that would work for me.

We go first to the family home where Tom lives and has his tiny office for a quick bite to eat. The mother of the household welcomes us with a big smile, clearly pleased and proud to have *Padre Tomás* there as part of the family. After we are seated at the roughly hewn wooden table, I looked around at how little they have compared to what I was used to in the US. No cupboards to speak of, no paint on the cement block walls, everything is utilitarian—stove, table, benches for seating at the table, pots and pans hanging on the walls wherever there is room. Yet compared to the lives of so many in the area, they have a lot. What most touches me is the wealth of warmth and love that I see in the interactions among the children and their mom and dad. They speak tenderly to one another and embrace easily. I'm reminded how that kind of open expression of family love and affection was not part of my childhood. Hugs or

"I love you" were not part of our family vocabulary. A longing for that kind of love and affection stirs somewhere deep within me.

By the time we finish eating, it is dark outside. We set out walking quickly through the street and turn down a walkway between some houses to attend to a family of a fifteen-year-old girl dying of tuberculosis. They had sent a message asking Tom to come to pray with her and anoint her with the holy oils. When we arrive, the young girl is almost motionless on a bed with no sheets. Everything the family owns is crammed into the close quarters. The air is muggy and starved of oxygen with the extended family crowded around. I am standing on their dirt floor, looking into their eyes and seeing the pain of poverty and sorrow, the face of God in the poor.

This was the briefest of my experiences of these past two months and yet the most profound. It was a deep dive into feeling compassion and solidarity with the people. Day-to-day life is struggle enough for so many people here who have so little. That in itself pulls at my heart. But the encounter with this family with so few resources to care for their dying fifteen-year-old daughter was wrenching. A certain feeling of helplessness to do much to change the big picture of so much poverty begins creeping into my soul and will only grow stronger as this journey continues.

The precariousness of people's lives is more than economic. The crime rate is high and the terrorists are active in recruiting young people in the area by offering an attractive vision of a more just and egalitarian society. I can sympathize with the vision, but the horror is in their methods. In Sendero's view, Peruvian society is totally corrupt, unjust, and irredeemable. Their solution is to destroy all existing structures of society and then build a new society out of the ashes of the old. This includes aid organizations, development programs, and the churches because their work to help people just slows down the progress of the revolution. The Church is to be the dessert in their banquet of destruction. They have no qualms about murdering anybody standing in their way. So much of the government response is to threaten, assault, jail, and kill people they deem to be in collaboration with Sendero, leading to the deaths and oppression of many innocent people, which ends up playing into the hands of the terrorists.

Since I arrived at the Maryknoll Center House in Lima, I have been hearing about Sendero activity and the increasing threat they pose. Three weeks ago on July 20, the terrorists ratcheted up their activity in Lima. Sendero called a *paro armado*, an armed strike, for the whole city. They demanded all activity be shut down under threat of violent reprisals. To show they were serious, they burned five city buses the day before the armed strike. On the day of the "strike," all privately owned buses stayed off the streets and only the relatively fewer city-owned buses were operating. It was only partially effective in shutting down the city as most businesses stayed open. But their "success" was in their ability to hang a darker, more threatening cloud over the city's inhabitants, including me.

3

A HOT AUGUST NIGHT

August 1989

On August 8 I passed the written test for my driver's license, the last step in the two-month process of getting my documents. I am still waiting to get the actual physical license. Manuel, the office manager, has promised to send it to the Maryknoll Center House in Puno where I will be getting my mail. I can finally leave Lima. I feel like I have drawn the "Get Out of Jail Free" card in the Monopoly game I loved to play as a kid. Eleven months have passed since I first arrived at Maryknoll, New York, to begin the orientation program. It almost feels like a lifetime ago. And in a way it is.

I checked on the availability of flights the day before the written test. The result? More waiting. There are no flights available until August 13. As I wait, I am beginning to second-guess my decision to work in the Altiplano. Would it make more sense to stay in Lima? In my ventures out to Ciudad de Dios and other areas around Lima, I have seen a lot happening in terms of organizing with parish programs and popular movements among the people. I find it attractive. It resonates with some of my past organizational work in US parishes and peace and justice groups. I think about how I led the process of establishing the Office of Peace and Justice Ministry in my diocese and taking on leadership with Pax Christi Michigan in my first years after ordination.

So why go to the Altiplano? Perhaps what I need to learn most in the Altiplano is not so much how to organize a barrio parish or a *comedor*, a soup kitchen, so much as a new style of being with people, of listening first, of entering into their experience, of being quiet and still before God, of being led more by the Spirit at work in the community.

I come back around to the feeling of being drawn to the "desert" of the Altiplano. The image of the Altiplano of Peru as "desert," as a place of testing and challenge, with its Southern Peruvian Aymara culture and language so different from the English-speaking world I grew up in, first emerged as a metaphor for the journey when I began to seriously consider working in Peru, then solidified when I traveled there to see it first-hand as part of my decision-making process.

Getting to the point of taking that exploratory trip to Peru began, unexpectedly, a couple of years after my 1980 ordination as a priest. Almost imperceptibly at first, the idea of doing foreign missionary work began to pop into my thoughts. Initially I dismissed it as a kind of crazy idea. But like dandelions in the springtime, it kept popping up until I couldn't ignore it any longer. So I started to take a serious look at it. One thing I felt clear about from the start: if I embarked on this missionary journey, I would do it in the Altiplano of Peru where my cousin Alberto worked as a Maryknoll missionary.

From my earliest years in life, I felt a connection to Alberto, who was a first cousin to my mother and from my same hometown of Fowler. His given name in English was Albert. Family members called him "Fr. Al." I was inspired by stories about him and other Maryknoll missionaries in the *Maryknoll Magazine* that always had a place of honor in the reading rack next to the toilet in our bathroom. On a few occasions I was privileged to hear him talk in person about his work in Peru and defending the rights of the people. The stories captivated my attention.

In April 1985, I took the step of going to Peru to see how it would actually feel to be there. I needed some direct experience of the land and its people. I asked my friend Dick Preston, who had been a missionary in Honduras, to go with me as my unofficial translator. I especially looked forward to visiting "Monseñor Alberto" as he was known to Peruvians. He had already been in Peru twenty years as a Maryknoll missionary and now was head of the Juli Prelature, a territory of four hundred thousand mostly Aymara people split into two areas north and south of Lake Titicaca. His formal title was apostolic administrator, which gave him the same job as a bishop but without being given the full title. He had requested that designation because he felt a local Aymara priest should be named as bishop one day and he hoped it would help pave the way.

Dick and I met up with him in Lima where he was attending meetings of the Peruvian Bishops' Conference. We had some privileged time with him at the Maryknoll Center House, and he personally showed us around Lima and the Bishops' Conference offices. I regretted that it wasn't going to work out to spend time with him in the Altiplano.

After Lima, we flew up to the Altiplano where Maryknoll missionaries welcomed us at the Center House in the city of Puno and offered to take us around. At one point, we headed south around the lake to see where Alberto lived in the town of Juli, with its colonial-style cathedral nestled in a small bay on Lake Titicaca. I began to imagine what it would be like to work with cousin Alberto in the prelature.

We were delighted to accept the invitation to go out with Jim Christiansen, a Maryknoll priest who ran the Rural Education Institute of the Prelature of Juli. Jim was a tall, soft-spoken man with a scruffy beard and, like me, from a farm background in the US. He took us to the communal harvesting of a potato field at the institute. The test field was part of the Church's outreach to help in the development of more productive farming methods. At first we stood off to the side, observing the potato fields lit up by the intense Altiplano sun. Men and women in traditional dress were working with hand tools to dig and harvest the potatoes and select out seed potatoes for the next planting season.

Meanwhile a *watia* was in progress for the celebration of the harvest later in the afternoon. Fresh-dug potatoes were baking, buried in the ground under a pile of hot coals. While the potatoes were baking, we were invited to visit another communal field a little higher up for a *bocadito*, a "little appetizer." They seated us at a table in a small, one-room adobe house. The *bocadito* was a full meal of rice, boiled potatoes, and a boiled quarter of something that I did not recognize. I whispered to Jim, not wanting to offend our hosts, asking "What is this?" Jim leaned over and whispered back, "I'll tell you later." After we left he explained it was guinea pig, considered a local delicacy. I was glad he didn't tell me before I ate it.

Afterward, Jim showed us around the office, classrooms, and small barns of the institute. It was my first time seeing a pen of llamas close up. I couldn't resist stepping into the pen of gentle and regal-looking creatures to have my picture taken with them. When the camera flashed, one indignant llama proceeded to spit a wad of freshly chewed green grass at me and scored a direct hit on my face and glasses. Jim commented with a little grin on his face, "They do that sometimes." It was a little more direct contact with the local reality than I had bargained for!

Over the next several days as we traveled around, I continued to be impressed with how the Maryknollers were respectful of the Aymara culture and committed to working collaboratively among them.

During our whole time in the Altiplano, the farm boy in me felt a natural connection with the rustic, rural life of the Aymara campesinos. I was fascinated to see them working fields by hand and shepherding flocks of sheep and llamas. The stark beauty of mostly treeless fields and plains surrounded by towering mountains and the shimmering waters of Lake Titicaca spoke to my soul. I saw wide-open landscapes where only a few types of trees grow at that altitude, and there are few of them. The sun is hot and intense in the daytime and the nights are very cold all year round. In the dry, winter season, the whole area takes on the appearance of a desert: there is very little green growth to be seen across the plains, fields, rolling hills, and the soaring mountains with their rocky and bare slopes. It remains desert-like until the rainy season comes and fields of green transform the landscape in a new cycle of growth.

I reflected on how Jesus was led into the desert for forty days to confront his demons and get a clear sense of direction about his mission in the world. The question looming over it all remained, *was God calling me into the Altiplano "desert" to change the direction of my life as well?*

The following year I attended Maryknoll's month-long Discernment for Mission program where I wrestled with my questions, doubts, and fears. At the end of the program, I made a list, and more positives than negatives emerged about going to work in Peru. Still, I was not sure.

A year later, I knew it was time to decide. Fish or cut bait as my dad would say. I had talked to my bishop and he was supportive. But I still had doubts. I wondered, *was God really calling me to do this or was I just attracted to the adventure of it?* An attraction to travel and adventure ran in our family. My grandparents Arnold and Irma Thelen traveled the world at a time when few people ventured far from our farming community. Grandpa Arnold wrote accounts of his travel experiences that appeared in the local paper. It all seemed pretty exotic as I was growing up.

I also questioned whether I was unconsciously looking for an escape from the growing demands and anxieties of parish responsibilities and my peace and justice work. I realized I needed some time apart to sort it out and hopefully make a final decision. I turned to Gethsemani Monastery where I had done a retreat once before.

Gethsemani Monastery is in the rolling hills of Kentucky. It has expansive hills and woods where one can roam and reflect. I was first attracted there by the writings of Thomas Merton, the famous priest and monk who resided there until his untimely death in Bangkok, Thailand, in 1968. His spiritual journey and writings on peace and justice inspired me. I made arrangements to spend five days there on silent retreat in hopes of arriving at a clear decision.

The clarity I sought came on a hot and humid August night. I had spent two days wrestling with the decision. My sense of adventure, embarking upon a new spiritual journey, and my heart for working among people on the fringes beckoned me. But could I handle the isolation and the separation from all the familiarity of life and people I knew in the US? The mail was slow and phone service was scarce and unreliable. Could I learn Spanish and enter into a whole new culture? I was finishing a Doctor of Ministry program. Did I want to give up the professional opportunities that might open up? Was this the right time?

On my last full day, I took a late evening stroll to ponder it all. Sweat started dribbling down my face in the muggy air as I headed down the long driveway toward the main entrance. The gravel crunched beneath my feet with each step I took. Anxieties and doubts rode down my forehead on the beads of sweat. In the distance I could see the entrance off the main road where a yellow caution light flashed overhead. Was it a sign? I sent my anguished question to the heavens, *Lord, do you really want me to do this?* Then a song I knew from church began playing in my mind, "Be not afraid, I go before you always, come, follow me…. If you cross the barren desert, you shall not die of thirst, if you walk amidst the burning flames, you shall not be harmed…" then again the refrain, "Be not afraid…" Suddenly, I stopped stone cold and cried out to God, "But I *am* afraid!" And in the articulation of it, my fears fell away, replaced by the peace and certainty that it was the right decision to go ahead and do this thing.

4

A PILGRIM'S JOURNEY

August into September 1989

If you're going to work in the Altiplano you need to know about coca leaf tea. The coca leaf has been revered since ancient times in the Andes for both its medicinal qualities and its ritual use. Coca leaf tea is a mild stimulant similar in strength to coffee. It is an antidote to the altitude sickness almost every foreigner experiences when coming up from the coast. Nausea and headaches are typical. When I flew up from Lima after finishing the process of getting my documents, I felt headachy for three days. At night I felt like I just couldn't quite get enough oxygen. It helped when I cracked open the bedroom window as I had been advised to do, in spite of the cold night air. If I walked too fast or went up steps, I was quickly out of breath. Lots of coca leaf tea helped prevent most of the nausea, but I had to let the headache part run its course. After four days, my body had kicked up its production of red blood cells to absorb more oxygen, and I felt just fine. Occasionally, a person discovers that their body won't adjust and they simply cannot work long term at this altitude of 12,500 feet.

Now I have the freedom to choose where I will live and work for the next four years. The bishop has already asked me to consider the parish in Yunguyo. When I meet with Fr. Ray Finch, the Maryknoll head of the region, he also lets me know that Donald, the pastor, expressed interest in having me come. He describes several other places where I could choose to work and encourages me to visit all of them before making my choice. Then he tells me, "It's our policy that you can take up to six weeks to decide." I think to myself, *that's a long time to be in limbo.* Nevertheless, we make a plan for me to start the visits.

First, I visit two places on the northwest end of Lake Titicaca, Huancané and Moho. I like the people I meet, but a big concern is how remote they are and how difficult travel and communication would be. It is hours on terrible roads to get there and the only communication to the outside world is by shortwave radio.

Next on the list to visit is Yunguyo on the opposite side of the lake. I like that it is much more accessible and I am getting anxious to make a decision. It is almost a year since I began with Maryknoll at their headquarters in Ossining, New York. I learned a lot by way of preparation during orientation in New York, then at language school in Bolivia, and while getting my documents in Lima. But all the moves and changes have made me weary. I feel the need to find a place sooner rather than later where I can settle in for the next four years.

Part of the weariness is that I continue grieving the loss of my brother Lester, the second oldest of my four siblings. He had surgery on an aggressive brain tumor and was about to begin radiation and chemotherapy treatments before I left for New York. He was diagnosed in late July. The surgery was in August. The program at Maryknoll was set to begin September 1 and continue through December 10. I anguished over the decision about whether to continue with the program.

Sometimes life decisions are crystal clear. This one never was. Either decision, to stay or go, was going to affect the course of the rest of my life. So much had led up to this. So much about it seemed so right. Until Les got sick. It was like an avalanche stopping the train I was on, asking me to reconsider. In the end, you have to make the best decision you know how to make. That's all I could do. I will probably never be able to adequately explain why I made the decision I did. All I can say is the impulse to stay on the train that was taking me to Peru was stronger than the one saying get off the train and stay home with family. The last day of August, I drove off alone in my car and headed for New York.

The week of Thanksgiving I came home early from the orientation program to spend time with family, especially with Les, and offered to help his wife, Pat, with his care. Their only daughter, and my goddaughter, Jennifer, was about to turn three years old. Since I was no longer in a parish assignment I had time to spend that I would otherwise not have had. Was that part of the cosmic plan? I am not convinced, as some say, that God has a plan for us, at least not some predetermined plan carved in stone. But I am sure that the extra time was a gift I will never regret having spent in that way.

I agonized over it all again when it came time to leave for language school in Bolivia the first week of January. With mixed emotions, I decided to continue the journey, feeling there was not much more I could do, and with no idea how long he might live. I naively hoped it would be a long time.

Ironically, maybe even providentially, because I decided to continue on to language school, I had one of my most cherished moments with Les. I was able to say a heartfelt goodbye while he was still aware and present to the moment. Tears welled up in my eyes as I told him, "You have been a good older brother to me all these years. I'm so grateful." At which point he smiled and said, "Now you're getting all emotional on me," true to our family way of deflecting mushy emotions. Then he and Pat presented me with a goodbye gift, a T-shirt with the words "Roamin' Catholic" printed below a caricature of a backpacking hiker. It was his way of saying goodbye. He never lost his sense of humor. Shortly after I left for Bolivia, he slipped into a semi-conscious state and we would never have been able to have that conversation. A month later, on February 2, I flew home for his funeral. It all happened so much more quickly than I ever expected. I have never worn the T-shirt. I cherish it too much and I don't want the memories to fade.

The T-shirt went with me to Bolivia, and now it is resting in my suitcase at the Center House in Puno as I continue my visits to figure out where I will live and work. Today is August 21 and the transportation van I took from Puno to Yunguyo has parked on the south side of town a few blocks from the main plaza. It feels good to get out and stretch my legs after the two-hour ride around the lake crammed in with a dozen other passengers. As I walk through the Plaza de Armas, I see a couple of money changers at their tables shaded by large umbrellas. It is a reminder of how close I am to the border with Bolivia. The church stands before me across the plaza. I try to imagine what it would be like to live in this town of eight thousand inhabitants with all its border activity compared to the isolation of the villages I visited on the opposite side of the lake. The church doors are closed so I head down the side street.

The doorway off the dry, dusty street is ajar. I enter cautiously and follow the narrow walkway between the old colonial church and the rectory. It quickly takes me into Donald's courtyard, lushly layered with plants, shrubs, and flowers. A stone cross stands in the center of a manicured lawn bordered by beds of plants and a circular crushed-stone walkway. I spot Donald on the far end tending the garden. Beyond him, the outermost beds of plants hug the high, stuccoed wall that encloses the whole garden area that would be the size of a small field for a local Aymara farmer. It seems like a world unto itself, like an oasis in the desert.

When he hears the crunch of my shoes on the walkway, he stands up to his full Napoleonic height and says exuberantly, "Federico, welcome!" He has a head of thinning white hair slicked and combed straight back across the top of his head, and a well-trimmed salt-and-pepper beard. He invites me in for a cup of chamomile tea that he makes with the flowerheads he was picking when I arrived.

As the tea steeps, he tells me, "You've come on a quiet day, but tomorrow we start the first course for my new project called Plan NIP, *La Nueva Imagen de la Parroquia*." He pronounces the Spanish title with an exaggerated emphasis on each word and rolls r's with a flourish. In my head I translate the title as The New Image of the Parish. "The founder of the program will be here with her team to train our first group of leaders," he adds.

"So, what's it about?"

He launches into an effusive description of the program, which involves forming a new leadership team in each of the forty-five communities in the parish.

"Sounds exciting," I offer. My mind flashes back to the last place I worked at in Michigan where we were organizing neighborhood structures within the parish. Perhaps I could bring some of that experience to this project. There is some comfortable familiarity about it.

At the same time, I have a twinge of a feeling that he seems almost too excited about this new project. But I tend to give people the benefit of the doubt, and on this day in the cold, dry season of the Altiplano, I am looking for a welcoming place to settle into. I decide to stay for the three-day course to learn more about the parish and meet the pastoral team. The team includes four sisters from Colombia who live in the convent and two Aymara men who have their own families. We seem to hit it off as I meet them during my stay. The team, the plan, and Donald's respect for and knowledge of Aymara culture make Yunguyo seem like the right place for me. Less than two weeks into looking at places, I decide on Yunguyo. What I don't see is that Donald's expression of warmth toward me and his enthusiasm for Plan NIP are like a layer of clothes covering up more deeply embedded personality traits destined to create conflict between us.

On my first day after moving in, we have supper together and, without declaring it as such, we settle into a mentor-mentee relationship. Donald is the mentor willing to teach me about this new world I have stepped into. I am the mentee ready to soak it up as I'm trying to get my bearings.

The dining room table is just off the kitchen in the parish house. As Silverio, the cook, clears the dishes, we both make coca leaf tea, pouring boiling water over the dried leaves in our orange plastic cups, adding a spoonful of sugar and stirring until it cools a bit. From Donald's side of the table, you can see into the living room, which is a step up from the dining room and has an open, fieldstone fireplace at the far end. I am on the other side of the table, facing a china cabinet behind Donald, and to the right of that the hallway leading to our bedrooms. When I ask about the china, Donald tells me about his predecessor, the previous Maryknoll pastor, who had the cook dress up in white shirt and black pants and serve him at the table covered with linen, china plates, real silverware, and cloth napkins in wood-carved holders. Donald has been at this parish for 20 years. His predecessor would have been here in the 1960s. It was a different era, and he obviously was a different style missionary who sought to recreate his US lifestyle (and then some it seems) in Peru. Times have changed.

The table now has a thick plastic cover over a plain white cloth. Huddled in the center are a jar of dried coca leaves, napkin holder, and small carafe of *esencia*, a black syrup made from boiled-down coffee grounds. It's the local version of instant coffee.

Donald knows a lot about the ancient Aymara culture and I am grateful he is willing to share his knowledge and wisdom with me. Somewhere into the conversation, I tell him, "At language school, Fr. Frank McGurn told us how in Aymara rituals an *awayu* is placed on the ground like an altar cloth over *Pachamama*, Mother Earth."

"That's right," his eyes light up. "The finest ones are handwoven. The rows of colors represent crops in the field."

In the coming days, we continue to have conversations like this over meals. He surprises me one evening when he brings a wide, tooled, black leather belt to the table and tells me with almost a tear in his eye, "This belonged to Alberto. I would like you to have it." When he hands it to me I hold the buckle end of it with my left hand and run my right thumb over the raised tooled letters that spell out *Alberto K-13*. K-13 is for the thirteen letters of his last name. It feels like the relic of a saint. Tears well up in my eyes as I hold it in silence. Finally I say, "Thank you."

The belt obviously meant something to Donald and I think symbolized an emotional connection to Alberto that he felt on some level deep down in his soul. My being there, Alberto's kin, seemed to evoke that and moved him to give it to me. I didn't realize it at the time but that would be the closest I would come to feeling some genuine affection between us before things deteriorated.

As the mentee in this new experience, I am in the posture of a child. Learning a new culture is not unlike learning a language. While studying Spanish in Bolivia, I felt like a child in the first years of life slowly catching on to the language. You first have to tune in to the foreign sounds and distinguish between them. Gradually the sounds become words and eventually sentences and paragraphs that you can actually understand and even use in conversations. In a similar way, the Aymara culture is new and unknown to me. I don't know how to act in new situations because I don't know the cues and expectations. I find myself doing a lot of looking around to see what others are doing and try to follow along.

Like my first Saturday morning in Yunguyo when Silverio invites me to go to the weekly "black market" on the border a mile down the road. He is a short and stocky man with the typical barrel chest and high cheekbones of the Aymara people and has been Donald's cook for many years. He lives in town with his wife and young daughters. Like most people in the town, Silverio has some small plots of land he cultivates out in the *campo*. In the house, he boils our drinking water for 20 minutes as instructed. But then I watch him wash salad vegetables and fruit under the running, unboiled tap water. So much for my German-American sense of logic and consistency.

I accept Silverio's invitation and we head off, walking the road that swoops down from town and then rises to the market on the border. On our left, Lake Titicaca is sparkling in the sunshine. Some good-humored conversation makes the walk go quickly. The market is on the Bolivian side but there is an easy flow across the border on market day and we casually cross over. I see rows of vendors with all kinds of goods from Chile, the United States, and other Latin American countries. Silverio explains that people can get things at bargain prices, some of which are not available in regular stores and shops on the Peruvian side. You can get things like Concho y Toro Chilean wine, a variety of clothing, and many packaged food products. They even have cartons of ultra-pasteurized milk from Chile. I take special note of that because I was told the locally produced milk is not safe. I grew up on the farm drinking gallons of raw milk drawn from the big cooling tank in the barn so I sometimes crave a cool glass of milk, the kind of craving I would come to have for foods I loved back home but could not get here.

The border market is a place for socializing as well as shopping. Shortly after we arrive, Silverio meets some friends and introduces me. Then he buys a *grande*, a liter-size bottle of beer, that is commonplace in Latin America. It is nine o'clock in the morning. Apparently the US saying of "don't drink before noon" doesn't apply here. He mischievously opens the bottle and hands it to me first as we stand around in a small circle. Everyone is watching and waiting to see what I will do. I hesitate for a moment, feeling the gaze of their eyes on me. Then, not knowing any better, I lift the big bottle to my lips and take a swig. They all laugh with great enjoyment at the new gringo who does not know how to conduct himself and is acting like a barbarian. Then, with a big grin on his face, Silverio takes the bottle back from me, produces a small glass from the cloth satchel hanging at his side, and proceeds to demonstrate the right way to do it. He pours beer into the glass and makes the ceremonial offering to Pachamama by pouring a few drops on the ground, and only then drinks the rest of the beer from the glass. He refills the glass and hands both glass and bottle to the person on his right, who drinks and then pours a full glass for the next person, and so on around the circle it goes. For them it was as natural as breathing. For me it was like being potty-trained.

Back at the parish house, I continue settling into my room by taping some photos I brought with me on the wall. I pick up the one of Mom, Dad, and me sitting together and smiling at a Maryknoll cookout in Detroit. I have my hand across Dad's back, resting on his right shoulder, and Mom is on my left. There are pictures of the many cousins, uncles, aunts, and friends who came to the big potluck we had under tents for my going-away party at the farm last summer. I can still taste the crispy-skinned barbecued chicken Dad cooked in quantity on grates over the open grill he constructed for the occasion. Such things have warmed my affection for him in my adult years. One picture from the potluck is of me and my good friend Kate in a side-by-side hug with laughter all over our faces. I have in my hand the bouquet of daisies she had just handed to me. Several other pictures are of friends from the mission orientation program in New York and language school in Bolivia. Another is of Alberto on the memorial folder from his funeral. I open it gingerly and look again at the dates printed inside.

Born: May 30, 1917, Fowler, Michigan

Ordained: June 10, 1945, Maryknoll, NY

Appointed Prelate of Juli: March 31, 1974

Died: Feb. 9, 1986, Qaritamaya ("place of rest"), Puno, Peru

Qaritamaya is the location of the monument built by local residents on the side of the road where he died when his jeep crashed into the back of a truck. Many suspected sabotage, though the investigation was inconclusive. I tape his picture near ones of Gandhi and Thomas Merton.

When I am done taping pictures on the once-empty wall, I gaze around again at the space I will try to call home for the next four years. It is a simple but solid room with tile floor, plastered walls, and ceiling. There is a single bed, wooden desk with drawers, a bookshelf, and a small closet. The bed has a plywood board between the springs and the mattress to keep it from sagging. There are four heavy blankets. Nights, I have already discovered, are always cold in the Altiplano. In the warmer rainy season months of October through April, Donald has told me, I should be able to sleep well with only two or three heavy blankets at night. Now, during the much colder months of the dry season, I am already making good use of the mummy-style sleeping bag designed for winter camping that I brought with me. I have three heavy blankets on top of that. There is no heat in the room and the window always needs to be cracked open at night to get enough oxygen from the thin air. The strong morning sun is a welcome source of warmth when I step outside after the cold of night. It's easy to imagine how worship of the sun developed. I'm becoming a convert.

For my early morning shower, I head outside in shorts and flip-flops with a towel draped over my shoulders and shampoo in hand to walk around the house to the shower room by the parish medical clinic. The parish complex is enclosed by an eight-foot wall so I don't have to worry that I'm putting on a show for the neighbors. There is a water tank on the roof and an instant electric water heater unit just above the shower head. It is worth the risk of electrocution to feel the hot water streaming over me after walking through the cold morning air.

On weekdays, Silverio arrives early and makes breakfast. Having a cook is not my preference, but it came with the package when I moved in. As I get to know him, I find I enjoy his good-natured company. He always greets me cheerfully saying, *"Buenos Días Padre Federico."*

And I respond, *"Buenos Días Silverio. ¿Cómo has amanecido?"* How's the start of your day?

"Bien no más, ¿y tu?"

We continue the morning ritual until we run out of banter. He either fries eggs or cooks locally grown quinoa into a hot breakfast cereal.

We live next to the back door of the church. The main entrance at the other end opens onto the central plaza. The massive stones around the doorframe are still in place from the Inca temple that once stood on this site. I feel an ancient presence when I press my hands against their cold, damp surface, trying to imagine the Inca rituals that took place here. In the time of the Inca Empire, this was where pilgrims purified themselves before approaching the more important Inca temple in what is now the nearby town of Copacabana across the border in Bolivia. Its importance had to do, no doubt, with its proximity to the Island of the Sun, the legendary birthplace of the first Inca. Each successive Inca reigned supreme in Cusco from approximately 1200 AD until 1533 when the Spanish Conquistadors brought the Inca rule to a violent end. At its height, the Inca Empire spanned from Ecuador through Peru and down to northern Chile and Argentina. To this day, pilgrims come in large numbers to Copacabana to visit what is now the shrine of *El Santuario de la Virgen de Copacabana*, the Shrine of Our Lady of Copacabana.

I think about how I, too, am on a pilgrim's journey.

5

WALKING ON
HOLY GROUND

September 1989–March 1990

It is September 3 and I am riding with Donald in his Toyota pickup as he swerves around the biggest holes and washouts on this long-neglected dirt road. It is slow going as we make the two-and-a-half hour trip to the isolated community of Sicullani. On the way, we picked up Alejo Choque and his new Plan NIP team members. Alejandro is the Aymara catechist-leader of the Zepita parish, about an hour's drive south from Yunguyo. They will be staying in Sicullani and promoting Plan NIP over the next few days.

When we arrive, we meet with leaders of the community inside their small adobe and thatched roof chapel. They seat Donald and me like visiting dignitaries up front on a raised wooden platform behind a small wooden table. Everyone else sits or stands on the dirt floor. I feel uncomfortable elevated above the people who by now have filled the chapel. In my vision of Church we should all be seen as equals.

The meeting in the chapel begins with songs and prayers in the Aymara language. An occasional gust of wind through the door refreshes the air. Donald gives an initial introduction to Plan NIP and ceremoniously presents the leadership with a cross that has a figure of the resurrected Christ, a symbol of the new life he hopes will come with this initiative. It is a contrast to the bleeding and dying Jesus on the cross that is hanging on the wall behind me.

When the opening session concludes, they bring out a meal of boiled potatoes, *habas* which are fava beans, and morsels of a hand-rolled mixture of ground quinoa the size of a marijuana joint. They bring two heaping plates to the table for Donald and me. The rest sit around a long, narrow white cloth on the ground as food is poured out in abundance in the traditional communal style for a special event. We use our fingers as utensils. I feel privileged to be part of this richly communal event.

An elderly woman with a brown weather-beaten face is sitting quietly in a spot close to me. She exudes ancient wisdom and the presence of Pachamama, Mother Earth, with which women are deeply connected in Aymara culture. While people finish eating, the chatter among them grows louder and children begin running about. No one seems to pay attention as I step outside the chapel door to be alone for a moment. I stand transfixed before the absolute quiet that hangs over the expanse of plains punctuated by hills and mountains on all sides. There is not a motor or sound of any machinery to be heard, not a single power line strung across the landscape. An awareness of Pachamama washes over me like a wave of spiritual energy. I feel a bit like Moses before the burning bush in the desert when God told him, "the place where you stand is holy ground."

A week and a half later, with my experience in Sicullani of the sacredness of Mother Earth still fresh in my mind, I take a walk through some of the compact fields just outside of Yunguyo. Everything is quiet and I easily drift into contemplating the sacredness of the earth upon which I am treading. Each little field has its paths and footprints. There is such a sense of intimacy with the land here. Each inch is known and personally claimed. Each *chakra*, or field, is a different size and shape. As I walk along, a feeling of peace comes over me, a feeling of kinship with the land. I hear some sheep bleating in the distance and remember the sheep of my childhood on the farm. The land at this time is so brown and dry before the start of the rainy season, this "desert" land the Lord had called me to.

My contemplation of Mother Earth takes me back to our family farm where I first felt enfolded in God's presence in nature. One day when I was ten years old, an intense discussion of some sort among family members in the house was overwhelming me. I slipped outside unnoticed, mounted my Huffy bicycle and rode a half mile south on the gravel road.

At the crossroads, I took a right turn to the steel bridge hanging over the creek and stopped under the big oak tree that shaded it. As I stood still, straddling the bike with my feet on the ground, a heightened awareness of God's presence came over me. I remained mesmerized there for some time before riding back home, feeling I had been touched in some special way. I kept it to myself.

One day when I was fifteen, I was out working our twenty-acre field of gently rolling land. The alfalfa had been cut and left to dry two days earlier. I was turning it into fluffed up windrows with a rake hitched behind our gray 1940s Massey Ferguson tractor. A gentle clack-clack-clack sounded from the rake's rotating tines. The tractor engine purred as I drove up and down the field in a repetitive rhythm with the sun-warmed breeze brushing against my face. Suddenly the spiritual gears shifted and I felt drawn upward into God's presence and carried along as if I were sailing through a cloud. Time slowed as I drove along until my expanded spirit contracted again and rejoined the rest of me sitting on the gray metal seat of the tractor.

That same rolling field is where my grandfather Arnold regularly found old stone arrowheads and knife blades during spring plowing. One was dated by an archeologist to 7500–7000 BC and two others from 500 AD. It was likely a Native American campsite. I can't help but think they too felt a sacred presence in that place. The earth is sacred, holy ground upon which we tread. The name Pachamama more and more speaks of that for me. Those experiences of the sacred on the family farm helped open my soul to what I am experiencing more intensely now in Peru, with more to come.

I am looking forward to introducing my parents to this land of Pachamama. They made plans with me to come for a month starting in February. I am hoping the visit will help dispel some of their fears for my safety that have come with hearing news reports of violence in Peru. Their fears are out of proportion to the reality of my daily life. I have been reassuring them in phone conversations that coming here is no more dangerous than visiting high crime areas in the US. I'm trying to convince myself of that as much as them.

I fly down to Lima the first week of February to meet Mom and Dad at the airport. I first take them to the Center House in Miraflores for a couple of days. Then we travel to Arequipa, Cusco, Machu Picchu, and on to Yunguyo. I have felt us growing closer together, traveling and sharing conversations over meals. The most precious moment came when I was sitting side by side with Dad at the top of the terraces overlooking the sacred Inca ruins of Machu Picchu. Mom stayed below to rest while we climbed the steep slope. As we sat there transfixed by the beauty of it all, Dad said, "I never thought I would be sitting here in my lifetime with a view like this."

"And I never thought I'd be sitting here like this with you. I'm so glad you and Mom could come." We both gazed out, misty-eyed for a moment, before going back down to where Mom was waiting for us. That mountaintop moment brought our hearts closer together and closed a wide swath of the emotional distance between us that had so marked my childhood.

By the time we arrive in Yunguyo, it is the time of carnival and, more importantly, time for *Jatha Katu* ceremonies in the potato fields. February is well into the growing season. Potatoes are a major crop and the staff of life in this land where all the potato varieties of the world originated. The potato is sacred, as shown by the practice of kissing the first potato harvested from the earth. Special ones are called *mamata* in Aymara, meaning "mother seed."

My parents are staying with me in the parish house in Yunguyo. I introduce them to Silverio who later invites us to join in a ritual of *Jatha Katu*, a ceremony intimately connected to Pachamama (*Jatha* is pronounced "hata," meaning seed).

The day before Ash Wednesday, we walk with Silverio down to the parish field next to the convent. The sisters join us in the middle of the plot where we form a circle around Silverio, careful not to trample the potato plants that are in full flower. We watch as Silverio carefully digs up a whole potato plant to see how it is doing. As he holds it up for all to see, he has a big smile on his face because there is an abundance of small potatoes forming on the roots. We watch as he carefully replants it and then celebrates the plant by uncoiling ribbons of colorful streamers and wrapping them around the plant. From his side pouch, he produces a plastic bagful of *mistura*, confetti of colorful dots of paper. He tosses this by the handful over the potato plant and over the plants around it, then all over us where it collects in our hair and clothes. We laugh as it tickles and trickles down the insides of our shirts.

The festive spirit continues as he opens a bottle of beer, fills his glass, and pours a few drops in offering to Pachamama. Then he raises the glass saying, "*Salud!*" "Cheers!" before drinking it down. He refills the glass and passes it on to the next person in the circle who drinks and refills it in turn, and around it goes until all have partaken. When we finish, I give Silverio a big thanks for inviting us, especially my parents, into this ritual.

The next day I head out with Mom and Dad to a campo community for a *Jatha Katu* Mass of thanksgiving. It is Ash Wednesday on the Roman Catholic calendar, but in rural communities, Ash Wednesday pales in significance to *Jatha Katu*.

We are riding in my 1970s-era white Toyota Land Cruiser that originally belonged to cousin Alberto. I feel I am carrying on a piece of his legacy by lovingly maintaining it in service to the people to whom he dedicated his life. After a half-hour ride over bumpy dirt roads, we arrive at the chapel at the agreed-upon time. The only person there to greet us is the catechist.

It is only after we arrive that the people start to gather. A modest wooden table is brought from the chapel and placed outside the door to serve as an altar. I set up some of my things for mass as we wait. I invite my parents to relax and enjoy the view because it can easily take half an hour or more for everyone to arrive.

I have learned not to be in a hurry. Shortly after I began going out to the communities, I threw away my watch so I wouldn't offend people. I was habitually looking at my watch, noting how long we were past the agreed-upon "starting time." I finally realized I had grown up with a very different sense of what it means to start something "on time." I began to use the time to connect with the people as I waited. I would talk with the local catechist in charge and meet some of the community leaders, or accept an invitation to bless a house that had been struck by lightning. Initially I would ask, "How far away is your house?" I would get an answer like, "just over the hill." After several experiences of "just over the hill" being a twenty minute or longer walk, I learned to ask, "*How long* will it take us to walk there?" in order to gauge whether to go before or after the mass. I'm slowly learning how to navigate in this culture.

Gradually, people make their way to the chapel from their houses scattered across the landscape. Some twenty or thirty women arrive with young children and babies wrapped in *awayus* tied over their backs. They sit side by side on the ground in a semicircle a short distance from the altar. Each one unwraps a small handwoven *awayu* and places it on the ground like an altar cloth in front of them with items to be blessed, things like seed grains, herbs, new potatoes, jugs of water, salt, and coca leaves. The men, as is custom, stand behind them. When we are ready to begin the mass, Aymara songbooks are passed out. I introduce my parents and the catechist welcomes us on behalf of the community. At the point when I give my reflection on the Gospel reading, the catechist translates it from Spanish to Aymara, freely adding to what I say. I just let it go, figuring he is the local leader and he can have his say too.

The climax, as far as the people are concerned, comes at the end of the mass. I bless a large container of water and then go around blessing all the items on the *awayus*, sprinkling and splashing water abundantly over everyone and everything. There are smiles on the women's faces and glee in the eyes of the children. This is a moment of true intersection, a moment when our very different lives and religious sensibilities are joined in this ritual action. They will take these blessed items to their families to use for healing remedies and home rituals.

After mass, the community shares in a meal of new potatoes, rice, and roasted guinea pig, which they bring to me and my parents in metal bowl-like plates. As we eat, I explain to my parents how the way we celebrate mass here integrates aspects of Aymara culture. The Aymara always ritually ask pardon of each other at the beginning, the songs and Scripture readings are in the Aymara language, women sit on the ground because of their close relationship with Pachamama, and the blessing with holy water imbues everything with the life-giving energy of the Holy Spirit. In today's mass we have given thanks for the promising signs of a good harvest seen in the *Jatha Katu* rituals in the fields.

It has also been our last major event together before my parents head back home.

≈⌒≈⌒≈

W hen I return from seeing my parents off safely to Michigan, I have a class to teach starting the last week of March. Last December, I agreed to teach a course on Faith and Spirituality at the pre-seminary. The bishops of the Southern Andes established their own major seminary in Juliaca as a place to prepare students for priesthood in a way that respects their Aymara and Quechua cultures. The primary and secondary schools often leave students inadequately prepared for seminary study. To help remedy that, a residential pre-seminary program was set up in the town of Ilave, about an hour's drive around the lake from Yunguyo.

I walk into the classroom for the first session on a Wednesday morning. I am nine months out of language school and about to begin teaching a class in Spanish with seven students whose first language is either Aymara or Quechua. While their cultures and languages differ, they share the deeply rooted sense of Pachamama. They all grew up in small, rural communities steeped in their local culture. There are some outside influences such as from entrepreneurs who make trips to the coast to bring goods to the local markets or from TVs in some houses. While most communities do not have electricity, it is not unusual to see an adobe house with a TV antenna on the roof and a small television inside powered by a car battery. Still, the rural communities are tight-knit. Aymara or Quechua is the first language of the home. Children usually start learning Spanish when they enter the school system.

I have my doubts about how much I can bridge some of the cultural divides that separate us. The students are seated in wooden chairs around the rectangular table in the middle of the room as I take a seat at the head of the table.

In my preparations over the previous weeks, I had decided to start with themes that I hoped would connect with their experience. I drew ideas from Creation Centered Spirituality that takes as its starting point the goodness of all of creation, rather than starting with concepts of sin and redemption. It highlights the first chapter of Genesis where God looked over the works of creation and "saw how good it was." Creation Centered Spirituality develops themes of our connectedness to the earth and the cosmos and a reverencing of nature. This seemed to fit with the central place of Pachamama in the Andean world. The formal theological term closest to this is panentheism, which holds God is present in and through all of creation, but is not the same as creation. I found in this concept a way of staying within the bounds of Catholic theology while talking about Pachamama.

I offer a warm smile to the students and begin with introductions. Then I start talking about themes of creation and the very agrarian nature of so many stories and rituals found in the Old Testament. From there, the next week, I draw some connections with Pachamama. By the third class on April 4, we have developed a level of trust and openness, which is not easy for an outsider to achieve, especially in Aymara communities, which tend to be very wary of outsiders and reluctant to share personal aspects of their lives. It is a defensiveness that helped them resist the domination of the Inca Empire which imposed the Quechua language on conquered peoples. The Aymara, however, maintained their distinctive language and culture within the empire. It is a defensive strength that is currently helping them resist terrorist encroachment.

One example of this resistance to outsiders came alive for me when Bob Hurteau, a young Maryknoll priest from the US, wanted to live in one of the Aymara communities outside of Yunguyo. He had finished extensive study of the Aymara language at the Maryknoll Language Institute in Cochabamba, Bolivia. He wanted to gain more fluency by immersing himself in a community. Donald, the pastor in Yunguyo, helped him make initial contact with an Aymara community he thought would be receptive. At first, Bob got "the Aymara no," which went like this: when Bob asked the community leaders if they would be willing to have him live among them, they said yes, of course, but they would first have to find a room for him with a willing family. After waiting several weeks, he asked again and the response was they had found a room but it was a storage room and needed to be cleaned out. After waiting several more weeks with no word, he inquired again. The response was that the room was cleaned out but there was no furniture yet. He waited again. They may have hoped he would just give up. In the end, they did accept him to live among them. Apparently, the community needed time to discuss his proposal and work through their reservations before finally agreeing to let this outsider in.

As I begin the third class at the pre-seminary, I invite them to share some of their prayer experiences. I am pleased when they readily talk about a number of ritual prayer experiences tied to Pachamama that they have witnessed in their respective communities. I decide to take a risk and explore more directly how they understand Pachamama.

I ask, "How do you understand Pachamama in your life; what does Pachamama mean to you personally?"

One student responds: "Pachamama is the source from which all life springs."

Another says, "Yes, all the plants grow from the earth."

They talk about this for a while, expanding the reflection to how animals, birds, and fish all have life because of Pachamama. They also refer to her as Virgin Pachamama, a reflection of how closely the Virgin Mary is identified with Pachamama, both being givers of life. Festivals of the Virgin Mary that originated with the Spaniards are at one and the same time celebrations of Pachamama.

Then a student asks, "But does our human life come from Pachamama?"

One answers, "Yes."

Another questions, "But how can that be since we are born of our parents and do not grow out of the earth as plants and trees do?"

The discussion continues and gets very lively around this question. It clearly touches on something deeply embedded in their lives. I stop them for a moment and invite them to listen as I read in Spanish the second biblical story of creation in Genesis chapter two, that states, "So the Lord God formed man out of the clay of the ground and blew into his nostrils the breath of life and so man became a living being."

With that I invite them to reflect on the connections between the two, between the language of the Bible speaking of human life being formed out of the clay of the earth and the language they use to talk about life coming forth from Pachamama. At this point in the class, I am wondering how directly they connect God to Pachamama.

I ask, "Does Pachamama equal God?"

The answer is, "Yes."

It is obvious that in their experience it is a pretty direct connection. I suspend any judgment about whether they are fitting into the categories I was taught in seminary. There is also the question of how much gets distorted in the translations going on in their minds from their primary language of Aymara or Quechua to having to express their thoughts in Spanish to me whose first language is English. Often there is no direct word-for-word translation from one language to another, especially when it involves more abstract stuff like metaphor and mythology, or jokes and wise sayings.

By the end of the class, I am filled with wonder and gratitude at this opening into their lives. I can't help but think how their reverence for Pachamama has much to teach the rest of us about the sacredness of this home we call earth.

I get into my Toyota Land Cruiser and pull away from the pre-seminary, head down the driveway and onto the main road along Lake Titicaca. I am driving, looking across the wide-open expanse of land around me, thinking about the conversations we just had in the classroom and what a privileged experience it has been. Suddenly I am filled with wonder and awe in the presence of Pachamama, and drawn up into what I can only call a mystical kind of experience of Pachamama. My soul, my whole consciousness, is floating above my body and it is only with effort that I keep my hands on the steering wheel and keep driving down the road. Eventually my soul returns to my seat and I am back to "normal" again.

Is Pachamama God? Or is it that God is present in and through Mother Earth and all of creation? Theological distinctions don't seem adequate at this point to talk about the experience I've just had. What I know for sure is that I have been lifted up on eagle's wings in a dance with Divine Presence, and that to walk in this land of Pachamama is to walk on holy ground.

December 1989–May 1991

I am sweating from my half-hour walk up the base of *Cerro Khapía* on this hot, sunny afternoon. It is the highest mountain in the area at well over fifteen thousand feet and home to Yunguyo's protector spirit, *Achachila Khapía*. The mountain base is an upward sloping plain, like the train of a wedding dress where it sweeps upward from the floor behind the bride. Finally, I reach the path that cuts sideways across the slope. It is a treeless expanse of brown earth and grass as short as a putting green from the overgrazing of sheep and alpaca. Occasional rock outcroppings dot the hillside. The rock formation I have come to investigate is not unusual in and of itself. But a local resident told me a man from a nearby community became very ill after walking past it in the evening darkness last week. He warned me that it is a place where evil spirits emerge in the night to attack unsuspecting passersby. The hairs on the back of my neck start to prickle as I approach this place where the Aymara underworld intersects with life above.

In the Aymara cosmology there are three levels of pacha. *Manqhapacha* is the realm of the underworld, where the dark forces of the devil, demons, and a hierarchy of malignant spirits reside. The surface world, *Akapacha*, coincides in many ways with Pachamama. *Alaxpacha* is the realm above—the sun, the moon, the stars, and spiritual entities that include the Creator and the saints.

As a child I was taught that hell is "down below" where the devil reigns and where evil people who fail to repent go after death. Heaven is "up there," the realm of God, the saints, and angels. Life on earth is between the other two realms which compete for our souls. This strikes me as similar to the three realms of the Aymara cosmology. The similarity must have lent itself to how the Aymara have incorporated Christian personalities into their cosmology. For instance, they include God the Father, Jesus, and the saints as part of the realm above, of *Alaxpacha*.

The Aymara are attuned to the forces of evil at work in the world. I compare it to the way the Bible talks about Satan, demons, and evil spirits. In the world I grew up in, scientific explanations increasingly displaced belief in these forces of evil. Yet fascination with the spiritual forces of good and evil remains in Western culture. Consider how the Star Wars movies talk about *the Force*, a kind of spiritual energy at work for good in the fight against evil in the universe. It essentially portrays a spiritual energy or mysterious life force that exists beyond the explanations of observable science, a portrayal that has fascinated movie goers of multiple generations. Or consider how the movie *The Exorcist* became a box-office hit in 1973, and how movies portraying personified evil have had a lot of popularity ever since.

There clearly are forces of evil and darkness at work in the world. Some of the evil can be explained rationally. Human decisions and behavior cause much of the evil in the world. But some of the evil is bigger than that. As I continue my journey in Peru, the terrorism is steadily increasing. So are the human rights violations committed by government forces. At some point, social structures, organizations, and institutions seem to take on a life of their own. Destructive decisions of people in power become patterns that become "normalized," institutionalized, and defended. They become social injustice, institutional violence, systemic abuse, evil at work, and ultimately, evil personified if you will. Some call it the devil. Interestingly the word devil is evil with a "d" attached. Some refer to Satan and his minions. Many names have been used in many religious and cultural settings through millennia. In the history of art, all kinds of images have been conjured up of what people imagine the devil to look like. Our human qualities get projected onto the images of the devil we create, even as we tend to anthropomorphize our images of God. Both the mystery of God and the mystery of evil and evil spirits are ultimately beyond our human comprehension and our ability to give logical or scientific explanations or ultimate proofs of their existence. Yet experience is our best teacher, as William James elaborated so eloquently in his 1902 book, *The Varieties of Religious Experience*. And experience tells me that God in all of God's mystery is real. And that evil is a reality at work in the world. When the forces of evil in their many manifestations impact you personally, they can undermine your sense of safety and security. I feel that happening to me. The evil of violence is attacking my internal neural network, slowly damaging and taking parts and pieces of it prisoner. But I have a fighting spirit, and I know the best defense and the antidote to feeling powerless in the face of evil is to take action for justice and speak out for peace. It is the ancient battle of good vs. evil, and I am in the thick of it.

On Thursday, December 7, 1989, in Yunguyo we hold a public march against the violence. Our parish pastoral team, and especially the sisters, organized it as a youth and children's march for peace. They drew on their connections with the elementary and secondary schools in Yunguyo where they teach religion. We start the March for Peace at noon with some one thousand children, youth, and adults walking in unison around the central plaza. The children are wearing their best school uniforms and waving small Peruvian flags. Youth and adults carry banners with slogans like *Si a la Paz, No a la Violencia*—Yes to Peace, No to Violence. People have turned out in large numbers and the event concludes peacefully.

The following Tuesday, as part of the campaign, *Los Jóvenes*—the parish youth and young adult group—hold a vigil for peace. It begins with people filling the town theater for the program of songs, skits, and chants on the themes of peace and justice. Then the youth move to our parish hall for a dance with live music. The lights are bright and a joyous spirit fills the hall. Suddenly, at midnight, the lights go out and our sector of Yunguyo is plunged into darkness.

After some inquiries around town, the conclusion is that Sendero cut the electricity to send us a message to stop activities in opposition to them. In my journal I note these events, my growing fears, and conclude by asking myself, *"Where does it all lead?"* The fears are increasingly bubbling up and causing anxiety. But true to form, I push the fears back down, unresolved, and march on with my work here. But those fears will only stay down so long before they push back up with greater forces than ever, like trying to cap a volcano that has already started erupting.

I take another step into action, accepting an invitation from Sr. Pat to join the team of the *Vicaría de Solidaridad*, the Church Human Rights Office of our Prelature of Juli. It was founded in 1988 by Sr. Pat, its director, Maryknoll Sister and, by my estimation, warrior woman for justice.

I felt a connection with Sr. Pat and her passion for justice from the start. I often see her at breakfast when I am in town for an overnight stay at the Maryknoll Center House in Puno. We are both morning people and often sit together at one of the blond-colored wooden tables in the dining room. There's a large, furry wall hanging depicting a llama on the back wall. On the other side, a bank of windows looks out on the courtyard with its bed of cosmos flowers around a little patch of grass. A stone fireplace is at the opposite end from the kitchen door. Pat, who was born in Jamaica, New York, typically arrives for breakfast in her jeans and brown and white patterned Alpaca wool sweater overlaid with a down vest to defend her slender body against the cold. Her energy for the coming day's work is contagious.

The morning cook always comes out and greets us with, "*Buenos Dias,*" and asks, "*¿Que quieren para desayunar?*" "What would you like for breakfast?" We in turn greet him and ask how his day has begun, then order our breakfast. I usually request either pancakes or eggs and toast, with a side of split fried hot dog substituting for sausage. Pat orders all of those because, as she says, "I never know when I will get time for lunch if at all." She often talks about the many ongoing investigations and court cases, and the frequent walk-ins seeking help on cases of military or police abuse. I listen in awe, thinking this work is her *life*.

As part of the *Equipo Responsable*, the Vicaría support team, I attend the monthly meetings. The Vicaría office is a converted fifth-floor apartment in central Puno, a location chosen for security reasons. Today, I head out from the Center House at 8:30 a.m. for the 9:00 a.m. meeting. I pass through the Center House parking lot with its adobe walls and open the metal doorway to the street. The door squeals and clangs shut behind me as I begin the ten-block walk to 181 Moquegua St. The streets are alive with people walking to work and street-corner vendors selling freshly baked breads the shape of my palm. The offerings include whole wheat breads known as *pan integral*, white flour breads, and ones called *pan de queso* with a hint of cheese baked inside. They stay warm packed in cloth-lined wicker baskets. The aroma transports me to the home-made bread my mother used to bake. There are also *empanadas*—meat-filled hand pies—and coffee and coca leaf tea to be had. Children with trays of gum, candies, and cigarettes call out, *"Chicles! Dulces! Cigarros!"* Crowds of people are navigating tight sidewalks that barely keep you out of harm's way from the cars, trucks, and buses moving along the narrow streets and old colonial buildings. I welcome the warmth of the sun as it ascends over the buildings.

As I approach my destination, my shoulders tense. The poured cement structure where the office is located looms before me. The fading pink and green paint on the outside walls does little to soften its harsh appearance. Sendero recently bombed the Vicaría office, which is similar to ours, in the Ayaviri Prelature. We are just as likely to be targeted. There is no el-evator, so I begin to climb the five flights of bare cement stairs, one step at a time, stopping occasionally to catch my breath. The exertion at this altitude always feels like the first day of high school track practice. With each step, I am in a wrestling match between my fears vs. my rationaliza-tions that it is unlikely a bomb would go off here at this exact moment in time. I am vigilant, scanning every dark space that could be harboring a bomb with a timer about to go off.

At what point does one become terrorized? Or traumatized? In my case, it is like the slow drip of the IV bag you see when visiting someone in the hospital or have landed there yourself. In this case, it is the steady drip of the poison of terrorism entering my bloodstream a drop at a time and slowly frazzling my nerves. I am starting to notice the cumulative effect in my heightened state of always being on the lookout. I would later come to understand this as hypervigilance, a state of constantly being on guard in places of potential, or perceived danger, or among people you don't know or trust.

I think of the time I was on the train from Puno to Cusco. I was constantly looking around, on the alert for someone who might try to steal my bag in the overhead rack. I couldn't doze off for fear of someone picking my pockets. It was especially the case when the train stopped at stations along the way. Passengers would be boarding or getting off and vendors would be working the aisles selling food. Suddenly I spotted someone in the act of stealing someone's bag. I was like a tightly wound spring ready to be triggered into action. I yelled out in Spanish pointing my finger, "That man is a robber! Watch out!" At which point he fled. My heart rate was elevated most of the rest of the trip and I couldn't rest from my vigilance. The longer you are in an atmosphere like this, the more you are affected by it. And I was constantly in it one way or another in Peru. You are rarely really at rest and it gets exhausting.

It starts to alter one's brain and nervous system. You more quickly go into high alert and are much slower to calm down after an adrenaline rush. It starts to disrupt sleep patterns at night, making it harder to get a good night's sleep without waking up in the middle of the night thinking about the dangers and threats around you, or things you have "heard," which can easily get amplified in one's mind when thoughts run wild thinking about it all. And even more so if there is not a way to process it in an ongoing way with someone like a professional counselor or the assurance of supportive relationships that help one maintain a sense of safety and well-being.

I'm in this heightened state of vigilance as I walk up the stairwell to the Vicaría office. It is a relief when I arrive at the top of the stairs. No bomb has gone off. At least so far. I knock on the door of the Vicaría office. After I identify myself, a team member opens the door and greets me. There are six to eight of us who regularly gather. Today, Sr. Pat is here of course, along with Sr. Mary Ann "Mariana" who I also work with on the Seminarian Formation Team, and four others. I say hello to Mariana as I step around her in the kitchen to make some instant coffee and pick up a couple of cookies. The kitchen has bare-bones countertops made of poured cement—definitely not designed for a fashion statement. A small window above the sink looks out at an opposing gray block wall. The remaining tight space is occupied by a simple gas stove, a refrigerator, and some roughly constructed wooden cupboards.

We settle into the dining-room-turned-meeting-space next to the kitchen. It has a plain wood-frame couch with two cushions, a couple of similar looking chairs, and four metal folding chairs around a low wooden table. I take the metal chair option in deference to those who have been here longer, even though it is a little uncomfortable with the dull pain I have been feeling lately in my left hip. I make a mental note to get that checked out next time I get back home. Pat lights the candle on the table for the opening prayer. We pray a Psalm that was printed out for us and listen to a reading from the Gospel of Matthew: "Blessed are the poor in spirit…Blessed are the peacemakers…Blessed are those who hunger and thirst for justice…" The words speak to my heart and our gathering feels like an oasis of comfort and support against the growing violence in the country. Perhaps even more, being here soothes some of the intense loneliness that has hit me lately.

After the prayer, we continue with the formal part of the meeting, reviewing both terrorist activity and abuses on the part of government forces that have taken place since our last meeting. This flows into a discussion of how we can better support the people affected and advocate for their human rights.

A case in point is Sixto, who was assaulted by the police. Sixto is a campesino from one of the Aymara communities in the Province of Yunguyo. On August 28, 1990, he sold cattle at the Desaguadero border market south of Yunguyo on Lake Titicaca. As he was leaving, the police stole his money. They detained him in their local prison and proceeded to torture him through the night and shoot him in an attempt to keep him quiet. It is not uncommon for people to be ripped off by police and military personnel, but this was a more extreme case of brutality. They typically get away with their crimes. If a charge is ever filed, the perpetrators just bribe the judge and have the charges dismissed. The common person has little hope of ever receiving justice. But this case is different.

At some point, Sixto was taken to the local hospital in Yunguyo. It is a sad place with few resources for treating serious cases. Sixto was fortunate to have a powerful advocate. After he arrived at the Yunguyo hospital, a family member went to the convent and reported Sixto's situation to Sister Leticia Posada, a member of our parish team in Yunguyo. Sr. Leticia, the oldest sister at the convent, is from Colombia and has been a member of the Dominican Sisters of the Presentation since her youth. She has a big heart for defending the rights of the people and reaching out to the vulnerable. Because of their outreach, the sisters have the trust of the people. One example is their work with a group of Aymara women who make *bordados* to sell to tourists coming across the border. The embroidered pieces depict scenes of life in the Altiplano. While they work, the sisters hold discussions on topics like human rights and the dignity of women.

I assisted Sr. Leticia when she wanted to help the father of a large campesino family who had been electrocuted while working on a local construction job and could no longer work. There is generally no compensation in cases like this. She asked me to buy a hand-operated weaving machine in La Paz, Bolivia, so she could teach him to use it to help support his family. I happily did that, only later to be puzzled at why she did not give him one of the similar machines sitting idle in the convent. She was enthusiastic about helping people, if not always practical. But in the case of Sixto, she was a force to be reckoned with.

When the report about Sixto reached her, she swung into action. She immediately and fearlessly went to the hospital to be with Sixto and protect him from further harm at the hands of the police. He was seriously injured and it quickly became obvious that he needed to be taken to a bigger hospital in Puno. The police were preparing to take him to their own hospital in Puno where they could cover up the situation. Sr. Leticia, with bulldog ferocity and determination, refused to allow that to happen and made sure he was taken to the public hospital in Puno where they could treat his gunshot and torture wounds, and where the case would not be covered up. She faced off with the police authorities and told them in no uncertain terms what was and what was not going to happen, not brooking any objections. So it was that Sixto was moved to the public hospital in Puno.

We notified the Vicaría as soon as possible. Guido, a full-time Vicaría lawyer, began a legal investigation. He began collecting evidence, first by interviewing Sixto. Sixto, with the support of the Vicaría, was courageous in telling the truth of what happened and sticking with his story as the case progressed through the legal system. This was no small matter for a campesino with few economic means and no political connections to ensure his safety. It would not be unusual for him to receive threats and offers of bribes to retract his statements and drop the case. Sadly, such bribes and threats usually are effective, which means people in positions of power are rarely held accountable.

As I have learned more about how the system has not worked for the people, I have become less surprised that the terrorists have been able to exploit people's anger at the injustice and gain supporters in spite of their brutal methods. It convinces me all the more of the importance of the work we are doing in the Vicaría. Holding the guilty accountable, especially people in power, is the best thing we can do to undercut the appeal of the terrorists. I can't help but reflect on any number of government lies and cover-ups in my own country that have taken place in our history, and how that has undermined democracy and human rights. Holding people in positions of power accountable is vitally important for the future and well-being of a country and its people.

A critically important factor in the case of Sixto was that people in his community were willing to testify and collaborate in putting together the case to take to court. Friends and family in Sixto's own community could have easily let themselves be intimidated and stayed silent. The support and reputation of the Vicaría and our pastoral team has made a difference in how people perceive their options.

I helped where I could in the case of Sixto, both as part of the Vicaría team and our parish pastoral team. By this time I was known enough in the communities to have gained some trust from the people. I drove Guido out to the community when he wanted to interview Sixto's family and other witnesses, and introduced him to the people. With that, the people were willing to open up to him. I was also in a position to provide some of the finances needed to help move the case forward and to help with medical expenses thanks to the support of people back home.

To offer more weight to the side of calling for justice, our pastoral team in Yunguyo prepared a petition that was signed by a large number of people from our parish. One result of all these efforts is that six members of the police force have spent some eight months in jail awaiting sentencing. Just having police spend time in jail is already a huge victory for the people.

Sr. Pat asked our pastoral team in Yunguyo to write a summary of the case for publication. We did this and concluded it by saying, "With everything that has happened, the people are more conscious and aware of their rights and that, yes, in solidarity, it is possible to prosecute a case and promote justice in our society." It has shown how the system can actually work for the little guy when the broader community comes together. It has given me a sense of purpose to take an active part in a case making a difference in people's lives. It is a step forward in the longer project of helping people receive some measure of justice that, historically, has been systematically denied them.

Am I being idealistic? Surely. But what ever gets changed without working toward an ideal, without holding up an image of the possible in the face of the seemingly impossible? One person receiving justice because he had the courage to stand up and say "NO" to just giving up after being brutalized, and saying "YES" to taking on a whole system stacked against him. One person willing to trust and accept the help and support of a community of people working with him and his family in solidarity for change makes a difference. Yes, I am an idealist, but a practical one who looks at the concrete steps needed to move forward, while acknowledging that perfection will never be reached in this lifetime. One of my images of the ideal comes from the prophet Isaiah in the Hebrew scriptures who set forth the great vision of the peaceable kingdom in chapter 11, the opening lines of which read, "Then the wolf shall be the guest of the lamb and the leopard shall lie down with the kid," even as he lived in an era of more wars and violence than we have today relative to the size of the populations of his time.

Being a "practical idealist" came into my vocabulary thanks to a comment from my cousin, Fr. Ray Rademacher, at a conference during a small-group discussion. After he listened to me talk about how we can use the modern methods of nonviolent action to help build Jesus's kingdom of peace, love, and justice, he looked at me and said, "You are an idealist, but a practical idealist." That stuck in my mind like an arrow hitting the bullseye. In the case of Sixto, I was able to be part of living that out in a way I could never have anticipated back then.

Eight months later, at a Vicaría team meeting, I report that the previous Thursday night, two dynamite blasts went off in Yunguyo at 10:45 p.m. and 2:30 a.m. Also at 2:30 a.m., three gunshots were heard. I went out after the first blast that went off by our parish meeting hall next to the police station on the main plaza. The police were even more startled than I was. Early the next morning, the flag of Sendero Luminoso was found up the flagpole in *Plazo Dos de Mayo*, the smaller of the two plazas in Yunguyo. My first thought was that terrorism had come to town and we could expect more violence. But later in the morning, in visiting the police captain and then the sub-prefect, the suggestion was made that, given the conflicts between the main police and the *Policía Técnica*, the latter may very well have done it.

Even though in the end it seems to have been a relatively "minor" incident in that nobody was injured and there was little property damage, it has taken a psychological toll. Was it one police force against another, or was the suggestion of it just a way for town authorities to deflect their fears of the growing reality of terrorism? A question left unanswered.

At the Vicaría team meeting, we discuss the likelihood that it was Sendero testing the waters for how local officials would react. It raises my already growing anxiety. At the end of the Vicaría meeting we take time, as we usually do, to share how each of us is feeling and how we are coping with the growing violence.

I have been struggling to be more open about my growing fearfulness. I usually am the last one to share and tend to cryptically share something about my fears, and then move on to something more positive, like sharing my gratitude for this space where we can share our anxieties and find some support. I still tamp down my fears much more than share them.

Lately I am leaving the meetings with mixed feelings. On the one hand I am grateful for an emotionally safe space to talk about what is happening and to find some collective ways to take action. On the other hand, the detailed discussions of violence and atrocities are having the cumulative effect of making me feel even more fearful for my safety and struggling with how to cope.

7

LOSS, LONELINESS, AND CONNECTION

March–May 1991

I am walking through the community of Pilcuyo on its main dirt road. A ribbon of Lake Titicaca is visible beyond the flat expanse of the peninsula. All around are adobe and cement block houses with sunlight flashing off tin roofs on this cloudless day. Small plots of land, chickens, and sheep are interspersed among the houses of the several thousand inhabitants.

Fr. Mike Briggs, a Maryknoll priest, is walking beside me wearing his newsboy hat and sunglasses. The rounded features of his face and figure project the gentle warmth and calm he is known for. This is our first meeting since he agreed to be my spiritual director. Shortly before I arrived in Peru, he had completed three years as interim head of the prelature after my cousin Alberto's death. He speaks Aymara and spent time during those three years traveling and listening to the people to see how he could best serve them. Through it all he continued to live in his simple adobe house where I came to meet him today.

As we walk, Mike explains, "My idea of spiritual direction is not to direct you or try to tell you what to do, but mostly to be a listener and companion on the journey. And what we talk about is confidential between us."

"That's great," I respond. "I really need someone to share my journey with. It has been a real struggle lately." I go silent. The tears are welling up in spite of my attempt to hold them back.

As I have grown into adulthood, dealing with my feelings has been a challenge. I vividly remember an experience during my first year of graduate-level seminary when we were required to start doing field ministry. I chose to work with a local youth program. My supervisor, who was in charge of the youth program, met with me weekly to help me reflect on my experience. He challenged me to share my feelings and not be so stuck in my head. He would say things like, "OK, you described the activity you were doing with the kids and how they were not very cooperative. Now, how did that make you *feel*?" I froze up every time. My defenses went up like the Great Wall of China. My anxiety shot through the ceiling as he tried to pry me open. But through his patient prodding, I began to find words for the anxiety and the disconnect between my head and my heart. I felt the un-freedom of it and the desire to unlock the door to my imprisoned emotions.

"Tell me what's going on," Mike says, ready to listen. We continue to walk as Mike patiently waits for me to speak. A surge of anxiety courses through me at the thought of sharing what has been so painful for me these past months. The old defenses start slamming into place. I should just detour and talk about more general things and pretend I am doing just fine. Take the safer route. *No! I need to do this.*

I take another deep breath, exhale, and send out a trial balloon, "I have been feeling a lot of loneliness and sadness these past months." I pause and wipe tears from my eyes and blow my nose with an old fashioned white hankie I pull from my pocket.

"It sounds painful. Where do you think it's coming from?"

I stare into the distance. Finally, words begin to flow. "Well for one thing I have been grieving the loss of my brother Lester. February 2 was the second anniversary of his death from the brain tumor. This year it really hit me. I sat all alone in my room in Yunguyo looking at his picture, sobbing, and just wanting to hug my parents. All the feelings of loneliness and missing people these past months came pouring out."

"That's a lot of sadness," Mike says gently.

"In the afternoon, I took a walk along the road overlooking the lake. I talked to my brother, telling him how sad I was feeling, how much I missed him. Then I asked 'Les, are you ok?'"

As much as I had tried to dismiss it, a small voice within kept questioning whether he had made it to heaven or if he was still languishing in purgatory. As a kid in Catholic school, I had been taught that your soul could be in purgatory for years after you died. The more sins you had, the longer it took to get purified before gaining entrance to heaven. It was described as a fiery place, not as bad as hell, but not yet heaven. In seminary I grew to believe that "purgatory" as I had been taught does not exist. At most there is a final purification that happens in a flash on your way to heaven after you die. Yet the stuff we grow up with has a way of persisting, like the deep roots of the quack grass in our garden on the farm. No matter how many times we hoed deep to cut out the roots, it always came back from the remnants that ran deeper still. So I needed to know if my brother was ok in the afterlife.

I continue with Mike, "As I walked along the road, all of a sudden I felt his presence in a way that you just know is real. In my mind I heard him say, 'Don't be sad, I'm ok.' In my mind's eye I could see him with his wry smile looking down at me. Then a deep peace came over me."

"Quite a blessing," Mike tells me.

I forge on, "I remembered him in the masses I had that day, the regular nine o'clock morning mass, then I had a funeral mass at two o'clock and an eighth-day mass in the evening. I took comfort in being with families who were also grieving the death of loved ones. I invited Sr. Marta from the convent to come up for lunch. It helped just to be with someone. Later in the afternoon, when I was alone again in the empty house, I went to my room where I sipped on some scotch. I took out one of the last pictures taken of Les. He was holding his little daughter, Jennifer. She was just three years old at the time and now barely remembers him. The memories came flooding in, most of all when I said goodbye before I left for language school in Cochabamba. That was the last time I saw him alive. A month later I flew home for the funeral and then returned to language school."

"You were doing some good grieving," he says. "Sometimes it gets delayed. Maybe that's what happened when you went back to language school so soon after the funeral. Sooner or later the feelings come out."

I think about that for a moment, then continue, "When these kinds of feelings surge up, I find it helpful to walk along the lakeshore in Yunguyo, or the ocean coast when I am in Lima. I say to myself, like a mantra, 'waves rolling over time.'"

"Kind of like saying, 'time heals,'" he adds.

"Yes. You know it's kind of ironic. Before I came to Peru I was starting to get a little better at sharing my feelings with some of the people I felt closer to. But now that just makes it harder to be away from them. I don't have those kinds of closer connections here."

"It takes time," Mike offers.

"I'm finding it especially hard lately with Donald. He seems more distant than when I started out in Yunguyo. Instead of our relationship building over time, it seems like just the opposite is happening. The more he gets involved in his new grain mill project, the more distant he is from me and the rest of the parish team. He just went ahead and launched it on his own with no discussion or input from us. It is a good project, but it seems to be consuming most of his energy these days. Maybe he just operates much more in his own world than what I saw when I first arrived."

Mike shifts the conversation by asking, "How has prayer been for you?"

"Well, lately I have been praying with Psalm 27, 'Wait for the Lord with courage; be stouthearted and wait for the Lord.' Those words are stirring up something within me. It's just not clear yet what it is. With the growing violence in the country, I am getting more fearful about what could happen to me, or to any of us. Sometimes I wonder why it doesn't seem to impact others as much as me. I see how connected the Aymara people are to their families and communities, and I think maybe that's it. I don't have the family and community support here like they do."

Mike suggests, "It might help to think about where you do find positive energy and connection with people and try to build on that. You are doing some good work here and people appreciate it."

"Thanks. Yunguyo was a good place for me to start and settle in. But now I find myself more energized in my work with the Vicaría and with the seminarians."

"It would be good to pay attention to that. There is nothing wrong with shifting your priorities."

~∽~

In our next session, I discuss my two-month furlough coming up in mid-June that will mark the halfway point of my five-year commitment with Maryknoll. I am excited about seeing people back home again. I've been missing them so much. At the same time, something fundamental is shifting in my life here. As I think about being gone for two months, I realize the people and their way of life here have been seeping into my DNA. Some part of me will very much miss being immersed in this Aymara world while I am away.

One thing that has helped me feel more part of the life here is that I recently began studying the Aymara language at the Institute for Aymara Studies in Chucuito, a town not far from Puno. Learning the basics is giving me insights into the Aymara mindset. Some of the ways the local folks speak Spanish always puzzled me. Now I am seeing how native Aymara speakers frequently use Aymara speech patterns in the way they talk Spanish. This six-week course, and the discussions of culture that come with it, are taking me a step further inside of life here. One of the reasons I decided to take this introductory course was to see if I even had the capacity to learn this language that is so different from English and Spanish. I would want to gain some fluency if I decided to make this a longer-term missionary commitment. Would I actually want to make that commitment? Really hard say at this point.

Connecting with the youth and young adult group in Yunguyo has also helped the cause of feeling more connected to people here. Still, at this point, it is one foot in the door and one foot out. Like when I gathered with them the other night. I really enjoyed myself with them as we laughed and joked and were serious together. I yearned to continue being with them as I walked the "older" ones to the door after wrapping up, something I haven't felt in quite that way before. But it is complicated: the parting at the street door brought deeper awareness of a feeling of belonging, but also of the reality of still being in two different worlds.

The door is both the entryway to coming together and the divide that separates. The young people stepped out the door into the town plaza and I stayed inside. For all that we were able to share during the evening because we had come to feel more comfortable with each other over time, we still come from two different worlds of culture and experience. At the same time, it is clear that we can come together through that door, and that after my two years in Peru, some closer relationships and connections to people here are possible. How much will I be able to step through the door into relationships with people in the Aymara world during my time here and feel less like I'm on the outside looking in?

8

THE FIST OF FEAR

August–September 1991

I made it safely back to the Maryknoll Center House in Lima after my two-month furlough in the US. It was hard to pull away again. Mom commented on our time together with a touch of irony, saying, "You know, since you joined Maryknoll we have spent a lot more time together than when you were in Michigan."

The time in the US made me all the more aware of how much Peru has become a part of who I am. I felt both "at home" and disoriented in the US. People I got back together with had grown and experienced new things in hundreds of little ways that I had not been part of. I felt a dissonance between things like highways full of shiny cars in the US and the relatively few and older vehicles in the Altiplano. And overwhelmed by huge stores full of 20 choices of everything compared to small storefronts families operate out of their homes in Yunguyo where they either have the one Peruvian brand of what you want or it just isn't available. So here I am back in Lima asking myself, where is "home" now? After returning last night, I am aware of a feeling of being "at home" here, a familiarity of place and people. In the past week before returning, I especially felt a growing intensity of a longing to return to Peru.

It is a return to what has become familiar in Peru, but also to the reality of the violence. At mealtimes at the Center House, I have been asking people how things had been going while I was gone. They've been telling me stories of Sendero's ongoing assaults. Clearly, the violence has only gotten worse. I feel the fist of fear punching my gut again, almost as if I had not been away for two months. The stories I'm hearing bring the threat of violence ever closer to me. I hear an account of what happened in Moho, one of our parishes on the opposite side of Lake Titicaca. Sendero entered the convent and rectory and then sent the townspeople in to ransack it. I'm told of a priest of our prelature receiving a death threat letter. Two Polish priests in the diocese of Chimbote north of Lima were killed and their bishop, Bishop Bambarén, was told to resign under threat that they will kill four gringo priests if he does not. One of our catechists in hiding, another shot. It goes on and on. It seems clear that the violence is zeroing in on the people and the institutions of the Church that I am intimately a part of. I'm starting to feel like I have a big target on my back. It makes the possibility more real that I or any of us could be next.

The next day I fly back to the Altiplano and stay overnight at the Puno Center House. I have learned to not rush around the first three days it takes my body to adjust to the altitude. I can't help but think of how, on the day Alberto died when his jeep crashed into the back of that parked truck, he had not done that, and some think he may have blacked out. He was in a hurry to get to some urgent business. So I rest.

The next morning after breakfast, I make my way back to Yunguyo. I note how there is a feeling of coming back "home." Many things are familiar now. When I landed in the Juliaca airport, walking out of the plane, I felt a great joy in being back to this place of pampas and hills. These past two years, I have made my entry into the parish life and team, into being part of the support team of the Vicaría, into the Seminarian Commission, and into life in general in the prelature and with the Aymara people.

But just one day later, I am feeling a great sadness, so distant from family and friends in the US after so much quality time with them. My feelings these days are like a ping pong ball going back and forth across the net from the world here on one side and the US on the other.

For some reason, Andrés has been on my mind since I got back to Yunguyo and I go to visit him. I head off, walking down a maze of side streets solidly lined with walls that shroud houses and courtyards. Shards of glass cemented on top of the walls glint in the sun. I knock on the cold, gray-painted metal entrance door to his house and go in. Since he has little that would be of interest to thieves, as he has told me, he leaves it unlocked so visitors can just walk in. Sadly, there are few visitors.

"Hola Andrés! ¿Cómo estás? How are you?" I greet him.

"Aye Padre, gracias por venir," he answers, thanking me for coming. Andrés is blind, elderly, and now partly lame in his right leg. His wife died over a year ago and he misses her terribly. They were never able to have children so he is mostly alone. I find some comfort in being together in our loneliness.

The next day, August 29, is the Feast of the Beheading of John the Baptist. In my morning prayer, the image of John the Baptist losing his head gets juxtaposed with thoughts about the terrorist threats against Church workers in Peru. It feels like a premonition.

After breakfast, our parish team has gathered for our mid-year evaluation. We are seated in the living room of the parish house on the eclectic array of chairs that have long inhabited this place. Two new members of our team are bringing some fresh energy. Ricardo is an Aymara seminarian who is starting a pastoral year at our parish to get practical experience of parish life. It is part of his formation program. He has an upbeat, outgoing personality, easily given to laughter. As a member of the Seminarian Commission, I am his supervisor. The other new member is Sister Lucila Chagua, who has come up from Lima to join the sisters at the convent. Lucila is a young and energetic Aymara originally from the nearby town of Juli. After some introductions and catching up with each other, we start reviewing the goals we had set six months ago for our pastoral work. It all moves along undramatically in the early stages of the meeting. But, another dynamic emerges.

One thing that at first stayed mostly in the background comes to the fore—the fact that in Peru we are in a state of civil war. In a subtle but powerful way it affects all of us. We fear for the future, even for our personal safety. We see the disintegration of social institutions all around us. Mistrust increases because of infiltration by terrorists in institutions, including the Church. There is concern about whether projects and programs will draw more violence to us and the people we serve.

Eugenio, our office manager and pastoral worker, first speaks of it. He is afraid that putting comments or testimonies about violence, or communities addressing injustice, in our Plan NIP newsletter, will draw violence to him, remote as that would seem to be. Then in the closing mass, several of us reflect on fears. I speak of how I came to acknowledge some of my deep-seated fears while home on furlough. Even as I speak, I feel those fears surfacing from where I had tamped them down. Lucila notes that the danger is growing for foreigners in the wake of the recent killings of a nun and three priests. I hadn't really acknowledged that before and am surprised to hear her say it. There is a truth there.

It is so good to be able to share our fears. As we conclude our meeting, we join in celebrating mass together—something that rarely happens with all of us together. In the moment of silent reflection after communion, I suddenly feel a great joy, like I want to stay in this moment forever. The mix of fear leading to joy seems paradoxical. But I'm just going to accept it as a gift from above.

It is three years since I started the orientation program with Maryknoll in New York in September of 1988. Fall was fast approaching when I left Michigan. It is my favorite season, and I do so miss it this time of year. I remember when as a teenager on the farm I drove the tractor with the chopper behind it, drawing rows of corn stalks into its head at the front and spewing the chopped-up stalks and corn cobs out the other end and into the wagon behind it. I can hear the grind of the machinery and smell the fresh-ground pungency of the silage. Leaves of mighty maples in Michigan will soon be changing color and blanket the ground in orange and red. I always delighted in hearing the dried leaves rustle under my feet and breathing in the rich, musty odor they gave off as they decomposed. In the Altiplano of Peru, the seasons are the opposite and broken more into rainy season and dry season. In September, the earth awaits the first rains that will announce an end to the dry season and the time to plant the fields. The seasons here seem upside down compared to Michigan. Indeed, since coming to Peru, my life has been turned upside down in many ways.

∽⁓↫

I have been wanting to write down the names and read more about the stories of the two Polish priests who were killed in the diocese of Chimbote in northern Peru. Before I came up from Lima, I bought a local paper and a copy of the magazine *Sí* featuring stories of recent murders of Church workers. I have been reluctant until now to open up the pages.

∽⁓↫

Their murders are a chilling reminder of my vulnerability as a foreigner in Peru in this time of terrorism. I feel hesitant but at the same time compelled to look at the pictures and pages telling of these people's lives and how they were assassinated. It feels like approaching a terrible accident on a highway back home. Traffic slows to a crawl. You hope and pray no one has been killed. As you get closer you realize it is a gruesome scene of blood and death. You don't want to look, and yet, you cannot *not* look. As you drive by, you are compelled to confront the fear that you ordinarily keep buried in some dark corner of your existence, the fear that surfaces with the unvarnished truth that yes, this could happen to you some day. Someone could randomly lose control and come at you head-on from the other side of the highway. As you drive on down the road, you tamp that fear back down. That's the only way you can keep driving, keep functioning, and not exit at the next off ramp, paralyzed with fear, and unable to get back on the highway.

As my fears have grown in the face of the increasing violence in Peru, I have been, unconsciously at times, tamping them down so I could keep functioning. The problem is the fears have not been processed and dealt with in an ongoing way. They have just kept building up below the surface until, like boiling water in a closed container, at some point something has to give.

With no small amount of trepidation, I open the glossy pages of the magazine and begin to make notes. Two Polish Franciscan priests were killed on August 9—Fr. Michal Tomaszek who began his pastoral work in Peru in 1989 at the age of 28 and Fr. Zbigniew Strzalkowski who was assigned to Peru in 1988 at the age of 29. They worked together in Pariacoto, Ancash. Sendero Luminoso had been sending them threats, demanding they stop distributing food they were giving out during the drought, and stop organizing people around their issues of jobs, food, and health care. Sendero considered their work, especially the food aid, to be part of the "imperialist system," putting the people's consciousness to sleep and slowing the advance of their revolution. When they refused to leave, they were abducted, along with Justino Maza Leon, the mayor of Ancash, taken out to the countryside near the cemetery, and shot in the head.

Fr. Alesandro Giuseppe Dordi, an Italian priest, age 60, was assassinated on August 25. He worked the last eight years in the parish of Santa, just north of Chimbote. He was close to the campesinos, the article says, helping build schools and churches in the communities. Most recently he was helping them develop their agriculture and find more ways to market their produce. He was friends with the two Polish priests. When he heard of their murders he told his friends that he would be next. He chose to stay with his people. He was returning from celebrating mass and baptizing children in an outlying community when Sendero terrorists ambushed him and shot him in the head and chest.

The next page recounts of the death of Sr. Irene McCormack, a Sister of St. Joseph from Australia, age 52. She was killed May 21 in the remote mountain community of Huasahuasi in the Department of Junín. Terrorists accused her of distributing food aid and shot her and four other town leaders in the plaza. She had been working in the community for two years and, along with her other pastoral work, distributed food aid from *Cáritas*, the Catholic relief agency. She stayed with the people when others on her team fled to Lima.

How does one make a decision like that to stay? I have fond memories of Sr. Irene from when we were both at the language school in Cochabamba. She was a gentle silver-haired soul with nothing but goodness in her heart and a desire to serve the people. Her murder especially jolts me. *All* these deaths jolt me. And to think of the thousands of Peruvians who have been killed by Sendero Luminoso and government counter operations since Sendero began its guerilla warfare in 1980.

What has jumped up my fear most of all is the attack on Moho that I heard about for the first time when I got back to Lima. All the violent deaths in this civil war are tragic. But there is something about people and places you personally identify with that strike the hardest. The violent deaths of the priests and Sister Irene fall into that category. They were Church workers like me. The Moho attack slides the marker on the fear scale closer to the word "terrified." It is one thing to hear about attacks in other parts of the country, but this is one of our parishes in our Prelature of Juli. Yes, it is on the opposite side of the lake from where I am stationed and in a much more remote area, but, if it can happen there, it can happen in any of *our* parishes, including *our* parish in Yunguyo. I can't get that thought out of my mind. It just sits there like a storm cloud hanging over everything else.

I hear more about it at a meeting in Puno with Bob Hurteau. Bob is a Maryknoll priest and the pastor of the parish in Moho that was attacked. He works with the team of sisters who ran the parish on their own before Bob accepted their invitation to join them. He is a few years younger than me. His thick, brown hair is cropped short, and he ordinarily offers a pleasant smile. Today he looks strained. He and I are meeting to plan a gathering of all the priests and sisters of the prelature. We soon diverge and talk about what is really on our minds, the attack on his parish.

"How are you doing with what happened in Moho?" I ask. "Are you ok?"

"It was pretty gruesome and I have not been back there a lot since it happened. I've been having more stomach problems lately. I think it's the stress. Honestly, I don't know if I can go back there full time. The whole team, the whole town really, is pretty shaken up."

"When did it happen?"

"Well, it was the afternoon of July 2, two months ago today in fact. I was in the home of a family that lived a couple of blocks from me; their grandmother had passed away. I was doing the final prayers of commendation when I heard bomb blasts go off in town. The family was very protective of me. They told me to stay put. They kept me in hiding for four hours until the terrorists left. Three of our sisters, Franny, Celia, and Gloria, were at the parish that day. The other two, Carmen and Genoveva, were away. Fr. Narciso was there too."

He goes on to talk about how they ransacked several buildings, including his parish residence, office, and the sisters' convent. They stole and destroyed things in the process. But the worst part, he tells me, was what he saw the next morning. Townspeople took him out to a hill where they had executed six local leaders who were involved in development projects or the *rondas*, a local civil defense group supported by the military to oppose the terrorists. Then he chokes up as he tells me how he saw their frozen and bloodied bodies that had been left on the hill overnight. The people had been afraid to move them. Sr. Franny took charge and had the people cover the bodies. "We prayed over them," he says, "and asked the people to come to church for a mass." Then after a pause, "I keep seeing those bodies … and I have been waking up at three or four in the morning full of adrenaline, hyper-alert for any danger, and not able to go back to sleep."

I ask, "How are you coping with all that?"

"Not very well I'm afraid."

How would I cope? I wonder. Would I leave? Would I stay? I have no answer.

A week later we're at the meeting of the Maryknoll priests, sisters, and lay missioners of the area. Part of the meeting is dedicated to reflecting on the violence. We start with Bob who talks about how he is trying to handle the Moho situation. The sisters have pulled back from the parish for the time being. He is going there periodically with Brother Leo Shedy to be supportive of the people, but finding it personally very difficult after the attack and executions. Sr. Pat Ryan reviews how representatives of the Vicaría went out two days after the attack to investigate and show support for Moho. The attackers had stolen the radio communication system, which was the only means to get communication out from that remote area in a timely way. So there was a delay in even finding out about the attack. She discusses alternative ways to communicate in emergency situations in remote areas, like sending a trusted messenger on the next bus or car going out. She makes the recommendation that there be more contact between the team in Moho and its closest neighbor, the team in Huancané. And for all of us, she suggests we need to develop more connected and supportive ways of being in relationship with each other and a system of more regular communication with those in remote areas.

Then we reflect together on the growing presence of Sendero in the country overall and their stepped-up attacks on Church workers. They seem to be entering a new and more brutal phase of operations. As the weight of this descends on us, someone finally verbalizes one of our deepest fears saying, "For the first time it seems possible that if things continue the way they are going, Sendero could actually pull this off and take over the country."

In the silence that follows, we all give some knowing nods of agreement. Then, for the first time, we begin to speak openly about our worst fears. We talk about the growing number of threats against Church workers. We talk about the "what if"—if any of us gets a death threat from Sendero. We ask ourselves: do we stay here no matter what because we have a commitment to serve the people? Or does there come a time to exercise prudence and get out? There is an uneasy consensus that each of us would have to make that individual decision and that would be respected. Or there might be a collective decision if, for example, the Maryknoll leadership decided to pull everyone out. We agree it is helpful to talk about it, and that that is something we have not done enough of, as much as we wish we could avoid having to deal with it. Someone punctuates the end of our discussion by saying, "None of us signed up to be in the middle of a civil war when we came to Peru, but here we are, and we have to deal with it."

~·~·~

Last night I dreamt I was about to conduct the graveside service for my father's funeral. He is still very much alive but in the dream he had died. I was preparing some Aymara ritual objects to use in the service back in my hometown. I was about to cry, thinking about how I would speak of the wonderful experiences we shared when he and Mom came to visit me in

Peru. As the dream continued, I recalled the intimate father-son conversation Dad and I shared sitting on the mountainside overlooking Machu Picchu, and how we had grown so much closer over these many years since my childhood experiences. What is the meaning of the dream? Love, death, and elements of my two cultural worlds are all mixed together. Eventually I'm going to need to find a new level of integrating these two worlds into the one world of my life.

It has been a whirlwind of activity since I returned from my furlough in the US. I have been investing time in establishing the supervisor-supervisee relationship with Ricardo for his pastoral year in the parish. I am finding I really enjoy his company. I have met with the Seminarian Commission of the Prelature of Juli and I've also gone to the seminary in Juliaca to meet individually with the three seminarians I work with on behalf of the Commission. And I feel good about the recent session I led for the monthly Pastoral Theological Reflection process I initiated with our Maryknoll group.

In the process of these various meetings and overnights in Puno, I have been able to talk more personally with those I'm working with. In spite of the growing fears, these meetings and gatherings have given me a feeling of accomplishment in being able to make some real contributions to life here. It is proving good for me to invest more in these connections beyond my parish work in Yunguyo, about which I have been feeling increasingly less enthusiastic. All of this is shifting the dynamic of how Donald and I work with and relate to each other. Or not, as the case increasingly seems to be. It is no longer the mentor-mentee relationship we had at the beginning. I have become more confident and competent in going about my work in the prelature, and more independent and less in need of Donald's mentoring. Unfortunately, the change is not a smooth one in our relationship. Much later in my journey, a psychologist would tell me that this kind of evolution in a mentoring relationship like we had "seldom ends well."

9

FIESTA

October–November 1991

I am getting ready to concelebrate the opening mass with Donald for the biggest event of the year. It will overtake everything for the coming week in Yunguyo. It is October 10, the Feast Day of *Tata Pancho*, the affectionate local nickname for *San Francisco de Borja*, a.k.a. St. Francis Borgia, who was born in Spain. He became the third Superior General of the Jesuits in 1565 and was the one who first sent them to Peru. His statue is positioned up front on a tall portable platform, the *andas*, designed to be carried in procession. The statue is adorned with an elaborate set of new clothes provided by one of the sponsors and is surrounded by tall candles competing for space with huge vases of flowers presented by devotees.

For the past week, I have been hearing music groups practicing in the streets late into the night in preparation for the festivities. Each night it seemed like they made a point of passing around the church close to our house so we could be awakened by the music coming through our open bedroom windows after bouncing off the courtyard walls. The repetitive high-pitched melody of their flutes, their *quenas*, is playing like a recording in my head as I put on my vestments for the mass.

I see the *alferados* processing in before mass starts to take their front-row seats. They are the sponsors of the week-long festivities. This means each sponsor family spends more money than they can afford to bring together a large group of elaborately costumed dancers accompanied by an equally large band. Each group goes on public display in the procession of folkloric dances in the plaza after mass. It is a sign of prestige and social advancement to be an alferado. There is a lot of competition and social pressure to be the best sponsoring family. Alferados also host their musicians and dance group, extended family, friends, and anyone who happens to appear all week in their house, providing lots of food and a truckload of beer. Many cases of beer are brought as gifts by family members and associates. The name of the donor and number of cases are carefully written down in a notebook because the host is expected to reciprocate one day in this Aymara system of reciprocity.

The expense of being an alferado, in some cases, tragically means children suffer with insufficient food and clothing afterward. Seeing this, the parish team has had an ongoing campaign to get the alferados to scale it down to a more "reasonable" level. It never works of course. The culture of fiesta as a time to pull out all the stops has deep roots. Fiesta is a time to step out of the harshness of life and renew the sense of joy and the bonds of family and community. It is a time to honor your patronal saint and seek favors and protection. For all these reasons and more, you just don't go halfway.

Initially, I embraced the doomed team efforts to get the alferados to be more "practical." But this year I am approaching the fiesta with the theme of "let it be." I'm trying to live more in the spirit of the Serenity Prayer that begins, "God grant me the serenity to accept the things I cannot change."

The change in my approach has come with how I've been wrestling with the virtue of humility and trying to be less controlling in my approach to life. It is part of the new spiritual journey I began last month with the writings of St. Teresa of Avila, the sixteenth-century Spanish mystic and Doctor of the Church. I had been searching for something to get me out of the dryness I was experiencing in prayer. It felt blocked, like I had lost my connection to God and was wandering in the wilderness. Then one day, I was poking around the Center House library in Puno and discovered the three-volume set of Theresa's writings. When I randomly opened one of the volumes and read a few pages, it was like discovering gold. I began reading from her writings every day. In the *Interior Castle* she teaches that to advance in prayer, you need to grow in humility, to honestly examine and know yourself deeply, and acknowledge the faults and failings you need to work on. I've had to recognize the controlling and judgmental part of me that can be hurtful to others. It has been a hard reckoning, and depressing at times. In the next line of the Serenity Prayer one asks for "courage to change the things I can." Not an easy or quick process, but this feels like steps in the right direction.

At the conclusion of the opening mass, those honored to do so act in unison to lift the *andas* holding *Tata Pancho*. They take hold of the poles that extend out from the front and back and rest them on their shoulders. The solemn procession begins down the long church aisle. They pause just outside the church door as someone climbs a ladder and places a wide-brimmed hat on *Tata Pancho* to protect his balding head from the sun. It is a tradition to let him know he is being taken care of as a beloved member of this community. We walk in procession around the plaza to the cadence of religious songs, interspersed with a pause for blessings and prayers at each corner. When we arrive back at the church entrance, *Tata Pancho* is parked outside prominently facing the plaza. Donald and I remove our vestments in church and return to sit with local officials next to *Tata Pancho*. Ten groups of dancers and musicians are lining up around the plaza. They will perform as they pass by *Tata Pancho*, who is holding court over it all.

The most striking dance is the *diablada*, named for the devil figure. The dancer representing the devil is ornately costumed with a huge winged cape and elaborately ornamented pants and shoes. Covering his head like a helmet is an outsized mask with red flames curling outward, big bulging eyes, and flaring nostrils. I am attracted like a child to fire as the figure dances and spins, freely weaving in and out of the phalanx of costumed dancers who move in rhythm to the music, a big step forward, a half step backward, a full twirl, twenty dancers moving as one. St. Michael the Archangel with sword in hand weaves through the dancers pursuing the devil who has come up from the silver mines of Potosí deep in the earth. It's a reminder of the demons of the underworld of darkness and death. It is a dance of good vs. evil that in a chilling way evokes the deadly dance of the terrorists spreading like a cancer across this land.

The *diablada* is followed by nine other groups that come around the plaza to perform in front of *Tata Pancho* over the next three hours. After the dance, Bridget Meagher joins me for a walk through the festivities that continue informally all over town. She is a Maryknoll lay missioner working in Juli where she started a women's cooperative to help market their embroidery work. I am enjoying our walk, enjoying being able to relax with someone from my own culture.

Lately I have been questioning if I can ever really have a place in this culture. For all that I have learned about the culture, I realize more than ever that I will never be fully part of it. I will always be, to one degree or another, an outsider, a person connected to another world with resources that people here cannot access. My white skin is like a billboard that says, "Foreigner from Rich Country." The language and culture will never be the ones of my birth. I will never be able to speak and act within the Aymara world without having to think about or second guess whether I am getting it right. These questions about my cultural competency and my place here add another layer of stress to my life. There are times lately when I find myself counting the remaining months of my contract, wondering if I will be able to see it through.

The last day of October has arrived. I'm thinking about how Halloween will be celebrated tonight back home. Here, it is the beginning of three days of honoring the dead and letting them know they are not forgotten. From the courtyard outside the parish house I can see kites flying over the cemetery to help guide the spirits of loved ones to earth where their families are waiting for them. Tombs are being washed, weeds pulled, and debris cleaned up.

On November 1, families bring lots of food and drink to the cemetery. It is a festive atmosphere. They carefully arrange the favorite foods of loved ones on their tombs and place flowers all around to let them know they are part of the gathering. Today, as I enter the area, music and laughter are floating over the cemetery like the unseen spirits of the dead. One family after another beckons me to offer prayers and a blessing with holy water at each tomb. The family celebrations will go on through the night and into the next day. I have developed a deep appreciation for these days of family solidarity, days to gather and commune with loved ones who have died, days to share, to love, to reconcile, to cry and laugh together.

It is a stark contrast to the poverty of customs I have known in the US around remembering our deceased loved ones.

This is the third year I have joined in these Days of the Dead since my brother Lester died. He is much on my mind. The third year is one that families mark in a special way in the Aymara culture. I have often been asked to go to a family home in town or in the campo to celebrate a mass on the third anniversary of a loved one's death. The mass is followed by a celebration with music and dancing to mark the end of the formal time of mourning.

During the Days of the Dead, families who have lost loved ones in recent years set up memorial altars in their homes. Taking a cue from this, I set up a little memorial to Lester in my bedroom with his picture, flowers, and some candles. I spend my time there between celebrating masses in the church and doing blessings at the cemetery. I wish I had some of my own family around me. But, in the midst of my tears, it feels comforting to be with my brother in this way, and in that sense, I am with family.

In the evening, I join a small group of folks from church going house to house to visit the families with memorial altars. Light spilling into the darkness from an open door is an invitation to come in. At each house, we sing one of our familiar songs from church and offer prayers honoring the deceased. Then the family invites us to have a seat and serves us hot fruit punch and a small dessert before we go on to the next house. As we leave, another group comes in. This goes on in the homes well into the night. It reminds me of children going house to house trick-or-treating back home. In a way, this is the Peruvian version of trick-or-treat, but with a lot more heart and soul.

I am learning how to grieve communally, and how important it is to ritualize grief and take *time* with it. A measure of comfort has come to me through walking like a pilgrim with my grief into the sacred spaces of these families who have lost loved ones. Back home, when someone dies, we have a vigil the night before and then a funeral service and burial the next day and that is about it. There is an expectation that you will stop crying and just get on with your life after that. But grieving takes time. We have much to learn from the way people grieve in this culture. I am blessed to be here to experience it. It is in moments like this that I realize why I came, and why I am still here.

Experiences like this were bringing tremendous growth in my life, growth into a deeper realization of how important a strong network of supportive family and community relationships are for me to have the strength to carry on with my life and work, especially in times of grief and crisis. Increasingly I would find myself struggling with the question of whether there was enough to sustain me going forward or was it time to get out.

10

DEFLATED

December 1991–January 1992

A gust of fresh air came to town when Ricardo, who is an Aymara seminarian for the Prelature of Juli, began his pastoral internship with us last August after I returned from my two-month furlough in the US. In his first all-day pastoral team meeting, he seemed happy to be with us, outgoing, not afraid to join in the discussions, and his ready laughter was like fresh leaven in the mix. He expressed an enthusiasm for working with youth in the parish, which we happily encouraged him to do. Indeed, since he started with us three months ago, he has shown himself to be very capable and self-motivated in his work with them, even charismatic. Donald as pastor agreed to Ricardo coming to live in the parish house with us. I was assigned by our Seminarian Commission to be his internship supervisor and have weekly supervisory meetings with him.

I was happy to take this on. I might not have articulated it as such at the time, but it was another step into coming into my own as a pastoral worker in the prelature. I had a feeling of confidence about entering into this professional relationship. I wanted it to go well and to do it right (there's that perfectionist streak popping up again!). And, looking back, I was also unconsciously hoping Ricardo would bring a fresh and more relational dynamic to the living situation in the house. What I couldn't see was that with their opposite personalities it was almost inevitable that there would be conflict. I had no idea how damaging and discouraging those conflicts would turn out to be.

At one point, Ricardo pursued a friendship with a young lady at the convent who was exploring becoming a sister. There is always the possibility for a seminarian to fall in love and go in a different direction with life, since priests are not allowed to get married. I saw it as part of life for a seminarian who has to sort these things out in his life. Donald was disturbed by it and reported it to the bishop. I was furious that he had gone over my head and I told him so. He did not respond, so the tensions just stayed hanging there between us. It probably was just as well he didn't respond to me. He surely felt my anger and the situation could easily have escalated into a shouting match with my tendency to explode in anger like my dad did. It's an explosive anger I grew up with that got baked into my personality.

I remember all too well the time when my dad exploded in an argument with my oldest brother Bill, a teenager at the time, and physically threw him out of the house. He landed face down on the gravel driveway which left him bruised and bleeding. I was a little boy standing just outside the house the whole time, hearing the shouting inside and then watching horrified as Dad ejected my brother from the house. As children we learn behavior from our parents and eventually have to sort through it as adults.

Unfortunately for Donald and me, since neither one of us was willing or able at the time to address the tension between us, it would only get worse as more conflicts inevitably came up and were not resolved. I really liked Ricardo, and my supervisory relationship with him was meeting some of my need to have someone in the house I could relate to more easily. But the conflicts were quickly overshadowing that as things got more and more negative between Donald and Ricardo and, as a result, between Donald and me.

~~~

So now it's December and I am struggling to figure out how things have taken such a turn for the worse among us. I can't help but think that one of the reasons for the growing conflict comes from the fact that I am Ricardo's supervisor and Donald is not. Donald is not in the "father" role as mentor to Ricardo like he was with me when I first arrived, and Ricardo has no inclination to take on the role of the obedient and deferential "son" to Donald. I see more and more that Donald is an extreme introvert with a lone-ranger disposition at his core. Ricardo is the extreme extrovert who needs to have people around him and to interact with them as much as possible. The tensions seem to be exacerbated by their seeming inability to talk directly to each other about whatever is going on between them and my inability to effectively mediate.

Christmas does not overtake life around here like it does in the US. I got a clue my first Christmas here when there was no scheduled arrival of Santa Claus coming to town on a fire truck, or even on a sleigh pulled by a pack of llamas for that matter. It is mostly a nonevent in the rural communities. In town there are at least some activities. At the church in Yunguyo, we have an expansive manger scene including scenes and symbols of local life brought to us this year by Ricardo and the youth group. We sing Christmas carols in Spanish called *villancicos*, including a warm-spirited *villancicos* competition on Christmas Eve. Christmas morning there is a community-sponsored free cup of chocolate with a *pancito* the size of an English muffin for each of the thousand or so children. They stream into the main plaza from both town and countryside to receive what for many is a rare treat. It is the children that touch me the most. Watching them sit in little groups in the plaza consuming their treat, smiling and laughing, you'd think they'd just been gifted gold from the magi. And it did not take a thousand gifts under a tree to bring this moment of joy to town.

The day after Christmas, our parish team begins our annual two-day evaluation and pastoral planning session. I can't help but think to myself, *What parish team in the US would ever meet for two days right after Christmas!?* None! Never! I would be declared certifiably insane if I were to suggest this in a parish back in Michigan. Two different worlds, two different rhythms of parish life.

On New Year's Eve, there are some visiting sisters at the convent and we are all invited to join in a New Year's Eve celebration. The evening unfolds with music, laughter, good food, and libations, and even some dancing as we bid farewell to 1991 and welcome 1992. The fact that we were all able to celebrate together in the same room gives me a sliver of hope that we can all get along.

A few days later, however, I am riding with Donald in his truck on the way to Puno where I have a meeting of the Seminarian Commission. On the way I share some of the plans the Commission has for the coming year, including some formation events with the seminarians in February. His immediate reaction is, "Who's going to pay for it?" And then he proceeds to question the value of holding those events at all.

Money clearly is not the real issue. We have a very small budget from the prelature and are careful with it. So where is this negativity really coming from? Does Donald resent that I am spending more time with the Commission and less time at the parish? Or is it just more negativity about Ricardo showing itself in another way? Maybe some of both.

It makes me wonder what am I doing in Yunguyo. Why am I putting up with this? I should just leave and move to another place to finish out my contract. But what would happen with Ricardo? Is my commitment to working with Ricardo toward priesthood reason enough to stay? I am not one to back out of commitments easily. So for now, perhaps it is.

I continue to pray with the works of St. Teresa of Avila that call for humility, as I try to let go of my anger and frustrations, and trust what God can bring out of the conflicts. I am just the clay and God is the potter. But really, God, I would much rather be the one punching and shaping the clay. Can we go half and half on that?

Some days later there is an explosion of anger on Donald's part over youth having been in the parish hall and his judgment that they had left it in total disarray. He is putting the blame on Ricardo. In reality it was a high school religion teacher there with his class of students. I am furious at what I judge to be the injustice of putting the blame on Ricardo without waiting to get any other sides of the story. Like a mother bear protecting her cub, I tear into Donald and conclude with, "If you are going to turn this into another campaign against Ricardo, I'm leaving." At which point I abruptly turn and go to my room.

Well, so much for humility. When my anger button gets pushed, I can get just as explosively angry as Donald just did. The whole situation feels like the straw that broke the camel's back. It has shattered my hope that a new spirit might emerge in the house with Ricardo's presence. Just the opposite has happened, leaving me feeling more emotionally distraught than ever. I am sitting on my bed, head in my hands, depressed like never before, tears running down my face. What was I even thinking? What the terrorists couldn't accomplish, Donald has. I have no heart for being here anymore. I want to flee from it all like an emotional refugee. Instead of having a growing spirit of community and support in the house in this atmosphere of terrorism in the country, just the opposite is happening. I am feeling emotionally drained and all the more vulnerable to the impact of fear of violence. Instead of feeling more emotionally nourished, I'm feeling malnourished and all the more weakened. As a malnourished child is way more susceptible to disease, I'm all the more vulnerable to having the effects of living in a time of terrorism and government oppression overcome me and take me down.

～〜ゝ

A weekend away from the parish gives me a reprieve. Ricardo and I are in Ilave for the gathering of young people interested in priesthood, planned by our Seminarian Commission. The energy is good and I am again reminded how important and life-giving my involvements outside the parish are.

Monday morning when I'm back in the parish I remember the article in *America* magazine I read last week that brought me to tears. The title is "Mr. Mike's White Mama, Here She Go." It's about a skeptical California mom who visits her son. He has chosen to work in an African American school connected to a parish in an underserved North Philadelphia neighborhood. As she meets the people there, she realizes that he has been accepted and welcomed into the community and is blossoming. Now she is in the church, listening to him sing a black spiritual with all his heart and soul. She had never heard him sing before. It deeply moves her and she realizes that the emotionally cold life he had growing up never allowed that part of him to emerge. She bursts into tears. People come over to her and she is overwhelmed by the warmth, understanding, and encouragement of this community of faith and love.

Rereading the story now, I realize what it was that brought me to tears. Like the mom in the story, God brought me to this place and culture so different from my own to soften my heart and teach me what is most important in life. I need community, warmth, love, and friendship if I am going to survive and thrive in life going forward. By my reckoning, Donald is not able to offer that in anything close to the degree to which I need that right now. He has given me much, especially in the way he mentored me early on, but precious little of any kind of emotionally supportive relationship beyond that. It is not his personality. I need to accept it and deal with reality.

I need to move on. I need to go home at the end of my contract, back to friends and family and to a place of ministry where terrorism is not a wrench in the works. I'm done with entertaining the possibility of renewing my contract with Maryknoll and continuing on in Peru. Case closed. I came with a desire to serve among the poor and marginalized. I chose to work in this parish because I put a high priority on working as part of a team. That has generally worked out. What I didn't understand then was how difficult it would be to live in a house that has turned out to be, from my side of the equation, too much of an emotional desert. In the past I coped by sending painful and scary emotions into deep freeze. I excelled at work and my studies to feel good about myself.

Now the tectonic plates of my life are shifting. Personal and nurturing relationships have moved way up on the priority list of what I need in life. The satisfaction and affirmation of doing good work and having some good working relationships are not sufficient. I don't see a realistic hope of finding sufficient relational nurture and support in Peru. Perhaps my relational skills are just too underdeveloped to make that happen here. Even more, the situation of civil war, and the fears and threats that brings, compounds the situation big time. It is time to make my way back home where at least political and social violence are not likely to be crashing in on me as I try to find a more healthy balance in my life that will allow me to survive emotionally, and hopefully, one day, even thrive.

11

MOVING ON

February–March 1992

How do you continue to stay once the decision has been made to leave? I have been doing some calculating. My contract with Maryknoll goes through August of next year. The plan with Maryknoll is that I go back to New York next year at the end of May for the re-entry program. That leaves me with a year and four months in Peru, including some travel away from Yunguyo that should help me keep my sanity. I could pursue terminating my contract early, but it feels like I would be taking off the backpack of my responsibilities and leaving it on the side of the road for someone else to pick up. I would be running away from commitments I have made with the Seminarian Commission, the Vicaría, and of course with Ricardo. It seems to be baked into my DNA that you don't break a commitment, except as a last resort after everything has been tried to make the commitment work. Still deeper is the spiritual journey, the inner growth that continues in the mystery of it all. God called me to this "desert" place and I said "yes," and with that yes I made a commitment.

~~~

I get a break from Yunguyo with my month of altitude leave this February. Maryknoll requires us to get down to sea level for four weeks after every five months in the Altiplano to recharge our batteries. Foreigners tend to get run down working at 12,500 feet and I have not been the exception. Since there are no meetings I need to be at in Lima, I am going to

Argentina to get together with Fr. Brian Sheridan who was my language partner in Cochabamba. After the last clash with Donald, I wrote a three-page letter to him, laying out how I was feeling about our conflicts. I expressed my deep discouragement and ended by saying, "I hardly know anymore what to think or feel about the conflicts we have been having." To date, he hasn't given me any response or even acknowledged receiving the letter. Maybe he just finds it overwhelming. After all, he didn't bargain for all this conflict either when he invited me to join the team in Yunguyo. If nothing else, it was good therapy for me to write the letter and express my feelings in a more measured and thoughtful way. Having done that, I feel a little more peace as I head off on this trip.

After a bus ride to La Paz, Bolivia, I fly to Buenos Aires where Brian has come in for some meetings with his fellow La Salette Missionaries. We are similar in age and our friendship grew in the crucible of our Spanish classes. A "class" in Cochabamba was two students with one teacher. There was no place to hide while the instructor drilled us in class. It was four hours each morning with a different instructor each hour.

When I see him, he looks trim as always with his sandy, brush-cut hair. The day after my arrival, his meetings end and we make the two-day bus trip to the parish he pastors in the town of Clodomira in northwestern Argentina. The warmth and welcome of the people Brian introduces me to is like salve on a wound. Their warmth is on full display when Brian celebrates a wedding mass—starting, as is customary, at 11:00 at night no less! At the part called the Sign of Peace, people freely flow around the church, hugging and kissing each other. Even as a visitor, I am hugged as much as anyone else.

After two relaxing weeks in Clodomira, I take a bus trip to visit places in neighboring Paraguay and the spectacular Iguazu Falls. By the final days of my altitude leave, I am feeling rested. Much of my tension has drifted away with the miles traveled and the hospitality I have received from Brian in Argentina and from the Jesuits I stayed with in Paraguay. I am ready to return to Yunguyo, come what may.

I arrive back in Yunguyo on March 3 with a feeling of resignation. I take a short walk to the shore of Lake Titicaca and all I see is dull water. The diamonds I have always seen sparkling on the waves in the sunlight seem to have sunk to the bottom of the sea. As I celebrate masses over the weekend, I feel some comfort in the familiarity of the music and ritual. And Ricardo's laughter buoys my spirits some. But other than that, my emotions seem to have flatlined, like the line you see on a heart monitor screen when a person's heart stops.

The next morning in our little prayer chapel, I meditate with Psalm 26, "Lord, teach me your ways, show me your path." I thought about how when I said yes to the missionary call and set out on this journey, I couldn't have known in advance where exactly the path would lead or what the journey would be like. In the midst of the difficulties I have encountered, I can only walk on with a sense of trust in God, even a blind trust at times. The path forward only unfolds in the walking. There are too many unknown consequences of one's decisions, too many circumstances beyond one's control for it to be otherwise. So onward I go.

~~~

In mid-March I am on my way to the airport in Juliaca to catch my flight to Lima. The Seminarian Commission asked me to represent them at a national vocations meeting. On the way, I stop in Chucuito where Mike Briggs has agreed to meet me for spiritual direction. It is a beautiful day so we decide to sit outside on the grounds of the retreat center overlooking the waves of Lake Titicaca lit up in the sun. A gentle breeze wafts through as I begin talking about the turmoil of my life in Yunguyo. I tell him about the letter I wrote to Donald before I went on altitude leave and my frustration with his lack of response. Mike wisely encourages me to set up a time with Donald to talk face-to-face about the things I brought up in the letter. It's the kind of thing I would rather avoid, but I tell him I will give it a try. It is a helpful push in the right direction. But still, I hate dealing with conflict.

I tell him how I have been trying to figure out and better understand Donald's personality. In the parish teams I was on back home, we did some work on personality differences as a way to help us appreciate and accept the different styles and gifts of each member of the team. I tell him how it seems that Donald operates a lot in the realm of ideas and projects and seems to be most energized when starting a new big project. The downside is that he tends to move on from the previous project, like he did with Plan NIP and then left it mostly up to the staff to carry on as he moved on to his grain mill project. There is a tendency to connect with people more according to how they can help with his projects. Feelings and attending to relationships seem to be low on his felt needs and he has a high need for privacy.

Mike comments that my observations seem to mostly fit with what he knows of Donald, that he seems to have kind of a "Lone Ranger" style of operating in the prelature. But then he adds, "Still, I think it would be good to have that conversation with Donald about how you are feeling as we talked about earlier."

"Well, you are probably right. With my personality, I would rather avoid dealing directly with the conflict. When I get back to Yunguyo after this trip to Lima, I will ask him for a time to meet. Hopefully that way we can sit down and talk more calmly. I need to do this for myself if nothing else. He is not likely to be very responsive. In his mind he has probably already just moved on. I'll just have to accept that."

With that, we wrap up and I am off to Lima.

A week later, I return to the Altiplano and go directly to the four-day formation program we have for our seminarians. I feel again the positive energy that comes as I engage in this work. This year, I will continue to work with five of our theology students at the seminary in Juliaca. After I arrive back in Yunguyo, I set up a time to meet with Donald.

I finally sit down with him at our dining room table and share as best I can my thoughts and feelings about our conflicts. He sits calmly in his chair, listens, and seems to take it in, but offers no response. I maintain my outward calm even though my nerves are jangled. After a pause with no reaction from Donald, I state rather matter-of-factly how I see things going forward, that I see myself working half time in the parish and the other half of my time in the work with the Seminarian Commission and the Vicaría team. He makes no objection.

We both get up from the table and head in different directions, he to his office-bedroom down the hall and I out the kitchen door to take a walk. I can't help but think how my talk with Donald was so different from the mentor-mentee and sort of father-son dynamic we began with at that same dining room table when I first arrived. I wonder what the shift means for Donald; what does it feel like from his side? I doubt I will ever know. From what I can tell, processing feelings is not his thing. He just moves on and doesn't dwell on the past. That's his world. Apparently it works for him and I need to acknowledge that. It's one style among many in the mix of life.

For my part I feel some calm after the storm. I have carved out more space to work in outside the parish and feel a little more at peace, for now at least, and better able to continue on with my life and work here in spite of the violence swirling around us in the country.

12

FEAR SEEPS INTO THE PORES OF MY SKIN

April–May 1992

Alejo Choque, an Aymara leader, just arrived with the news that three presumed terrorists are operating in Zepita, our neighboring parish to the south along the lakeshore. He runs the parish and wants me to inform the Vicaría. I invite him into the house. He declines my offer for some coffee and we sit down at the dining room table. His stocky frame, solid from a life of hard work, more than fills the chair. Fear is etched in his weather-beaten face.

A sense of urgency has overtaken Alejo's normally calm demeanor. "Some of my trusted people told me that strangers are gathering information in the area and have been asking about me. They think it is Sendero. They could be planning an attack on Zepita. I have to face the possibility that they could execute me like they shot those leaders in Moho. But I am determined to stay. I was born and raised there among the campesinos. I have done my best to serve them all these years and I can't abandon them now."

"You are a good man, Alejo," I try to assure him.

He continues, "And it is not just the terrorists. People in positions of power could take this as an opportunity to attack me and my family and blame it on the terrorists. Some of them are upset that I have been talking about human rights in the communities and bringing in the Vicaría to give courses. Townspeople who see themselves as superior resent that a campesino like me is leading the parish. It is getting harder to be sure about who are my friends and who are my enemies."

"We are here to support you in any way we can," I say, yet knowing there is no way to guarantee his safety. "You are welcome to stay here if you need to get away from Zepita for a while."

"Gracias, but I need to be there. Rumors spread fast and people are afraid."

"*Cuídese*, take care of yourself," I say. "And keep me informed. I will pass this on to the Vicaría, and to our team here in Yunguyo."

I feel shaken by this news that the terrorists may be closing in.

~~~

On April 6, I awake with the rest of the country to the news that late last night, President Alberto Fujimori suspended the constitution and dissolved the Congress and Judiciary. It is a move to concentrate the power of the state in his hands. This would not have been possible without the support of the military. The news media are calling it an *auto-golpe*, a self-coup. Fujimori is justifying this move by saying it was necessary to fight terrorism and corruption. Democracy is the loser. It's a constitutional crisis causing heightened anxiety across the country. God help us. I will call my parents tomorrow after I get a better read on things to reassure them I am ok. They will most likely hear the news about it in the US and be worried.

The next day I assure my parents that, for the moment, things are relatively calm after the self-coup. I don't tell them the full extent of what is happening, or what we fear may happen. It is a calm by force. The president and his military supporters have all the key opposition leaders in the capital under house arrest. President Fujimori has named a new cabinet. Now they will start issuing decrees as they choose. It probably means more repression is coming. The military will have a freer hand to do what they want under the banner of fighting terrorism and innocent people will suffer. It unnerves me even more than Alejo's news about terrorists in Zepita.

~~~

Last week I attended a three-day workshop at the Chucuito conference center on dealing with violence. Pastoral workers from across the region packed the conference room. Two psychologists from Lima, both women, facilitated. There was a mixture of foreign missionaries like myself and local Aymara religious leaders. The facilitators talked about the nature of violence and how, as the levels of violence have increased in the country, people's fears have escalated along with it. They stressed that in order to deal with the violence in a healthy way, it is essential to support one another. They emphasized the importance of talking about our feelings and emotions. A key issue that emerged in small-group discussions and feedback to the large group was that, for the most part, we have not had those kinds of conversations between Aymaras and foreign missionaries.

It is a question of trust, the psychologists told us. They put the challenge to us, "Can you trust each other with your fears and emotions?" I thought about how differences of culture and language make that more difficult. The fact that I am only able to speak a few words of Aymara is one of those barriers.

Near the end of the workshop, a marvelous thing happened in the small groups, which were intentionally culturally mixed. As we faced each other in the small circle I was in, we were able to talk about some of our feelings in my group, especially the fears of violence and terrorism. I felt the barriers drop. Tears of gratitude welled up in my eyes. In the large group feedback it was obvious other groups had had similar experiences.

In a closing reflection, the presenters commented that, "It is a sign of a community's health and strength if it can continue to celebrate life, even in a time of violence. If a community stops celebrating, the people have lost their will to survive. But that is not the case here," they noted. "The people of this area still know how to celebrate! We affirm that and we thank you for the opportunity to be here." A round of applause broke out for them and just as much in affirmation of ourselves. I felt some renewed hope and strength about continuing my work here.

Today I am on my way to just such a celebration like the psychologists talked about. The sun is shining brightly as I drive my Land Cruiser with three team members to the community of *Quimsa Cruz* to celebrate their feast day mass. *Quimsa*, three, refers to May 3, the feast of the Exaltation of the Cross, or *Cruz*, for which the community is named. It is a relatively short drive to the chapel perched on a hill overlooking the sparkling waters of Lake Titicaca. A large cross stands prominently next to the chapel. After the mass, we are taken to the nearby house of the fiesta *padrino*, the sponsor for this year. We are seated on benches arranged outdoors in a big square where we have a view overlooking the lake and the snow-capped mountains of Bolivia. There is a moment of reverential silence as the opening libation is offered to Pachamama. Then as food and drink are served, laughter bubbles over like the foam spewing out of the big bottles of beer being popped open. Before long, the music begins and people are dancing on the patch of dirt that has been cleared for the celebration. The fiesta is on, and the tensions of recent days fade into the background. This is what a fiesta means to do, take you into a different time, fiesta time. If you let go and jump in, it transports you out of the ordinary drudgery of life and reminds you how good life can be. And today, in this community, life is good.

~~~

Near the end of May, I fly down to Lima for the annual Maryknoll assembly of the Peru Region. I arrive at the Center House on May 23. All the talk is about the massive car bomb that was set off last night in the neighboring San Isidro District of Lima. The news outlets are all over it, reporting that 400 kilos of dynamite were detonated by Sendero Luminoso in the high-rise business district. The next day, I open the Sunday morning paper and stare in near disbelief at the huge spread of pictures and stories detailing the horror of it. I look off in that direction for a moment, aware that it is not all that far from where I am sitting. I read on: up to $40 million in damage, thirty-two people hurt, sixty-eight businesses and seventy-seven apartments damaged, many severely.

I am eerily drawn to go see it. The feeling takes me back to the time on our family farm when our neighbor's barn went up in flames. You could see the plume of smoke from three miles away and hear the sirens of the fire trucks approaching. You knew it was bad, but there was an irresistible urge to go see it for yourself. People from miles around, our family included, got in their cars and trucks and headed to the scene of destruction. We were like moths drawn to a flaming torch on a summer night.

When I finish reading the article, I calculate it's about a ten-minute walk from the Center House to downtown San Isidro, twenty minutes at most. I head off alone, walking down the streets, feeling a growing dread at what I am about to see. A chill runs up my spine at the thought that terrorists could still be there. But no, I reason, they would have done the deed and fled long before the police arrived. *Why am I doing this?* No good answer comes. I just feel drawn there, almost compelled to go, as if a demon from the underworld were pulling me forward. What is it about evil and disasters that attract us? I think of how some people are attracted to horror movies. Except this is real. I walk on.

A few minutes later the scene of the blast comes into view. Pictures I saw years ago of bombed out Beirut, Lebanon, flash through my mind. But this is not a distant war zone on a television screen. It's as real as the train that hit my car when I was sixteen. I stop in a stone-cold stare. A few feet ahead of me a crater crouches in the street where the car bomb went off in front of the hulking remains of a bank building. A charred and twisted chassis is all that is left of the car that cradled the bomb. The crater is easily fifteen feet wide and rimmed with the tar-like remains of what became molten asphalt in the fiery bomb blast. The vehicle's gas tank must have exploded along with it. My gaze moves across the street and creeps up the blown-out front of a ten-story apartment building. The apartments are open like a movie set, naked and vulnerable. Twisted remains of window frames hang in the air. I see kitchens where someone's mother might have been washing dishes when the blast went off. And living rooms where children might have been playing. A shiver slides down my spine as my gaze descends back to ground level. Then the dead silence registers in my brain. Where are all the people? Where are the police? Is everyone except me staying away in fear? A burst of fear seeps into the pores of my skin like radiation after an atomic blast.

I need to get out of here before some terrorist in hiding comes after me or someone thinks I was involved in this. I turn and walk as quickly as I can back toward the safety of the Center House. Even the Center House and the area around it feel more vulnerable now. The House is only a block away from the Óvalo Gutiérrez, a sprawling traffic circle with a small park in the middle. I pass through it on walks I take to the bluff overlooking the ocean. Around the Óvalo is a grocery store I have been to, a movie theater I have sat in, a large church, and other businesses. A car bomb could just as easily be set off in front of any of those places. A shudder courses my body from head to toe. I gotta stop thinking about it. The regional meeting starts tomorrow.

The next morning I am lingering over a cup of coffee. The others who were sitting at my table have left to take a break before the meeting begins. Tom Burns, a Maryknoll priest, comes through the dining room doors and sits down across from me. He came in for the meeting from Ciudad de Dios where he lives and works. I first got to know him while I was getting my documents to start working in Peru. He looks tired and drawn. His thick black hair and beard are in their usual scramble. "Good morning Tom, how are you?" I ask, concerned and not just making polite conversation.

"Hi Fred. Things are bad. The terrorist activity is getting worse in our area. The violence and infiltration of youth groups in Lima are on the rise. They're getting bolder every day."

"I heard María Elena Moyano was murdered out in your area last February. Horrible."

"Yes, I knew her personally." His face turns ashen and his eyes glass over as he sinks into the memory.

It was national news. María Elena Moyano was a local heroine among the people in the *pueblos jóvenes* around Lima. She was a political and social activist who had been helping the poor organize community services like the *Vaso de Leche* program to feed the children, and community kitchens where neighbors organize to feed their families. Local leaders emerged from those programs, especially among the women. María Elena was known to give fiery speeches at events in the neighborhoods that inspired people to keep organizing. Most dangerous of all for her, she promoted nonviolence and spoke against the violent methods of the terrorists.

"It rips me apart that this good woman is dead," Tom says, as he cradles the side of his face in his left hand. "It still seems like it was just yesterday. She was a leader who brought hope and inspiration to the people."

"How did it happen?" I softly ask.

"She had just given a speech the day before in the barrio calling on the people to organize, calling for justice, and denouncing the violence of the terrorists. She had been receiving death threats for some time, but she never backed down. That night she was attending a baptism party. It was a big celebration with a lot of family and friends from the neighborhood crowded together in the family's home. Suddenly a shot rang out and a bomb was tossed at her in the midst of the party. She and others around her were blown to bits."

I recoil at the horror of it. Images of body parts strewn about pour into my mind like water rushing into a torpedoed submarine. Here was the hero, hope for the people, someone working nonviolently among the poor, bringing palpable change for the better. Here was light against the darkness. Her life of heroic goodness violently snuffed out. Where will it end? Is nothing sacred anymore? I go back to my room and the dam bursts, sending a river of sorrow down my cheeks.

There seems to be no limit to the means of destruction these terrorists will use to pursue their goal of tearing down the existing order so they can build some imagined utopia. Yes, there is much corruption and injustice in the country. Yes, the existing system is rotten in many ways. But I believe with all my remaining ounces of strength that nothing good can come from this embodiment of evil, and that whatever else is wrong with the existing order of things, what the terrorists have to offer is exponentially worse. They offer terror in a rage against the system. Terror that leaves no one feeling safe anywhere at any time. Terror that will never make our world a better place.

I look at the clock. It is time for the week-long meeting to begin. I collect myself and go down the wooden staircase to join the others already seated in the chapel.

13

DEATH STRIKES LIKE A TERRORIST

July 1992

I have often heard people say death comes in threes. *Is it true, really?* I would ask myself. Generally no, but often enough there are those times. Today would be one of those days.

～～

It's July 3 and Ricardo and I are just finishing breakfast when the phone rings. The old black rotary phone sits on a slim wooden stand by the dining room table. Ricardo picks up the handset. I can tell by the grim look on his face and his rapid responses in Aymara that something is wrong. After a brief conversation, he hangs up and tells me, "My cousin died, the one who was badly burned in the house fire last week. I need to go and be with my family."

"By all means, go. I'm so sorry," I say to him. We give each other a quick hug. He hurries down the hall to gather up a few things from his room and is off to catch the next transport out of town.

At 11:00 a.m., three men from a nearby campo community ask me to come right away to their house. A family member is near death, they tell me, and could I come to anoint him and pray with the family. I keep my ritual book, simple stole, oil for the anointing of the sick, and a plastic bottle of holy water in my Aymara-style shoulder bag. I sling it over my head and let it drape down my right side, prepared to celebrate what apparently will be last rites. It is not very far so I hop on my bicycle. When

I enter the house, they introduce me to Felipe, a man in his fifties who is lying in bed flat on his back, covered with a blanket, and barely conscious. I pray with him and the family, anointing his forehead, hands and feet, and then remain at his side to keep vigil with him. After a few minutes, he slips away. There he is. One minute alive among us, the next minute he is not. I bless his body with holy water and offer the prayers for the deceased with the family gathered around. When I arrive back at the parish, I slip into the church and say a prayer for Felipe and his family, grateful I could make it in time to accompany them in that liminal moment of his passing. Two deaths and it is only midday.

At 2:00 p.m., we start our scheduled parish team meeting with a mass marking the second anniversary of the death of Sr. Maria Gabriela's brother. She is from Antioch, Colombia. If she were home, she would attend mass with her extended family and spend the day with them. It is part of missionary life that often one cannot be with family at such important moments. And so we fill in for her family as best we can.

The team meeting finishes at 5:00 p.m. and we stay to have coffee with Sr. Maria. Suddenly, one of the children of Eugenio, our parish secretary and office manager who is with us, comes running in, scared and out of breath, to say that Javier, his older brother, is fainting at the house. We immediately get up and run to Eugenio's house a few blocks away. Javier is barely conscious, seemingly unaware of what is happening around him and unable to respond when we ask him what is wrong.

His body is convulsing with his jaw clenched shut and saliva is flowing from his mouth. There is no such thing as an ambulance so I lift him in my arms and carry him the short distance to what barely passes for a public hospital in Yunguyo. A doctor makes his best guess that it is an epileptic attack and gives him a shot of phenobarbital. As we keep vigil with Javier in the cold and stark hospital room, the doctor is nowhere in sight. When we ask for him we are simply told that he left because it was the end of his shift. Not a word to us or the nurse about what might happen next. It makes me furious—it seems like he just doesn't care, with a demeanor as cold and stark as the hospital room.

Javier continues to spew forth large quantities of saliva and then what appears to be globs of coagulated blood. It is all I can do to keep from throwing up at the sight of it. He remains unconscious, and then, suddenly, he is gone. It is less than two hours since he first told his younger brother that he was not feeling well. Death itself can strike like a terrorist.

We stand there in disbelief. None more so than his parents who had tragically lost another son four years ago. How is it possible that such a fine and talented young man, with so many possibilities for the future, so suddenly dies? I can't help but think that so much more could have been done for him at a good hospital in Lima or in the US.

We carry his body in slow motion back to the house and place him across the kitchen table, where relatives tenderly begin to wash the body. His parents struggle to make decisions about preparations for the funeral. Neighbors and family begin drifting in as word spreads. They speak of how he studied hard, was never one to roam the streets or get in trouble, how he was always helpful in the family. Eugenio and his wife, amid their sobs and tears, cry out to God, *"¡Dios mío! ¿Por qué, por qué?"* Their unanswerable "Why?" rings through the heavens like the ripple from a stone cast into the ocean until it dissipates into the vastness of the universe.

We stay with the family, offering what prayers and consolation we can until close to midnight.

The next evening, I go with the parish team and parish council members to the house for the vigil service. It is hard to believe that the young man I carried in my arms to the hospital yesterday is now laid out before us. Arrangements of flowers and tall candles stand vigil with us around the coffin. A bucket of holy water has been placed on the floor nearby. Those entering the house sprinkle the coffin, offering a blessing and a prayer in silence. Soon we start the vigil service of songs, prayers, and scripture readings. We struggle to find words that might help comfort the family. Moments of silence and our presence seem to speak best in the end.

After the vigil service, we stay with all those gathered and continue to keep vigil with the family. The room inside is packed so I sit with Donald and Ricardo on the patio where benches have been arranged in a big square. The winter night is cold as death itself. As the all-night vigil proceeds, the ritual sharings are circulated—a bottle of *pisco anisado* that is poured into a shot glass for each person, then packs of cigarettes, and small bags of coca leaves for each to chew. After a short stay, Donald leaves. Ricardo and I stay longer into the night for several rounds of the ritual sharing. My head is buzzing from the cigarettes. There is a subdued hum of people talking to one another and some occasional laughter. Most will remain through the night. I take some small comfort in knowing the family will not be alone in their grief.

The funeral mass is scheduled for 2:00 p.m. Sunday in the church. At 1:00 I go to the house to offer some prayers. Then all who have gathered carry the coffin, the flowers, and the weight of their grief to the church. A cross bearer heads up our informal procession. Donald is the main celebrant for the funeral mass and offers words of condolences to the family. With that, we make the short journey on foot to the *panteón*, the cemetery on the southern edge of town. Donald and I walk behind the cross-bearer followed by six men shouldering the casket. A dirge emanates from the musicians who accompany us. At the burial site, several people speak about Javier's goodness. His parents bless the site with their copious tears. Finally, the casket is lowered into the ground next to his brother Johnny. The soft thuds of the handfuls of earth we release over the casket intone the final farewell before two men with shovels fill in the grave.

The sadness of it all weighs me down, but for Javier's parents, their grief must be near unbearable. What do you say or do in the face of such a tragic death? Some of the answer is found in the rituals of the Aymara people, in the communal expressions that let us know we are not alone, and that some answers must remain beyond our mortal knowing in the *Alaxpacha*, the world above, when words fail us, in the depths of our grief.

14

PART OF THE FAMILY

August 1992

I'm looking forward to spending the first half of August with a delegation from Michigan led by Cris Doby, a friend and Director of the Office of Peace and Justice Ministry in my home diocese. With the tensions in my living situation, the tragic death of Javier that still haunts me, and the ever-encroaching terrorist activity in this remote corner of the world, having a delegation from the US visit and take an interest in what is going on means an awful lot. Plus, it will give me another much-needed break away from Yunguyo.

I make the four-hour bus trip to meet the delegation at the La Paz, Bolivia, airport. When they emerge from the plane, there are smiles and hugs from Cris and the other members of the delegation. We spend a couple of days in Yunguyo where I give them a taste of my life and work in the parish, then on to Juli, and the Vicaría in Puno. I am delighted as they make connections with the human rights work at the Vicaría and talk about ways of generating some funding and support from Michigan.

The day after the Vicaría visit, we take the ten-hour train ride across the Altiplano to Cusco, the historic capital of the Inca Empire. The next morning we head to Machu Picchu, which involves an all-day train ride through the Sacred Valley and along the Urubamba River. We descend from eleven thousand feet to sixty-seven hundred feet at the town of Aguas Calientes at the base of the steep mountains cradling the ruins. From there, we board a small tourist bus for the twenty-minute ride up the steep switchback mountain road, taking us to the entrance of Machu Picchu at eight thousand feet. As we snake up the mountain, it feels like at any minute the bus could slip over the edge of the narrow road that has no guardrails and crash in the rocky ravine below. Finally, safely at the top, we settle into our comfortable hotel rooms just a stone's throw from the entrance to the ruins.

I have been to Machu Picchu three times before this. Each time, the mystery and beauty of it has captivated me all the more. Nobody knows for sure why the Incas built this complex in such a remote area on the edge of the jungle. The speculation is that it was a resort for Inca royalty. I can never get enough of it. It is an incredible complex of intricate and masterful design. It has its own Temple of the Sun, various ceremonial structures, a water system, and separate residence areas for royalty, priests, craftsmen, and laborers who worked the terraced fields, all perched on some of the steepest mountains of the Andes.

Early the next morning, we head for the entrance gate as misty clouds roll up like billowing incense from the steep valley below. Soon the sun is shining brilliantly over it all. It is going to be a great day.

With the delegation back in Michigan, I return to Yunguyo. When I meet with Ricardo, he recounts to me how Donald got on his case about something. After hearing the details of the story, I can't see where Ricardo did much of anything wrong so I am not sure what to make of it.

A couple of days later, I finally sit down with Donald and just ask him, "Donald, where are you at with Ricardo moving on to ordination?" I wondered, especially with this last incident, if he was still of a mind to do what he could to intervene with the bishop and possibly block that from happening. Ricardo had recently received the Ministry of Lector, one of the formal small steps required on the path to ordination. The ceremony took place with the bishop during the closing mass of the annual Prelature Assembly in Chucuito last month. To my happy surprise, Donald tells me that he recommended to the bishop at that ceremony that Ricardo be allowed to move on to ordination. It is a weight lifted. Of course, Ricardo still needs to decide for himself if ultimately he will go on to ordination or if he wants to take his life in a different direction. But at least he has the freedom to decide, and apparently Donald won't be working against him.

The next day, we have our all-day parish team meeting to evaluate progress on the goals and tasks we set last December, and to make any necessary adjustments. My usual mode as facilitator has been to control the flow of these meetings by pushing things along in order to stick to our agenda and timetable. This time, I am allowing myself to mostly be one more participant, letting the initiative naturally flow around the room as people speak and make suggestions. I have grown in understanding that, in this culture, taking time to allow everyone to speak and to listen to them is more important than a timetable. It is liberating. I am not feeling responsible for the outcomes of the meeting.

Maybe part of it is that I feel less enthusiastic. There is a strong undercurrent of feeling ready to move on from this parish. Paradoxically, the more I let go of my controlling style, the more ease and enjoyment I have in being with them. But clearly, I'm not feeling the level of investment, the drive and commitment that I originally came with. The emotional transition is underway. My inner self has already begun to make the journey home to Michigan.

Ironically, as I am emotionally starting to check out of life here, I get invited into a family. I am shooting some hoops on the church's basketball court when I see Segundo approaching with some friends. I know Segundo and the others from the youth and young adult group. I ask them if they could use another player. When Segundo says, "Yes, you can be on my team," I feel like the odd kid out in elementary school on the playground who gets chosen for the first time to be on the team. Then, to my great surprise, Segundo adds, "And you will play center."

When I played basketball in junior high and high school, I alternately played forward and guard. The position of center was always reserved for the tall, lanky kid. But as I look at Segundo's team, I realize that, at five foot, ten-and-a-half inches, I am by far the tallest player.

After we finish playing and the others have left, Segundo approaches me and begins making small talk. I can tell there is something on his mind and he is testing the waters to see if it is a good time to ask me something. In this culture, you take time and engage the relationship before getting down to the serious business. It is so different from back home where the expectation in the Anglo world is that you get to the point quickly and not waste people's time beating around the bush before saying what you really came to say. He eventually asks me, "Will you be the *padrino*, the godfather, for my daughter Fatima's baptism?"

It is the first time I have gotten such a request in Peru. I am taken off guard. I know it is a commitment to be taken seriously and not entered into lightly. I think for a second about the fact that I will be leaving Peru in a few months. But, I reason, Segundo would know it is unlikely for missionaries like me to stay around permanently. So I answer, "Yes, it would be an honor." With that, a feeling of joy splashes across my heart. It means I will be part of the family. I promise myself I will stay connected with them one way or another. He goes on to say that he wants the baptism to be on Sunday, August 23, Maria de Fatima's first birthday. Since it's her first birthday, he tells me, they will also be celebrating the Aymara ritual of *ratuchi*, the first hair cutting.

When I share the news with Eugenio and Silverio, they advise me I will not be able to make it back in time to celebrate the 7:00 p.m. Sunday mass at church. The celebration will go on well into the evening, they tell me, and it would be an insult to the family if I were to just pick up and leave early. I know Donald had plans to be gone that day and will not be able to cover the mass for me. So I accede to their culture sensitivities and accept the suggestion to have Victor, the parish council president, do a Service of the Word in my absence. This is something that regularly happens whenever both Donald and I are gone. Eugenio tells me he will ask Victor to do it. All seems well.

~~~

I t's a beautiful Sunday afternoon as I joyfully celebrate the baptism in the church in the role of both priest and *padrino*. Then we all go to Segundo's brother's house for the party and the *ratuchi* ceremony. As the festivities continue past 7:00 p.m., I am feeling a little guilty that I am not in the church doing the mass. I rationalize to myself that this is a once-in-a-life-time event for me to actually become part of a family here and that skipping out on one mass will not be the end of the world. Besides, everything is taken care of.

But on Monday morning a sister from the convent who had just recently joined our parish team comes storming into the parish house and angrily accuses me of irresponsibility and giving a bad example. She dresses me down in Spanish, "How could you not show up for mass when you were right here in town!?"

Apparently there was miscommunication, or lack of it, with Victor. When he arrived at church, he claimed he knew nothing about being asked to conduct the Sunday evening service. At first I am really upset, but then I think, screw it. I acted with good intentions and I'm not going to let her destroy the joy.

I feel bad. I hate conflict like this. I could have communicated more with the whole team and made double sure the bases were covered. On the other hand, being a *padrino* is really important to me to feel a deeper sense of belonging, and I had good reason to think things things were all set. Oh, well. Life is not perfect. And I am part of a family.

15

A MOUNTAINTOP
EXPERIENCE

September–November 1992

The light of dawn is barely creeping out of the darkness on this Saturday morning. It is early spring. Some seventy of us are assembled at the base of *Cerro Khapía*, the tallest mountain overlooking Yunguyo, and residence of the guardian spirit *Achachila Khapía*. Donald offers a prayer of blessing over the people and we begin our pilgrimage to the top. I have my colorful woven *ch'uspa* hanging at my side containing my supply of coca leaves, lime mineral, and water bottle. Khapía rises to 15,777 feet, more than three thousand feet above Lake Titicaca. A strong case of altitude sickness in the form of nausea and headache is almost guaranteed. I am counting on chewing coca leaves combined with little chunks of lime to give me energy on the way up and hopefully keep me from vomiting.

At the summit, we will pray for blessings on the spring planting season. Farming is precarious in the Altiplano. There can easily be too much rain, or too little, too late. Damaging hail can come in an instant any time in the growing season. Making offerings to Pachamama and seeking protection from the heavens above in this springtime is deeply rooted in Aymara culture. Donald initiated the idea for this pilgrimage and put out the word to leaders of local communities who readily responded. I marvel at Donald's knowledge of ancient Aymara religious practice and his sensitive integration of it with Catholic tradition.

Last evening, Donald shared with me how cousin Alberto made this pilgrimage for the first and only time just three months before he died in the jeep accident. Donald recounted how he went up in a great spirit of prayer and fasting for peace. Now I will follow in his footsteps. Khapía, standing over us strong and tall, evokes a mixture of calm and awe as we begin our ascent. As Alberto walked this path, I imagine he would have had the budding terrorism of his time on his mind as he prayed for peace. I feel close to his spirit as we take our first pilgrim steps. *Walk with me, Alberto, and intercede for your people that this may be a good year for the crops and an abundant harvest of peace with an end to the violence.*

The initial trek is fairly easy as we walk up the gentle slope at the base of the mountain. I have the sensation of walking up Pachamama's long flowing garment sweeping up from the floor. The further the sun rises above the horizon, the more the cold air loses its bite. The path soon gets steeper and we find ourselves winding around rocky formations. When I start to feel short of breath, I begin chewing a small wad of coca leaves. I soon feel a lift, like drinking a strong cup of coffee. All the way up, the view of the surrounding fields, lake, and distant snow-capped mountains is spectacular. The hikers have gradually spread out during the long ascent, and I find myself out of sight of the others much of the time which lends itself to a mood of meditation.

I reflect on how I have been feeling disillusioned about working with Donald in Yunguyo, and my temptation to just get out of the parish scene. It has gotten worse lately, with Donald largely absent from the Plan NIP work that so inspired me when I first started, and supposedly was a high priority for our parish efforts going forward. Lately, he has invested most of his creative energies in his grain mill project. The grain mill seems like a good thing, but it is Donald's personal project. He seems to be increasingly disinvested from operating as a parish team, making decisions independent of input from the rest of us.

Yet here we are on this incredible pilgrimage initiated by Donald. I have to give him a lot of credit for things like this. The rhythmic walking turns my thoughts to what I have been reading of St. Teresa of Avila these past months. Her constant call to prayer and humility has pushed hard against my North American arrogance and tendency to try to exert control. As I have tried to put things more in God's hands, there have been surprising moments in prayer of feeling lifted up in God's presence. I try to quiet my mind and walk to the rhythm of words drawn from her writings, "Let go, let be, be silent, be still in gentle peace."

The closer I get to the top, the more I am feeling the effects of the altitude: the shortness of breath, nausea, and headache. When we reach the summit, I sit down on a rock to rest and pull more coca leaves from my bag to chew. The nausea and headache subside somewhat and I am relieved I no longer feel the impulse to vomit. Donald and I soon begin setting up to celebrate mass on top of a flat rock formation. We place an *awayu* over the rock as an altar cloth and then lay out the other accouterments. Next we prepare Aymara incense vessels and call people together. Lifting the burning incense to the heavens, we ask forgiveness on our knees, and pray for a good planting season and for peace in the country. Throughout our celebration of the mass, Aymara prayer leaders are making burnt offerings together with their prayer chants in small rock formations that are portals into the sacred mountain. Alberto's spirit wafts through it all.

By midday we are ready for the descent. I am mostly walking alone as people have dispersed and are walking down in different directions at different speeds. I frequently stop to rest. My left thigh and hip are sore. The pain has been getting worse over the past three years. I need to get it checked out when I go home on vacation in November. With that thought, a longing for home bubbles up. I am the last one to make it back down and I'm exhausted. A few hours later I fall into a long and deep sleep through the night.

In the days following, I feel an afterglow from the pilgrimage, like I have been blessed and some of the dross has been purified out of me through the experience. Something very special happened on a level deeper than what words can name. I feel more deeply connected to this land of Pachamama and its people.

A pilgrimage does that. It grounds you and ties you to the place. Step by step you feel the earth and stones beneath your feet. The experience becomes part of you. When you arrive at the sacred place, out of breath with every muscle exhausted, something transforms it into a unique joy as the place speaks to you and echoes the presence of all the pilgrims who have made the journey before you. It is only after completing the journey and even more in the days that follow that you begin to feel some clarity and deep *knowing* about why you embarked upon this pilgrimage in the first place. I own a part of Khapía now and Khapía owns a part of me. I look up and feel the comfort of Achachila Khapía, the Grandfather Spirit of this place, in some way joined with Alberto's spirit, watching over and protecting me in the midst of the violence that is roiling the country.

On Sunday, September 13, I awaken with the rest of the country to the news that government forces have captured Abimael Guzmán, head of Sendero Luminoso. President Alberto Fujimori has finally achieved something I can applaud. It came as a total surprise and almost seems too good to be true. After Sendero's twelve years of terror causing over twenty-five thousand deaths and billions of dollars of destruction, this is momentous. At the same time, it is more threatening for those of us involved in human rights work. President Fujimori, in his address to the nation after Guzmán's capture, attacked human rights organizations, accusing them of aiding the terrorists. This strikes close to home as I think about my work with the Vicaría. Will the military raid the Vicaría offices or even detain us? It feels like he has declared open hunting season on us. On the other side of the equation, it is also troubling to hear that graffiti from members of Sendero appeared on the walls of the university in Puno directly attacking human rights organizations for supposedly supporting government "genocide" against them. We are getting it from both sides, squeezed in the middle.

The news is reporting how the capture of Abimael Guzmán took place in Lima through good old-fashioned detective and surveillance work. A branch of the National Police called DINCOTE, the National Anti-Terrorism Directorate, began surveillance in early 1992 on suspected safe houses in Lima's upper class neighborhood of Surco. Four years earlier, Sendero began extending its reach from the countryside into urban coastal areas. One of the suspected safe houses was located above a dance studio that officially had only one person in residence. DINCOTE searched the garbage on a regular basis and concluded there were several more people living there. They also found empty tubes of a cream used to treat psoriasis, a condition Guzmán was known to have. With this information, they conducted a surprise raid and arrested Guzmán and eight others. They also captured his computer which contained detailed information on his operations.

～·～·～

The raids have continued through September; a total of fourteen of Guzmán's top commanders are now in prison with life sentences. This has dealt a serious blow to the terrorist organization since Guzmán operated as the charismatic head of Sendero with no heir apparent to replace him. There is finally some hope that the terrorists can be defeated.

News stories talk about it as the decapitation of the movement. It reminds me of scenes from my childhood on the farm when we would butcher a bunch of chickens all at once. We'd chop off their heads with an ax on a chopping block, at which point their headless bodies would fly around for a bit, spraying blood around the yard as they went, until they came to a dead halt. Will this be what happens now with Sendero?

Many units of Sendero still exist across the country, even if headless for now, and so the death, destruction, and bloodletting will undoubtedly continue. The deeper, more fundamental problems of overwhelming poverty, social injustice, and government corruption that helped give rise to Sendero remain worse than ever. Life has grown increasingly desperate for the majority of the population. How much can one person do? Sometimes I just plain feel helpless in the face of it all. The tentacles of evil and injustice reach into every part of the country. Can the capture of Sendero's top leadership at least stop the worst of this terrorist movement? I pray it is the beginning of the end, preferably without the bloodletting.

～·～·～

The last week of September I am riding with Donald in his truck to our monthly Maryknoll group meeting in Puno. I use the occasion to tell Donald that I will be going back to my diocese in Michigan next June. I also relate how I have backed away from putting a lot of energy into Plan NIP as I have seen him distancing himself from it and redirecting his energies to the grain mill and other projects. I share all this somewhat matter-of-factly and at some length. As expected, he has no comment or questions about it except to thank me for letting him know after I add that I am telling him because I feel as pastor he should know about these things.

Telling him brings me some peace. It is a burden lifted. I realize I have been holding back on letting him know. Was I afraid to tell him? I don't think that is it. It has more to do with accepting for myself the finality of my decision to return to Michigan. Putting it into words with him makes it real and concrete. It also puts to rest my struggling thoughts about moving out for the last few months before I conclude my time here. I will stay put and continue the work I feel called to do in the best way I can in the time I have left.

The other thing bringing some peace is my plan to be on retreat and vacation in mid-November thru December. After our Maryknoll retreat in Lima, I will go home in time for Thanksgiving and Christmas on the farm. Until then, I continue plowing more time and energy into the Vicaría work, writing grant proposals and reports, and doing preliminary intake work on cases people are bringing to us. The first week of October is proving to be especially heavy and wearying with a large number of cases of violence and killings. Most of the time, the biggest thing I can do is listen with compassion and let people know that someone cares.

I feel the importance of this myself when Alice Walters and Mark Saucier of the Peru Peace Network in the US interview us at the Vicaría as part of their fact-finding trip. The Network does education and advocacy for human rights and is supportive of the Vicaría. They ask us to share what is happening on the ground here and listen with great attention. Just to have them here, people from the outside expressing solidarity with us in these dark and difficult times, brings me to tears of gratitude, tears that also testify to the emotional strain I am feeling.

On Sunday my parents call to tell me my grandma Thelen, at age ninety-four, has fallen and broken her hip. She is scheduled for a partial hip replacement tomorrow. I love my grandmother who was such a loving presence in my childhood and through all these years. Tuesday at 6 a.m. my dad calls in tears to say her lungs are filling up and they don't expect her to pull through. In the midst of my own tears, I mentally make plans to fly home for the anticipated funeral. I call home on Wednesday from the Center House and find out she is recovering and expected to pull through in good shape. What a blessing that we are given this extra time after the roller coaster of emotions these past few days. I can wait and fly home in November as planned and spend some treasured time at her side.

I had driven to the Center House to be able to more reliably make and receive phone calls about my grandmother and be closer to the airport if I needed to fly home right away. During these same days there has been growing apprehension in the country. We are approaching October 12, which this year is the fifth centenary of the arrival of Columbus in the Americas. His arrival five hundred years ago was the beginning of the oppression and slaughter of indigenous peoples. There is much speculation that Sendero will use the anniversary as a reason to unleash a wave of violence particularly targeting Spaniards, Church projects, and Church workers in general. Church workers—that would be me.

On Tuesday night, the same day I thought my grandmother was dying when I was in the Center House, all the lights in Puno went out. A few minutes later, around 8:00 p.m., we heard the explosion of a bomb going off not far from us, apparently the work of Sendero. It rattled our windows and my nerves. The noose of terror seems to be tightening.

November 15 arrives with a gentle all-night rainfall. It is a great blessing for the people and their fields of crops after several very dry weeks. Tomorrow morning I fly down to Lima for the five days of our Maryknoll retreat and then on to the US for my long-anticipated vacation that will close out this year.

I am on the left with my cousin, Al Koenigsknecht, second from right, during my 1985 visit to Peru as I considered the possibility of working there. He was the apostolic administrator of the Prelature of Juli and died in an auto accident the following year.

The solidarity march to Ayaviri I participated in the day after I arrived to work in Peru. The sign says, "For Life and Peace," protesting the terrorist attack on the Church's Rural Education Institute.

"Monseñor Alberto," as he was known among the people, served in Juli 1974–1986. I was inspired by his commitment to human rights.

To my right, Pat Ryan, Maryknoll Sister and head of the *Vicaría de Solidaridad*, the human rights office I worked with. Left, Larry Rich, Maryknoll lay missioner.

José Yantas with Volkswagen and me on the other side. He and his wife, Ginger, took me to Pamplona Alta in the *Ciudad de Dios* (City of God) sector of Lima where they worked.

Children in the Pamplona Alta zone of City of God. Behind them, houses built on the desert hills.

In the churchyard in Yunguyo with the Toyota Land Cruiser I drove. It was first used by my cousin Alberto.

The children's march for peace in Yunguyo, December 7, 1989. Their sign says, "Children. We want peace."

My parents during their 1990 visit, standing by the kitchen door of the house where I resided. On their right, Eugenio, the church office manager.

The picture my dad took as we sat together overlooking Machu Picchu.

I am blessing the first ritual harvest of potatoes after a *Jatha Katu* Mass of thanksgiving in a rural Aymara community.

Silverio, our cook in Yunguyo, led a *Jatha Katu* ritual at the convent potato field during my parents' visit. Mom places streamers on the potatoes selected for the ceremony.

Aymara women celebrating the potato and the promise of a good harvest in a *Jatha Katu* ritual. In the background are homes and potato fields.

Students I taught in front of the pre-seminary building.

In the church garden in Yunguyo. To my left, Fr. Narciso, Eugenio, Silverio, and at the end, Ricardo, during his internship.

I am with my spiritual director, Maryknoll Father Mike Briggs, at the Center House in Lima.

A *diablada* dance during a festival in Yunguyo.

Fatima's parents, Segundo and Tina, invited me to a picnic on the shore of Lake Titicaca.

The baptism of my goddaughter, Fatima, in the church in Yunguyo.

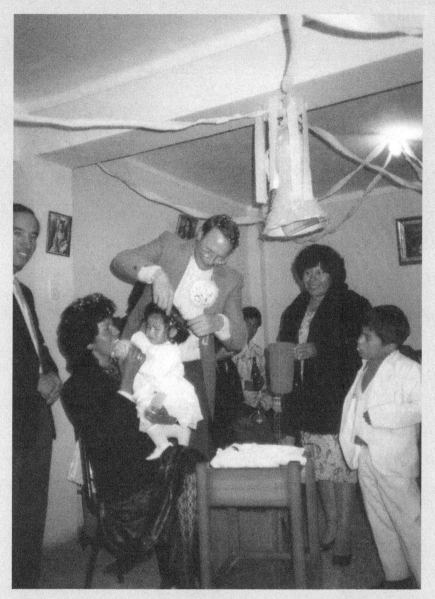

The baptism celebration was combined with Fatima's first birthday party and included the *ratuchi*, the symbolic first hair cutting.

Aymara leaders making offerings and prayers for a good planting and growing season after our pilgrimage reached the top of Khapía at 15,777 feet.

I'm standing at the top of Khapía with Lake Titicaca in the background.

After being covered with confetti and streamers, I'm dancing at my farewell party in April 1993.

My friend Felipe brought his music group from across the Altiplano to my farewell party.

I made a return visit to Peru in February 1995. Here, Father Narciso Valencia is celebrating the ninth anniversary memorial mass we held at the site of my cousin Alberto's death.

Standing at the monument after the memorial mass. The sign reads, "In Memory of Msgr. Alberto Koenigsknecht, Bishop of the Prelature of Juli."

Standing in front of Maryknoll headquarters in New York.

My parents on our family farm.

Aerial view of our family farm. The barn in the center was the setting in my nightmare of battling with the head *Sendero Luminoso* terrorist.

After my return from Peru, I became pastor of Cristo Rey Church. I am in the parish house with my cat Smokey.

HOME FOR THE HOLIDAYS

December 1992–January 1993

Five weeks have passed since I landed in Lansing and made my way back home to the family farm. It has taken every bit of that time, plus the retreat time in Lima before that, to recover from feeling worn out. Some of the exhaustion can easily be blamed on the energy drain from working in the altitude. Just as much of it, if not more, is from the relentless accumulation of stress from working in Peru in a time of terrorism and government counterviolence. Even in the two days leading up to my flight out of Lima for this trip back to Michigan, people at the Maryknoll Center House in Lima were speculating that Sendero might start setting off bombs at the airport and government buildings as the country approached the day of elections for a new constitutional congress. My anxiety was through the roof on my trip to the airport and then waiting to board my flight out, wondering if a bomb would go off at some point and I would be blown up.

It's late December and I'm waking up awash in memories at my parents' house. I'm upstairs in my childhood bedroom, lying on the bed with its wooden frame that dates from my grandparents' time when they ran the farm. I love the familiar feel of this room. It still has the same cracks in the ceiling, the same matching chest of drawers, and the old-style vanity with its big round mirror, bands of inlaid wood and little drawers on both sides. I get up with a stretch and a yawn, and realize I feel fully rested and awake for the first time since I got here. I look out the south-facing window at the snow-covered farm fields. In my childhood summers, they shimmered with lush green corn stalks, or golden wheat ready for harvest, or rich alfalfa sprinkled with grazing cattle. I turn to the east window where I see our woods off in the distance. As a child I loved to walk to the woodlot and engage my fantasies. I'd imagine a whole playhouse among the branches of a fallen tree, or driving the old car, the shell of which was left there to rust from a generation past.

It doesn't seem fair that I'm feeling so good and rested with only four days left to enjoy that feeling before I return to Peru. I'm already feeling nostalgic about our family gatherings over Thanksgiving and Christmas and the lavish meals Mom prepared, as always. We've never been able to convince her to sit down with us at these special gatherings for more than a few moments at a time before getting up to refill one of the bowls or platters of food.

During this time back, I met with the bishop and he said he would work it out for me to be named pastor of the local Hispanic parish. Then he said, "We have been waiting for you." It was nice to hear.

As I get dressed for the day, an edgy feeling creeps in as I think about returning to Peru in just four days. Fear and anxiety are beginning to surface in slow gurgles like the bubbles burping in the Cream of Wheat Mom cooked on the stove for breakfast when I was growing up. One of the feelings simmering in my gut is that something bad could happen to me just before my final departure from Peru in May. It's as if some demon is trying to dissuade me from going back at all. I don't want to deal with this invasion of my calm, so I do what I have always been good at. I push the feeling down into my emotional deep freezer so I can ignore it for the time being and continue the journey.

December 30 is my thirty-ninth birthday. My parents never miss a chance to get free birthday food. We meet up with some of my cousins for lunch at Kentucky Fried Chicken which offers, you guessed it, a free lunch for the birthday boy. At suppertime we have a family gathering at home with pizza on the menu because, as you may have already guessed, the hometown pizza place gives a free pizza to the birthday kid. The clincher is the birthday cake they picked up from the local grocery store, gratis of course on your birthday. With this triple score my parents are on freebie cloud nine. It was all a delight, including a visit with my beloved grandma Thelen in the afternoon.

Three days later I am on the American Airlines flight back to Peru. The goodbyes to my family at the airport seemed less dramatic this time, almost as if I were going back to a job in a nearby city, or like an interlude at a theater performance before returning to be seated again. I guess that's it, since the plan is to be back in Michigan in a little less than six months. As the plane is soaring through the skies, I wonder what my final few months will be like in Peru. It will surely be a time of transition one way or another.

17

BURN BARREL

February–March 1993

The fire is blazing in the burn barrel, the old fifty-five-gallon drum that's been standing in the back of the courtyard all these years. It is well rusted but still sturdy. One by one I feed sheets from a stack of papers culled from my files into the flames. As each sheet slides into the smoky inferno, I watch it curl at the edges, then blacken as it is consumed and turned into a fluffy white ash. I tried to put a whole stack in at once but it only caught fire around the edges and sent up a smoldering smoke before the flames went out, leaving most of it unburnt. This can't be rushed.

Sorting, organizing, and eliminating what is no longer needed are some of the ways I maintain the illusion of control in my life. During these past four years, I have systematically filed all my papers. I have all the notes, handouts, and general paperwork from meetings of the Seminarian Commission, the Vicaría team, our parish team, parish council, our Maryknoll gatherings, letters from home, materials from language school, and newspaper and magazine articles I clipped and saved. Sorting through the paperwork, deciding what to take back to Michigan and what to pitch, helps steady the emotional swings this time of transition is evoking. It is a calming, meditative exercise. Watching the pages burn one by one gives me a feeling of having my soul purged, a kind of earthly purgatory in which I release hurts, angers, mistakes, and frustrations from these past four years and send them into God's hands on the curls of smoke ascending to the heavens.

As the hot, smoky air shimmers and dances over the burn barrel, my thoughts drift back over the past month and a half. It seems ironic that as I have been preparing to leave Peru, I am enjoying life more than at any time since I first arrived. When I got back from my vacation in Michigan, it seemed almost effortless to jump back into the flurry of things-to-do that I have taken on in the prelature and engage the relationships that have grown up. With my departure plans in place, it is a time to focus on the things I enjoy and try to bring to fruition as much as possible the projects I have undertaken. I need to keep reminding myself to let go and just be in the moment. Nevertheless, there is no getting away from the fact that I am in transition. My move back home is clearly not going to be like an ocean liner sailing peacefully out of the harbor on the appointed day. Some days lately it feels like I'm in a rowboat being battered by an ocean storm and other days are more like water lapping peacefully on the shore where my boat is safely moored. I remember reading that the emotional move usually takes more time than the physical one, that you can be in a new place on a certain date but your emotions may take a while to catch up with you.

I think about Bishop James E. Walsh, one of the earliest Maryknollers in China, who said, "The task of a missioner is to go to a place where he is not wanted, but needed and to remain until he is not needed but wanted." As I tell people I will be leaving Peru in May, I am surprised by the intensity of feelings it surfaces. Suddenly people are telling me they don't want me to leave or are asking me if I will be back again. It is the first time I have felt such open warmth and appreciation from people here. It is really uncomfortable for this farm boy who grew up in a family that didn't do emotions. I dread the thought of going through four months of all these sentimental reactions around my leaving. My default mode would be to avoid these feelings as much as possible. But I know on a deeper level that I need to push myself to follow what Maryknoll Fr. Ed Byrne wisely advised me in his Christmas card. I came across it again as I was sorting through my papers. He wrote, "I pray that your final months are a time of special joy. Try to go slowly and savor the days and moments, the people and this special time to prepare your return. Give it time, celebrate it with the folks and let them tell you their thoughts and feelings." This time of transition has its own rhythm and energy. I need to respect that and not try to control it or run away from the emotions.

As the flames in the burn barrel continue to curl each page, I think back on recent travels that provided some relief from the tumultuous emotions of transition. I flew down to Lima in January to represent the Vicaría at the CEAS meetings on budgets and fund distributions. I felt especially proud to do this because my cousin Alberto was the chair of CEAS, the Social Action Committee for the Conference of Bishops. I fondly recall how he gave me a personal tour of the office during my first trip to Peru and talked about how CEAS helps support and coordinate human rights work. Along with the reports I had prepared for the CEAS meetings, I went with the feeling of having "arrived" as a capable member of the Vicaría team.

I cringe as I remember how talk of terrorism never let up in Lima. Particularly gruesome was the account I heard from a Maryknoll lay missioner who had come in from an outlying area for a few days. He told me how Sendero attacked a police station where he was working in Mañazo and went out of their way to throw a bomb in a bathroom where a pregnant woman and a twelve-year-old boy were hiding. If that isn't the face of evil, I don't know what is. It is hard to get an image like that out of your mind.

As I feed more papers into the burn barrel, I turn my mind to some more poignant memories. After the CEAS meetings, I stayed in Lima to receive six visitors from Michigan, including my uncle, Father Matt Fedewa, and good friends Brian Singer-Towns and Father Jim Eisele. Their arrival was delayed a half day after presumed terrorists shot bullets into the fuselage of an American Airlines passenger plane. As a result, American changed their flight schedules to have planes arrive from the U.S. in the morning instead of the middle of the night. When I heard about this, I wondered if my visitors would cancel their trip. To my great relief, they arrived just fine and I met them at the airport. We found a taxi-van big enough to take all of us and their luggage, including the two extra bags of medical supplies for our clinic in Yunguyo. As we headed for the Center House, I became aware of a car consistently behind us and commented I thought we were being followed. With the ever-increasing terrorist activity in the country, I had become constantly watchful for any signs of danger around me. Was I overreacting? Maybe. But as the saying goes, just because you're paranoid doesn't mean they aren't after you.

Their visit was a godsend for me. We toured Machu Picchu and the impressive Inca ruins around Cusco. At the El Inca restaurant in Cusco, we sat next to a stone wall built by the Incas and dined on delicacies like stuffed and roasted guinea pig. The Andean music group *Apu Marca*, Spirit of the People, was performing. My spirit soared with the music as patrons clapped to the music. I felt deep in my bones how much the music of the Andes has infiltrated my soul. When we were ready to leave, I thought, I won't find a place like this back in Michigan.

In Puno we visited the Vicaría and spent a day at the festival of Candelaria that goes on for two weeks around the central date of February 2. After that we made our way around the lake. Our first stop was at the monument on the side of the road marking the place where cousin Alberto was killed when his jeep crashed into the parked truck. It is built up of stone and cement in square whitewashed layers like a five-foot tiered wedding cake topped with a simple angle iron cross. Alberto's name and date of death had been hand drawn in large uneven script in the wet cement. Local residents constructed it to honor him and to ward off any evil spirits that might have conspired in his death. It stands as he did among the people of this land, providing a resting place for his soul. The location is known in Aymara as *Qaritamaya*, place of rest. Before we left, we gathered around the monument for a prayer and a moment of silence.

Further around the lake, at the cathedral in Juli, we were able to visit the crypt below the altar and pay our respects at Alberto's tomb. We helped roll back the heavy rug behind the altar where Alberto had stood so many times to celebrate mass. The hinges creaked as the heavy, wooden door to the burial chamber was swung up and doubled over to lie flat on the floor. A whiff of musty air wafted up as we carefully descended the narrow steps. They were barely visible in the dim light from the windows high above us. When I switched on my flashlight, it revealed the plaque marking Al's niche. As if on cue, we all stopped talking and stood there nestled in silence. Matt broke into tears and I began to choke up. It was Matt's first time to stand at the tomb of this family "saint" as he softly commented. I had been there before when my parents visited in 1990, but the emotions were strong as ever. I've had an empty place in my heart these years, feeling like life cheated me by not giving me the opportunity to work at his side. His death, three years before I arrived in Peru, was sudden and a shock to all. But standing in that crypt, I realized his spirit has been accompanying me all along and that I have been working alongside him. His courage in the face of the terrorists and his boldness in fighting for justice for his beloved people have inspired me each step of the way.

I add the last sheets from the stack of papers to the burn barrel and the flames slowly die down. Sometimes I wonder how I will make it through these next two and a half months. I am really not sure what to do about the tension that is building up. Exercise helps some as I take walks and ride my bike, sometimes for miles at a time. I really wish I could talk it through with Mike Briggs but, alas, he and others I might feel comfortable talking to are gone on altitude leave.

In March, the anticipation of leaving transitions to steps on the ground. I have talks with Ricardo and then with the bishop, discussing my concerns for Ricardo's future. In mid-March, the parish team sets April 13 as the date for my *despedida*, my farewell party. It will take place in Chucuito right after Easter, barely a month away. Suddenly, I have an expiration date. At the next Seminarian Commission meeting, we discuss who could replace me on the Commission and who will work with the seminarians assigned to me. For one last time I attend the annual Andean Pastoral Institute course in Chucuito. Then, in Puno, I facilitate the last of the Maryknoll pastoral theological reflection sessions I initiated two years ago and write up our conclusions. More endings, more letting go.

Early the next morning after the Maryknoll meeting, I pray in the window-lit chapel of the Puno Center House, now so familiar to me. The reading of the day is from Luke 12, "Do not worry about your life... if even the smallest things are beyond your *control* (the word gives me pause) ... why are you anxious about the rest?"

Control, I roll the word around in my mind. Can I ever really let go and stop worrying about all the pastoral problems around me and all the injustices in the world that fill me with anxiety? Can I stop feeling like I never do enough to try to set things right? Lord, help me to live more in the present moment, do what I can, and leave the rest in your hands.

At the end of March on a Sunday afternoon, at the invitation of the sisters in Yunguyo, Donald, Ricardo, and I are sitting around their dining room table to discuss whether it is possible for Ricardo to stay another year in Yunguyo after I leave. We talk around it for a while. Then, Donald finally opens up about how he has felt hurt and rejected that Ricardo has never confided in him or taken time to ask his advice about things. Ricardo responds with how he has felt rejected and not accepted by Donald and how he feels Donald never has shown any desire to form a relationship with him. It is tense, but at least they are finally talking to each other with some honesty about how they feel. No small thing. The general consensus is that Donald and Ricardo should get together, *talk* to each other, and arrive at some kind of mutual decision.

There is a glimmer of hope, but I have my doubts. It would take a small miracle for them to build an adult-to-adult relationship. From what I have seen, Donald would only be comfortable if he could be in the father-figure role. I have to accept that I can't control what happens. The two of them will have to work this out now—or not. I have done what I could. Donald will go on being who he is with his own distinct personality. He has done a lot of good in Yunguyo and I can see now with hindsight that Donald and Ricardo, with their very different personalities, cultures, and styles of ministry, were almost destined to clash.

18

TAKING LEAVE

April–May 1993

I'm sitting in my room this morning at the Puno Center House in a kind of stunned silence. It's April 13. Despedida day. My farewell party will take place this afternoon and into the evening at the Retreat Center in Chu-cuito. My mind drifts back to four years ago when I stayed there overnight before boarding the bus to the Ayaviri solidarity march. And it was where I spent four weeks at the orientation course for new pastoral workers the following spring. The place has embraced me in so many gatherings over the years. It radiates the sacredness of all the people who have come for one reason or another, like a place of pilgrimage awash in the holiness of all who have made the journey. How many times I have sat in the conference room with its rounded wall of windows overlooking Lake Titicaca and found my concentration dissipated over the sparkling waters. How many times we have ended conferences there with a mass or an Aymara ritual of blessings and offerings to Pachamama. Today, especially, I think of the times we have had despedidas for other missionaries who have concluded their time here. Now it is my turn. My heart is swollen with gratitude for the privilege of serving among the Aymara people and with my fellow pas-toral workers on this journey of faith. What an honor it has been to walk upon this land of Pachamama. For better or for worse I have been deeply marked by this experience and will forever carry the people with me in my heart. The spirit of life, joy, and resistance of the Aymara people is so much stronger than the demons of terrorism and corruption that have plagued this land. It has all impacted me and changed me in many ways.

It is in the celebrations of important life-moments that the meaning of our years is most revealed. In the late afternoon my farewell party begins with a mass in the conference room where way more people than I expected have filled the room. There are testimonies and more accolades than I could possibly deserve. It is both gratifying and uncomfortable. Growing up, it was deeply ingrained in me that you don't need to be recognized for your good deeds. You do good because that is what is expected. My uncle Matthew once told me how he grew up hearing his mother admonish him and his siblings in German saying, "*Mach nicht zu großartig*" (don't get a big head). Attitudes get passed on through the generations, even if not in the same language.

Interspersed in the testimonies is some good-spirited roasting which helps break up the seriousness. After the mass and speeches, mounds of food are brought out. There is music and dancing in traditional Aymara style, salsa, and even some good old rock and roll. Lots of colorful confetti is thrown over me and serpentine streamers are uncoiled around my neck. I am totally taken by surprise when Felipe arrives from the distant town of Azángaro with his *conjunto* of several musicians. They won first place in the Festival for Peace the Vicaría sponsored in December. I first met Felipe at the IPA orientation course for new missionaries that was held here in Chucuito. For some reason we really connected. I have seldom seen him since. I did help him once with some funding after there was a Sendero attack on the town where he was working. It obviously meant more to him than I ever realized. It is all joyfully and tearfully overwhelming.

A few days after the despedida in Chucuito, I am sitting on the steps of the parish house in Yunguyo after Sunday masses, looking over the courtyard. The back entrance to the church sacristy is off to my right, the door I have passed through so many times since I first settled in to work here. The warm afternoon sun on my shoulders has drawn me into a reflective mood.

All of a sudden, Wilber walks in unannounced, casually sits down next to me, and wants to talk. He must have entered through the main doors of the church and passed through the sacristy. Wilber is a member of the youth and young adult group. We have had conversations over the past year and a half about his interest in going to the seminary, but this is the first time he has approached me in this very informal way. I am pleasantly surprised. He asks about my leaving and wonders why I am not staying around longer. I explain as best I can in Spanish that the plan was always that I would be here for these four years and then go back to my home diocese, and that I feel the need to reconnect with my family there. He seems to take this in with some acceptance. Then he surprises me by lamenting that he hadn't taken more time earlier on to talk like this and get to know me more personally. There is a genuine sense of warmth and affection in his words.

After a while, Wilber leaves and then, as if on cue a few minutes later, another member of the youth group walks up and sits down next to me. We have a similar conversation, and he adds the note that he didn't think you could approach a priest like this in this kind of casual and personal way. It confirms the sense I've had that, along with the barriers of language and the natural reserve of the Aymara people, the image of priest as one-set-apart has impeded these kinds of more personal connections that have been in short supply in my years here. And being relationship challenged myself surely has not helped.

Then two more youths enter in succession and we have more of these conversations. This has never happened before. Are they passing the word? To me it seems marvelous, bordering on the miraculous, that they just came and sat right next to me, talking so personally. It is like messengers sent by God to let me know that something good has come to fruition in my years here. These experiences of more personal connections are coming with an unexpected frequency, ironically, just as I am preparing to leave, and, perhaps precisely because I am leaving.

It seems like what often happens when someone you personally know dies. The full impact of the meaning of that person's life comes into focus as never before and you realize how much you will miss that person. You wish you had had more time to spend together, and you think of all the things you wish you had taken more time to say to that person. Even though this time of my going away is not a funeral, feelings of loss and sadness are proving to be very much part of this time for me and those around me. It impresses upon me the need to attend to people, and myself, in this time of leave taking, by taking time with the leaving.

Two days later I am about to have my "last supper" with Donald. In a few days he will be leaving on vacation. He goes every year at this time like clockwork to spend a month with his mother in New York. I am going to Puno tomorrow for a few days to finish some grant proposals I have been preparing for the Vicaría. This will be our last opportunity to sit down, just the two of us, to talk before I conclude my time in Yunguyo. I prepared for it this afternoon by taking a long walk along the lakeshore to think it through. In the end, I took a deep breath to let go of any illusions of an emotional farewell or that we might reflect deeply on what our time together has meant. That is not Donald's modus operandi. When something is over, he seems to move on and not look back. I thought about some practical points to talk over, like leaving my jeep here for parish use, and about whether he sees Ricardo staying here for the rest of his internship. When Donald arrives for supper, we sit down at the table. Donald offers a prayer of blessing and we begin to eat. The conversation flows surprisingly well. Donald seems calm and accepting of Ricardo staying and we continue to talk about many things. It almost seems like old times, harkening back to when I first arrived. I am grateful and it brings some peace.

Before I know it, it is the end of April and the youth group, under Ricardo's leadership, has organized a despedida, their own farewell for me in the parish hall. After they install their new leaders for the year, they offer toasts, showering me with handfuls of confetti and embracing me with lots of hugs in the process. Their recent discovery of my approachability seems to have gotten a little infectious. They present me with some *recuerdos*, gifts that I will treasure. Then the music begins and we dance into the night. Near the end of the evening I put on my cassette of the song "La Bamba," from the movie of the same name, and we dance to that too. It's been a favorite song of mine since my time in language school in

Cochabamba, often lifting my spirits, and now it comes full circle to mark this ending time. With its old Spanish lyrics adapted to the new beat of rock and roll, it feels like a bridge between our cultures where we have met and learned to dance together. And it has been quite a dance. As I walk out with them at the end into the darkness of the night, I wonder, as I prepare to leave this place, what will the future bring for them in this time of violence and upheaval in Peru?

My most emotional farewell is with Ricardo. It is the morning of my last day in Yunguyo and my bags are packed. Last Thursday he invited me for the first time to his family home in a small community outside of Ilave. In effect he was inviting me into the innermost circle of his family. It was a beautiful, sunny day in the valley-like surroundings. We celebrated a mass to mark the one-year anniversary of the passing of his uncle Juan and then all shared in a meal together. They gifted me with a handwoven *inkuña*, a very special cloth used in Aymara rituals.

Now, on this sunny morning of May 10, Ricardo and I do morning prayer together one last time in the house chapel and then say a tearful, heartfelt goodbye. We bear hug each other, and then it is time to go. Ricardo helps me load my bags into my jeep, which I will drive to Puno one final time. I get in, start the engine as I have done so many times, and pull away with a lump in my throat.

19

WILL I MAKE IT
OUT ALIVE?

May 1993

I have five days in Lima before my final departure. My anxiety is growing by the hour. The effects of working four years in Peru in a time of terrorism have grown like a cancer in my bones. I suppressed the bulk of my fear and anxiety over the years in order to survive emotionally, like a dam holding back the floodwaters. That made it possible to continue functioning most days as if it were just another day. But now, as I am about to leave, I am finding it impossible to keep the dam from cracking open and the floodwaters of fear are pressing through the fissures.

On my third day at the Center House, Fr. Ray Finch, the regional superior, hosts an informal wine and cheese farewell for me. Most of the Maryknoll missionaries of Peru are here because they, like me, are flying to Caracas, Venezuela, to attend our Latin American Area Assembly. From there I will continue on to New York for the reentry program that starts the first week of June. There is a spirit of conviviality as people catch up with each other at the gathering. After a time, Ray clinks his wine glass with a spoon to call for everyone's attention. He offers a toast, thanking me for my time in Peru, after which all raise their glasses with him and say a hearty "salud!" He presents me with a small gift, a beautiful wood-carved *Iqiqu*, the good luck figure of abundance, and concludes with a blessing to send me off.

My final evening at the Center House, I'm sitting in my upstairs bedroom at the end of the hall, examining my plane ticket one more time. I am scheduled to fly out early tomorrow morning. Everything seems to be in order except the disarray of my feelings. As I do my final packing, irrational fears are coming out faster and stronger like flood waters breaching the dam. The question, *Will I make it out alive?* is overtaking my thoughts. My heart is racing. I begin to wonder if I am going to have a heart attack. Images flash through my mind of news reports I remember seeing on TV about soldiers in Vietnam who survived the terrors of war, and were finally taking off on their flight home to the safety of US shores when their plane was shot down, just as it made its initial ascent over the jungle. All were killed when the plane crashed. *That could happen to me,* some irrational inner voice keeps blaring. Or is it actually very rational? After all, terrorists shot a bullet into that American Airlines flight in January. What is to keep them from bringing down my plane just as it ascends over the shantytowns of Lima? It would crash and I would die in a burst of flames. I barely sleep during the night, tossing and turning. I try to pray. I tell myself the fear and anxiety is irrational and overblown. Nothing helps. The floodwaters of fear have burst the dam. Finally I just say it. *I am terrorized.*

I get up at 5:00 a.m. and get myself ready to go to the airport. After I descend the wooden stairway, I walk my bulging bags down the first floor hallway and make my way out to the sidewalk. The metal door clangs shut behind me. I don't see another soul as I wait on the curbside for a taxi. In the darkness, the street lights emit a halo-like glow through the dripping fog that has rolled off the ocean and engulfed the city overnight. My heart is pounding. *I might not even make it to the airport. A car bomb could be set off somewhere en route just as I'm passing by in the taxi.* Images of the bombed-out district of San Isidro I saw last year are playing like a movie trailer in my head.

A taxi driver pulls up to the curb in an old Toyota. It looks sturdy enough. But it is always the luck of the draw. You never know what shape the brakes are in or whatever else might be failing. Most taxi drivers operate independently on a shoestring and have little money for repairs. We agree on a price and he loads my luggage into the trunk. I climb into the back seat and we head off in the darkness to Jorge Chávez International Airport. The streets are mostly empty compared to the congestion that will appear in another hour. I crack open the window and feel the flow of sticky, humid air. My driver doesn't bother to stop when traffic lights turn red. It is easy to steer through the few cars and delivery trucks that are out. I am slightly relieved. We will get there sooner rather than later. Less chance for something to go wrong. Less chance for an accident. It would be easier for a terrorist to shoot at us if we stopped for a long red light. *These thoughts are irrational*, I try to tell myself. *What are the chances? But there is a chance. I could be kidnapped. Stop!* I tell myself. *Stop imagining the worst.* But it is no use. I grip the seat and just try to hang on. In the morning stillness I hear the city awakening around me and the not-so-muffled noises from the muffler.

We pass through the city center and head toward the airport on the northern outskirts of the city. High-rise buildings gradually give way to ground level structures of tin roofs and wood plank and cement block walls. As we get closer to the airport, I distract myself by reading signs on the rows of closed tourist shops that I know are piled high inside with handwoven items, alpaca sweaters, and other Peruvian crafts. The owners will soon open to vie for a share of the diminishing numbers of tourists coming in this time of civil war. It all looks familiar. I have been in these places. The makeshift nature of the structures, combined with the darkness, sends another wave of panic through me. Perfect hiding places for terrorists. One could jump out of a dark alley at any moment and throw a bomb in front of the taxi, or shoot at us from a dark corner hideout. My breathing is rapid, almost to the point of hyperventilating. *Dear God, please get us safely through this last stretch of road to the airport.* We finally swing into the airport entrance and are stopped briefly for questioning at the police checkpoint. Their job is to stop terrorists from bombing the airport or shooting travelers. We pass through easily. I am not reassured.

We come to a stop in front of the wall of clear glass entrance doors. My driver quickly gets out and lifts my bags out of the trunk. I pay him and give him a generous tip. *What will I need the money for if my plane is shot down?* I feel a little better standing in the check-in line buffered by the other travelers around me. I maintain my vigilance, constantly looking around for any sign of trouble. Finally my bags are sent into that black hole in the wall on the luggage conveyor and I wonder if I will ever see them again. I head to the boarding gate and wait. It seems like an eternity until I finally board the plane and buckle my seat belt, ready for takeoff.

As we lift off and begin to soar into the sky, I grip the armrests, wondering if that imagined bullet will materialize and take us down. It doesn't. I draw a deep breath, tilt my head back against the headrest, and exhale. The blue sky of the dawning day opens before me as the plane circles over the ocean waves and points toward Caracas.

20

MARGARITA NIGHTMARE

May–June 1993

My flight from Lima is sailing into view of the Caribbean Coast of Venezuela. From my window seat, I can see the blue-green ocean waters curving along the sandy shore. I'd love to be relaxing on that beach. We descend smoothly as a seagull gliding along the coastline to land at Simón Bolívar International Airport. I'm looking forward to taking part in the Area Assembly of all the Maryknoll missionaries working in Latin America. I will be seeing a number of people I went through orientation with nearly five years ago in New York. Now that I am half a continent away from Lima, the terror I felt as I left has subsided. But I continue to feel wired from the adrenaline as if I had drunk a gallon of high-octane coffee on the way. I will be in Caracas for two weeks before heading to New York for the Maryknoll re-entry program. My body tenses when the tires make that first little bounce against the asphalt as we touch down on the landing strip. We come to a halt without incident. I disembark with the other passengers and pass through customs with no problems. I draw a deep breath and exhale a sigh of relief.

When I get outside the airport terminal, I hail a taxi to take me, first, to the pre-Assembly gathering of the Maryknoll Associate Priests. We are meeting separately for a few days before the main event. With my bags in the trunk, I settle into the back seat. The driver is in his forties with dark brown, sun-soaked skin and an effusive personality. He is talking in what at first sounds to me like some language I never heard before. I soon begin to recognize it as a Caribbean coastal version of Spanish and listen carefully, trying to puzzle it out. He is speaking in a fast-clipped and high-toned drop-the-endings-and-contract-everything style. So the *¿Cómo está?* of "How are you?" comes out *¿Com'stá?* Gradually my ears tune in to the differences. The further we drive along, the more I'm understanding his Spanish and apparently he is understanding mine. That's a relief. I hand him the address of the meeting place in Playa Grande that I had written on a piece of paper before landing just to be sure. He tells me it is along the coast between the airport and Caracas. As we drive along the ocean beach, I sit back and enjoy the warm saltwater-infused air pouring through the windows.

When we arrive at the meeting place, its bright white exterior and lodge-like appearance stand out. It is a block in from the coast and up the hillside far enough that the spacious deck on the second floor provides an ocean view. The next day, a dozen of us begin to share our mission "life lines." There is an immediate feeling of comradery and openness as each of us shares, in turn, an overview of key moments in the journey of our mission experience. I hear common threads of the initial challenges that came with learning a new language and culture. There are stories of accomplishments and blessings, dreams and disillusionments. Many have had struggles with loneliness and challenges with building relationships in a new culture. Hearty laughter at some of our fumbling mistakes along the way is sprinkled through it all. It feels like bathing in warm sunshine on the beach after a dark and stormy night.

After three days together, we all pack up and go to the Caracas Center House for the Latin American Area Assembly which will take place over the next six days. At the top of the agenda is a discussion of the future direction and structuring of Maryknoll in Latin America. It is a liminal time as the numbers of people signing up for mission work is in decline and decisions need to be made to adjust to the new reality. Maryknoll was founded in 1911 by Fr. James A. Walsh and Fr. Thomas F. Price as the Catholic Foreign Mission Society of America. It was just three years after Rome no longer listed the United States as mission territory. Soon after, the Maryknoll Sisters were founded by Sister Mary Joseph Rogers. The first missionary work for both organizations was in China but eventually spread to other countries around the world. At its peak, the Maryknoll Fathers and Brothers had more than one thousand priests and brothers.

Now there are far fewer and the numbers are projected to continue to decline. In recent years, Maryknoll started the lay missionary program that has met with considerable success. Some of the discussions will be about how to structure this new initiative within the Maryknoll "family."

When the official gatherings end, I have a few days before my flight to New York for the re-entry program. I mention this in a casual conversation among a group of us who had been together in language school. We had hung out a lot together in a spirit of lighthearted friendship and much-needed laughter as we coped with the frustrations of learning Spanish.

We laugh again now as we recall one of our humorous moments with Casey, a slender, soft-spoken, reserved member of our little group. We had all gone out one Sunday morning in Cochabamba to get *salteñas*, which are savory hand-held meat pies in a thin pastry crust. As can easily happen in language school, Casey confused the words *salteña* and *soltero* when she said to the shop owner, "*Yo quiero un soltero,*" meaning "I want a single man."

When the laughter dies down, I mention I wouldn't mind getting away someplace to relax for a couple of days before my flight to New York and asked if anyone had any suggestions. Anita, the shortest member of our group, suggests Margarita Island which lies just off the coast from Caracas. When she says she too has a couple extra days to kill, we hatch a plan to go.

The next day we take a commuter plane to the island, find an inexpensive hotel and make our way to the hot, white sandy beaches awaiting us. Swimming in the warm saltwater, lying in the sun on the beach, listening to music, watching the waves roll in, is all a soothing contrast to the feeling of terror that had climaxed during my last days in Peru. After a late supper and long walk through the only town on the island, we return to our rooms at the hotel for a good night's rest.

In the morning I wake up, sinking into a deep sadness about leaving what has been my life with Maryknoll for nearly five years. There is a feeling of loss, almost as if I had lost a family member. When I flew out of Lima, I left behind the people in Peru that I have been so deeply part of these years. I will keep in touch with some of them, but it will never be the same as living there and working among them. Deep-seated feelings like this have been emerging lately in ways I hadn't expected.

A week ago, while I was still in Caracas for the Assembly, I dreamt that a monstrous machine was demolishing huge sections of buildings and terrain around me as it made circular sweep after sweep. The machine rotated on a center hub with huge destroying arms extending out endlessly in all directions. There was no escape from its reach. I was frantically dashing and zigzagging around in the dim light of the night to avoid being crushed to death. I woke up with the adrenaline still surging and my heart pounding.

I can see now that the dream was playing out some of my stored up fears from the intense experience of living in Peru in a time of civil war and terrorism. Once I made my departure from Peru and got some distance from it all, the lid started coming off of the stronger fears and anxieties I suppressed in order to keep functioning. My body was deciding it no longer needed to keep it all tamped down.

The deep sadness that I woke up with this morning passes as I get up and get moving. Looking out the window, I see the sun shining in the clear blue sky. We spend another day relaxing on the beach, reading and listening to music. I am drawn into the rhythm of the waves rolling in and receding back into the ocean. Waves rolling over time. I wonder what will wash up next.

I wake up early the next morning, remembering a dream of terror with stark clarity. In the dream I am maybe fourteen years old, standing in the barn on our family farm. I'm on the ground floor area where we bedded down the cows with a fresh layer of straw every night in winter. Over the winter, the straw had built high enough that my head could touch the hand-hewn beams of the ceiling above me. It is a spring day. The barn and barnyard are empty and silent. The cows are out to pasture. A single electric fence wire stretched across the wide opening of the barn separates the inside bedding area from the cemented barnyard on the outside.

Suddenly, Abimael Guzmán, head of Sendero Luminoso, appears along with two other terrorists at his side. All three are rough, imposing figures, especially Abimael with his heavy black beard and angry eyes. They are outside in the barnyard moving toward me. I am in the bedding area of the barn with two companions at my side. Everyone is brandishing a knife and a deadly skirmish appears imminent. Then the others in the dream disappear and it is just me and Guzmán. A paralyzing fear grips me as he approaches and crosses the wire. I slink back behind a partial wall that is open on both ends, hoping he cannot see where I am.

Originally, the wall was the exterior of the barn before the adjoining shed with its open front and the hay barn next to it were attached. I stoop down to hide, but he sees me and begins stalking me, coming closer and closer. I move around the wall, carefully matching his movements to keep the wall between us in a slow dance of terror. Suddenly, a rage swells up in me and, with dagger raised in hand, I turn like a cornered dog to attack him. I shout, "Get out of here!" and plunge toward him with the knife. He turns and flees toward the opening to the hay barn. I run after him and have a chance to fatally stab him in the back just as he reaches the hay barn. I hesitate to go for the kill and instead graze his back with the tip of the blade. His shirt is slit open and blood starts running out. He keeps going and slips away into the hay barn, seemingly into thin air.

As I lie awake in bed remembering the nightmare, an eerie aura of evil turns the air stale and stifling in the room. I go for an early morning walk along the beach to try to shake it off. Later, I meet Anita for breakfast at an outdoor café. We order eggs and toast with café americano and some orange juice.

At first I hesitate to say anything. My default defense strategy is to repress the terrifying dream. But the relaxed atmosphere of the island takes over and I say, "Anita, I had a really bad dream last night."

After recounting the dream to her, I sit in stunned silence with my hands wrapped around my coffee cup, holding it close to my chest like a security blanket. I'm staring out into space. But the space is not empty. I am staring evil in the face, a face with murky black and gray features set in a black swirling cloud. I'm staring evil in the face and evil is staring back at me. A cold shudder courses through my body and I become aware of an emotional numbness, my feelings shuttered up against the onslaught of this terror dream. In a flash of insight, I realize the emotional numbness started sometime back in Peru in response to the growing terror. I have not been feeling, not experiencing the normal register of emotions for quite some time.

I made it out of Peru alive, but evil and the effects of terror came with me. In my nightmare, evil symbolized by Abimael Guzmán and his terrorists mounted an attack on me, invading the space of my childhood. I'm going home, but there is extra baggage coming with me. In the dream, I fought back and prevailed against Guzmán. I hope I can continue to prevail against the feelings of having been terrorized as I make my way back to the US.

21

ADMITTING I HAVE PTS

June 1993

I'm an hour and a half out of New York City on American Airlines flight 1518. Earlier this morning, I left Caracas and South America for good. The flight has gone smoothly and with the growing distance from Peru, I'm feeling more at peace, at least for now. As I watch the changing cloud formations from my window seat, I wonder what shape my life will take going forward. I tilt the seat back and close my eyes to rest. The dream I had on Margarita Island starts playing in my mind like the old movie reels from my grandfather's travels I watched as a child. But unlike grandpa's reels, this movie is not easily tucked back into a metal storage canister. What more does it want to reveal to me? Some deeply embedded stuff from my four years in Peru is surfacing.

Even though I was never physically attacked by terrorists or members of the armed forces, the fear for my safety penetrated into the deep recesses of my being. It isn't something that I constantly thought about in Peru. But like breathing toxic air before you know just how dangerous it might be, you get on with your life without thinking about it all the time until the damage it can do catches up with you. There were times when violent events in Peru made me think about it a lot. There were times when I had to contend very directly with my fears. But most days, I packed the fears away and carried on with the mission work I had come to do. Now that I have made it safely out of Peru where I can let my guard down, things are surfacing that need to be processed, that are *demanding* to be processed. It seems like the effects of living in Peru in a time of terrorism has become like a submarine in the sea of my psyche, and the passengers are my repressed fears. After a long time in the ocean depths, it eventually has to surface. If my experience in Peru is affecting me this way, I can't begin to imagine how someone is affected who has experienced a direct violent attack. Shouldn't I be able to shake it off? I don't know. But I do know those dreams in Venezuela were powerful and foreboding.

After landing in New York, I take an airport van that drops me off at the front steps of the Maryknoll Motherhouse an hour north of the city. It is late afternoon when I walk up the sandstone steps and pass through the heavy wooden doors with my bags in hand. It feels both old and new to be here. I have a couple of free days to rest and regroup before the start of the Return Program. I spend some of the time making phone calls and catching up with folks like my parents and my friend Kate. I had forgotten how good it feels to be able to dial a long-distance call and immediately have someone answer on the other end, and be able to have lengthy conversations without worrying that it costs $5 a minute as it did calling from Peru. It was especially difficult in Yunguyo where I had to walk to the local phone company building across town. I would first hand over ten or twenty dollars' worth of Peruvian currency to the person at the walk-up counter, who would then direct me to one of the phone booths after waiting twenty minutes for one to open up, and then I could dial my call which might or might not go through on the first, or even the second or third try.

Two days after my arrival, our group of Maryknoll Associate Priests is meeting in the big conference room for our orientation to the Return Program. Everyone has had time to settle into their rooms on the fourth floor of this building, the same floor where we stayed five years ago when this all began. We started out together in this same conference room with its tall, wood-framed windows looking out on to the spacious grounds. That was back in September of 1988. It was all so new to me then. Now there is an air of familiarity about this huge stonework structure with pagoda-style embellishments on its roof that are reminiscent of Maryknoll's early work in China. At one time it was a full live-in seminary.

Earlier, I had taken a walk around the grounds and woodlands. I went past the communications building housing the magazine and book operations and, just beyond that, the building for retired priests and brothers. As I strolled around the grounds, I pictured my cousin Alberto who would have traversed these same pathways. I went across the road to the grounds around the Mother House of the Maryknoll Sisters, enjoying the spring flowers and thinking of those strong women who have dedicated their lives to serving the least among us. Then I walked back to the main building of the Maryknoll Fathers and Brothers for the start of the Return Program.

Among the associate priests gathered together in the conference room are Charlie Hardy, who worked in the poorest barrios of Caracas in Venezuela; Charlie Mulligan, who went to Chile; Lou Anderson, who landed first in Korea for a time and then went on to teach English in a remote area of China; Leo Huber, who ended up in the Beni River area in the jungles of Bolivia; and Fred Bugarin from Alaska, who served in his ancestral land of the Philippines. Some are returning like me, others are here to renew their contract. We greet each other with the conviviality of those who have become part of the Maryknoll Family and missionary culture. It is good to be with these guys. I have a little more energy today. It's been four weeks since I left Yunguyo and my body has slowly been recovering from working in the altitude.

Later, after supper in the cavernous but brightly lit cafeteria in the basement, we head across the street to begin a week-long course on missioners in transition at the Maryknoll Mission Institute.

On Monday morning, I get a call from Bishop Ken Povish letting me know I will be named pastor of Cristo Rey Church, the Hispanic parish in Lansing, Michigan. I am relieved to know I have a place to land. I don't do well when things are left hanging in the air. He gives me the option of waiting until my Maryknoll contract officially ends on August 31. But as when I first arrived in the Altiplano, I am anxious to get out of the "limbo" of transition and get settled somewhere. I suggest starting July 21 which will give me about four weeks with my parents after the Return Program ends. He agrees to set it up that way. The fact that I will be working in a Latino parish is also a relief. Ironically, when I first left for mission I remember thinking, *I hope I don't automatically get pegged for Hispanic*

Ministry when I come back to the diocese. Now I can't imagine going anywhere else. If I had to go to one of the more typical, White, middle-class parishes in the diocese, I would feel like a fish out of water. The parish life of White, middle-class America that I left behind seems totally disconnected from the reality of the Aymara people I have served in Peru. How things change. How *I* have changed.

In the afternoon, I meet with Teresa, a counselor on staff at Maryknoll, for a debriefing session. It is part of the program. Her office in the administration wing of the building has a casual feel to it with family pictures scattered among the volumes on the bookshelves. I settle into the soft chair across the coffee table from her, feeling nervous. It has never been easy for me to dive into the feeling side of life and talk about it, and even less so with someone I have just met. I remind myself, more like work at convincing myself, that this is an opportunity to get some nonjudgmental help with this process of transition. After introductions, I begin to share some of what I've been experiencing lately. I talk for a while about the dreams, the anxiety, and the emotional numbness. She listens attentively and along the way makes brief comments letting me know she is hearing me. Then I pause for a moment and say, "I really think I need to get more in touch with what's going on with me."

She agrees and says, "I know a good counselor I can recommend for you. I think it would be very helpful to meet with her while you are here. You may be experiencing some post-traumatic stress and she could help you explore that, and can take more time with you than I can offer."

I simply say, "Ok," at which point she writes out the name and phone number and hands it to me.

I hold on to the slip of paper, feeling some rising anxiety at the suggestion that I need more counseling. I recoil at the idea of having post-traumatic stress, thinking, *That's not me, I wasn't physically attacked by the terrorists. I am stronger than that.*

I want to move on to another topic of concern but I am having a hard time focusing; I am feeling disoriented and stumble around in my mind, trying to produce some words. Finally, I just sit quietly staring off into space with my eyes glazing over and my mind shutting down.

Teresa waits calmly for a moment and says, "What you are going through is not unusual for what you have experienced." That calms me a bit. Then I hear her say, "Maybe this is a good place to stop. I encourage you to make the appointment for the follow-up counseling. Take advantage of it while you are here."

After supper, I am still thinking about the debriefing session when I happen to see Pepe Aramburu in the fourth floor lounge down the hall from my room. Pepe is a Maryknoll priest a few years older than me from Puerto Rico. He was recently assigned to counseling work in the Personnel Department after finishing his counseling degree. He is heavy-set with jet black hair that maintains an unruly appearance. I first met him in Peru at regional meetings in Lima. We fall into some friendly banter over coffee and chocolate chip cookies that are stocked in the lounge's kitchenette. There is a counter between us where we rest our coffee cups close to the cookie jar.

Then he asks, "How are things going with the Return Program?"

"Ok," I respond. "I met with the counselor for the debriefing session today. She thinks I might be having some post-traumatic stress but I don't think that's really it."

"Why not?"

"Well, I have experienced a lot of more minor things during my years in Peru, but I was never directly physically attacked or anything like that."

"What are some of those things?

I mention some things, like the time I awoke in the middle of the night to a bomb going off near the Puno Center House, and the terrorist attack on the parish in Moho that left me more fearful that if it could happen there it could happen where I was living. I mention some of the threatening things that happened in Yunguyo, the San Isidro bombing near the Center House in Lima, and the general atmosphere of terror, poverty, and violence I was living in.

When I finish he says, "Well, when you put all those things together it really adds up. You have been through a lot. Having some post-traumatic stress would not be unusual."

With that, something clicks. I realize, yes, I *have* been through a lot. I am grateful to Pepe for helping me connect the dots and accept the naming of it. Post-traumatic stress. There is relief in having a name for it. It's like going to the doctor with some symptoms that are not like anything you have experienced before. When the doctor examines you and puts a name on it, there is relief in at least knowing what you are dealing with even though you may not yet fully understand it.

I make the appointment to see Susan Scheffel, the counselor Teresa recommended when I met with her. In my first session with Susan, I continue to explore what Pepe had helped me to see. I talk about living in the midst of the violence in Peru and how it is affecting me now, threading together the pieces of what I went through in Peru and how much I repressed and downplayed the impact on me. That becomes especially clear when I talk about the terror I felt as I was making my final departure from Peru. I downplayed it as "irrational" and had not talked about it with anyone. My unspoken response to the violence in Peru was to tell myself I should be strong, be able to be the "hero" who doesn't get afraid and who certainly doesn't run in the face of danger. As I am talking, I'm feeling an onslaught of sadness, like I could cry, sad that I couldn't be stronger in those situations, sad about all the violence and tragedy, sad that I couldn't do more to *stop* it, to say *enough!* I hold back the tears, still trying to be strong, still afraid of too much raw feeling all at once, afraid I might disintegrate and wash away in a river of tears, even as Susan assures me that it is ok.

Afterward, back in my room at Maryknoll, I reflect on how I have not felt much of the normal range of emotions since leaving Peru. I'm starting to see how a wall of numbness got built up and only began to crack open with the terror I felt on the way to the airport in Lima, and then with the terror dream on Margarita Island. Until now, what I primarily felt was relief to be out of Peru, and some excitement about making a new start as a first-time pastor at Cristo Rey Church in Lansing. It's becoming clear there is a lot more work to do on this post-traumatic stress business. I write these reflections down in my journal and add, "Perhaps I need to get more in touch with the pain of my loneliness in Peru and the deprivation of human touch and love."

When I go for my second counseling session with Susan, I continue to talk about the fears and anxieties that grew up around the violence in Peru. I also mention how when some of us went down to Lower Manhattan over the weekend I noticed myself being hypervigilant, constantly looking around and being on guard against any possible danger, watching for robbers who might attack us, even though there were no signs of anything about to happen. She affirms that that is another indication of post-traumatic stress, which we simply start referring to as PTS. I talk about my decision to leave Peru and the long transition time leading up to it, emphasizing how *clear* I felt about needing to leave, and *not* having any desire at this time to return, and of how *positive* I feel about my new assignment as a pastor in my diocese.

Then she says, "I sense you are really clear about wanting to leave and not wanting to go back." Her comment is followed by a long, silent pause on my part.

After a few moments she says, "It's *ok* to be leaving and it is perfectly fine to not want to go back. You have given of yourself generously for five years and now it is *ok* to return and stay."

As I listen to her, the floodgate opens and my tears start pouring out. I tell her, "It is so good to hear that and be affirmed in my decisions and feelings about leaving."

Late in the evening, writing about the session in my journal, I conclude, "It all brought me a step closer to freedom and relief...to release of the past as I move toward a new beginning."

I have one more session with Susan the day after the end of the Return Program. We talk about some of the typical symptoms of PTS that I can expect to have in recurring waves going forward, like sadness, loss, grieving, and depression. There will be sights, sounds, and smells that can trigger the trauma feelings. I need to learn what those triggers are for me and learn to take care of myself. There will likely be more trauma dreams. Going back home, things will be different; I may not feel like I fit in, she tells me. She encourages me to seek more counseling in Michigan. With that, we conclude.

I stay around Maryknoll three more days to give myself some breathing space in this time of transition. On Wednesday, my good friend Kate arrives to give me a ride back to Michigan.

My friendship with Kate grew up quite unexpectedly. We met years ago during my first assignment at St. Casimir Parish in Lansing when I was just getting my feet wet in ministry. I started there as a deacon intern in February of 1980. After my ordination in September, I continued on as a "baby priest," parish members liked to kid me. Kate began attending St. Casimir Church around that same time. Our lives intersected in a small discussion group I started that fall using a booklet from Pax Christi USA designed to help form local groups of the Catholic peace movement. When we introduced ourselves, Kate talked about her work as a special education teacher in the public school system. Her passion for working with kids on the margins of the institution matched her passion for the social justice issues we were discussing.

One of my responsibilities in the parish was working with the Liturgy Commission that helped plan services and decorate the church for special occasions. That spring, Kate was elected to the Liturgy Commission. A friend and commission member talked her into putting her name on the list of candidates. She had agreed only because she never thought she would be elected since she was so new to the parish. Our commission of six members had a lot of fun and laughter together. One time we made big plans to decorate for Easter. We decided to put up yellow billowing banners through the length of the church. Our idea was to have them swooping down from the high wooden ceiling beams to the side walls. After the material was cut and sewn to size, we gathered in church to put them up. Then we realized we had no plan for how we were ever going to get them attached to the ceiling beams. We stood there looking up like the dumbfounded disciples after the Ascension of Jesus. Finally, I took off my tennis shoes and attached the end of a long string to one of them and tied the other end to one of the banners. We took turns seeing who could get the shoe up over the beam with the least amount of throws for each banner. If any of the longtime members of the traditionally Polish parish had walked in, they would surely have been aghast at seeing tennis shoes flying through the air in the sacred space of their church and our little crowd sending up cheers from below.

A couple of years later, I started a Doctor of Ministry Program with St. Mary's Seminary and University in Baltimore. They had a creative approach where the professors came to our meeting place in Michigan to teach each forty-hour course over five days. I invited Kate to be part of the required Learning Group in the parish that was tasked with discussing my summary presentation of each course and helping design a pastoral application. The group jelled really well and I felt energized by the creative energy that came forth from it.

As time went on, Kate began to do things like put surprise birthday gifts and balloons for me in my office. It was not unusual for her to do spontaneous things like that for her friends. I, on the other hand, was "relationship impaired" from my upbringing in an emotionally challenged family. I pushed against the attention, feeling "smothered" in comparison to what I was used to. Yet the friendship continued even as, after five years, I was moved to a new assignment in Ann Arbor where I served for three years before going to Peru.

Along the way Kate got to know my parents and became part of the family. In 1988 she traveled with my parents and me from Michigan to New York for the December 10 Sending Ceremony for all who had gone through the Maryknoll orientation program together, after which we were sent off to our various language schools and countries of assignment. I was traveling with them from Michigan to New York because I had spent nearly a month away from the orientation program to be with my brother and our family as he was getting worse from his brain tumor. They had operated on it and were doing radiation treatments, but it was growing back.

I laugh when I think of the little family-run motel where we stayed for one night on our way to Maryknoll, New York. When my dad saw that the beds had a coin operated massage option, he put in some quarters and became like a little kid when it started vibrating. He sat in the middle of the bed cross-legged and proceeded to bounce up and down as if he had frog legs. We all roared with laughter.

~·~·~

Now, some five years later, Kate is here to take me on the ten-and-a-half-hour drive from Maryknoll to my parents' house. We agree to an early morning start and to switch off driving.

22

HOME BUT NOT AT HOME

July 1993–July 1994

By the time Kate and I pull into the driveway at my parents' house, it is late in the evening of July 2, just in time to wish Mom a happy seventy-third birthday. I don't have a card or gift but she assures me, "Having you home is the best present." A couple of tears trickle down as her face scrunches up with the emotion of this homecoming.

I sleep eleven hours through the night and wake up feeling more refreshed and relaxed than I have in a long time. After a late breakfast, I go for a walk down the road that runs north and south past our house. It is soothing to hear the familiar crunch of my shoes against the gravel. My eyes wander across the wide-open fields of our farm on both sides of the road where corn and wheat are in full growth. I draw in the grainy smell of the golden wheat waving in the breeze and glowing in the sunlight. It takes me to memories of my childhood, bottle-feeding baby calves when I was no bigger than they were, driving tractors and trucks long before I was old enough to get a driver's license, gathering nuts from the old hickory trees still standing tall and strong on the side of the road.... I look around with an awareness that I am here to stay this time. Michigan is my home. The solid ancestral ground under my feet is reassuring in the midst of my emotional swings of these days.

Three weeks later, I start my first day at Cristo Rey Church as their new pastor. The place is in shambles. The parking lot looks like a moonscape. Remnants of the annual parish fiesta that took place two months ago are strewn about and neglected outside the storage shed. Inside, there is a window air conditioner on a makeshift stand in the middle of the side section of the church where it would throw cool air over the people in front of it and extra hot air over the people in back of it. Go figure. In the office I meet Susana, the secretary-bookkeeper, and David, the finance council chairperson. I start up a conversation with them and learn there is a debt of some $200,000 and a history of missed payments for lack of funds. And, by the way, they have just been dealing with the discovery that the Men's Club president was siphoning money from the club's checking account.

In the afternoon I start moving into the parish house next door to the church just off the edge of the parking lot. It is a two-bedroom, premanufactured double-wide sitting low to the ground with no garage or basement. John and Lupe Castillo are there to welcome me. They are doing some last-minute cleanup. After they introduce themselves and give me a warm welcome, we sit and talk at the dining room table. "We are here to help in any way we can," they tell me. "We apologize for the wet carpets and floor fans. There was a leaking water pipe. Nobody noticed it until some of us came to clean the house after our last pastor moved out." Lupe goes on to tell me that she recently agreed to be the volunteer Youth Minister and adds, "So, like you, I am new to leadership at Cristo Rey." They go on to warn me that some of the more difficult members of the parish will "eat you alive if you are not careful." Not much comfort in that, I think to myself. At least I never had to deal with the threat of cannibalism in Peru.

In the following days, I slowly unpack some of my things while other stuff remains in my suitcases. I hang some Peruvian artifacts on the dark wood panel walls. The wood-burning fireplace looks promising for some cozy warmth in the wintertime. When I try out the La-Z-Boy recliner facing the TV, I notice there are cigarette burns and grease stains on the arms. When I examine the windows, I discover a number of the flimsy window locks are broken off. It is especially unsettling because the windows are a mere two feet off the ground. I shudder to think how easily an intruder could break in. With my PTS, I have a lot of anxiety around safety issues.

During my first days at the office, I start propping open the front door to let some fresh air into the stale interior. On my second day, a Latino member of the parish pulls into the parking lot and says excitedly, "It is so good to see the door open, like we are open for business again!" I am amazed at his enthusiasm over such a simple gesture. But when David, the finance commission chair, later tells me that rumors have been circulating that the church might close for lack of money, I begin to understand.

On Sunday I arrive early for the 9:00 a.m. mass in Spanish. I put on my vestments in the sacristy and then head to the back of the church to greet some people as they come in. Thinking of my experience in the rural communities of Peru where a mass never started less than half an hour after the appointed time, I ask the seasoned usher, "So, what time does the nine o'clock mass start?"

He looks at me like I must be the daftest gringo he's ever met and says, "Well, it starts at nine o'clock."

"Oh, ok," I respond. Then promptly at 9:00 a.m. the choir starts the opening song and the entrance procession begins. As I enter, I look around at the faces of the people and hope I can serve them well.

The next day we count the offertory collection from the three weekend masses. It is a total of $800, barely enough to cover some basic expenses with nothing left over for the monthly debt payment. The more I talk to people in the ensuing days, the more I hear of factions and power struggles taking place among some of the entrenched leaders and parish organizations.

It all adds to the challenges of my re-entry to life in the US. Sometimes I feel like a washing machine stuck on the spin cycle, swirling between the world of this new parish and the land of the Aymara people that still has a strong grasp on my heart.

I found a helpful concept in what is called the "neutral zone," that in-between space that William Bridges talks about in his book *Transitions* that I read and reread while still in New York. It is ringing true now more than ever. Emotionally, I am neither here nor there. The physical body can move quickly from one place to another, Bridges says, but the emotional move takes much longer. I feel like I am ready to project confident, professional leadership outwardly in the parish. But inwardly, I am afraid to let general parish members know what is going on for me emotionally with this transition.

In early August, I call a special meeting of the parish council, the main leadership body of the Church, so we can meet each other and have a discussion about where things are at with Cristo Rey. My idea is to tread slowly for the first year, thinking of what they taught us at Maryknoll in preparation for going into mission—when you step into a new place with people of a different culture, you should not start out imposing changes, but rather, be aware that you are walking on the "holy ground" of their lives. But as the discussions get going, the message I hear loud and clear from the parish council members is, essentially, *We have been suffering from a lack of strong pastoral leadership for the past five years. Let's get moving again!* By the end of the evening I suggest, and they agree, to embark on a process of writing a new mission statement which will lead into setting goals and action plans to guide us into the future. It fits right into my strong inclination to get decisions made and move forward with a plan. We'll see how it goes.

As I continue the journey of my entry into life as a first-time pastor at Cristo Rey, I feel the need to do everything right. That beast of perfectionism continues to rear its head. I want to be the successful, well-organized, collaborative, and visionary leader I aspired to become one day when I was in seminary. Becoming pastor of my own parish was delayed by the five years I spent with Maryknoll. So now, at 39 years old, I want to get it right and I don't want to appear weak in the face of the challenges before me. One challenge is a small group that has organized to get rid of me. They have long wanted a Hispanic priest named as pastor and are upset the bishop did not send one now. When they express their complaint, I tell them, "I would gladly step down if there was one available, but there isn't. So I'm afraid you are stuck with me."

I decidedly do not talk with parish members about the waves of grief, loss, and disorientation connected to my PTS and this transition. Some of the disorientation is that so many things are out of focus for me. It feels like looking at blurred images through an out-of-focus camera lens. So many things seem familiar and not familiar at the same time. A lot has changed and evolved during my nearly five years out of the country. New words and phrases have come into the vocabulary of news stories in the US that were not in common parlance when I left. There are new roads and businesses in the city. New songs on the airwaves. New brands of cereal on the store shelves. New political figures. On and on it goes. When you are living in it day-to-day, you are barely conscious of the little changes that are constantly taking place in what we call "culture" and "society." But after some five years away, it is like walking through a maze you used to be able to navigate without thinking about it and now someone has changed it around just enough to throw you off. They told us back in mission orientation that it is harder to make the transition back to the US compared to transitioning into a foreign mission assignment. It is proving to be true.

In mid-November, I finally pull out the two suitcases that have been sitting flat down on the floor of my bedroom closet. They still contain some of the wall hangings and other artifacts I brought back from Peru. I pull them out one by one and find places for them around the house. When I finish, I fit the smaller suitcase into the bigger blue one and stand it up against the back wall of the closet. A melancholy feeling comes over me as I look at the empty space on the closet floor that the suitcases had occupied. Those bags journeyed with me from the time I left Michigan five years ago, to New York, Cochabamba, Peru, visiting Chile, Argentina, and Paraguay, and finally making the return trip through Caracas, New York, and back to Michigan. Unpacking those things takes me one more emotional step forward into my life here in the US.

The journey of returning from mission is made one step at a time. You just know when it feels like the right time to take another step, as it did when I finished unpacking those suitcases. With each step I move a little further away emotionally from all that became so much a part of me in Peru, and a little closer to embracing my new life here. Just as I had to let go of my ties to the US enough to be able to step into the waters of the Peruvian and Aymara world, I have to do the reverse now. I hope that eventually there can be some integration of all that is Peru within me with what I am experiencing in Michigan as a "returned missionary" and pastor of Cristo Rey Church. I need a lot of healing from PTS. I also need to deal with a lot of disillusionment I am feeling with Church and liberal social justice movements that I have been part of in the past that no longer seem to jibe with my experience in mission. I feel sandwiched between two worlds, and belong to neither one.

A year has passed since I returned to Michigan last June. I am on retreat at Weston Priory. It is a small monastery in the forested hills of Vermont. I like the spirit of these monks who are gentle, welcoming, and aware of social justice issues in the world. I am here for five days seeking some peace. With all my journeys of these past years, my life feels unsettled. I start by taking some time to read my journal entries from January 1993 when I was still in Peru. I am moved to tears thinking of all the people I got to know and the life I shared with them. The tears tell me I am still grieving all that I left behind. I give thanks for these tears that help wash away some of the pain of loss. They give testimony to the fact that what I have experienced in the past is part of who I am today. But who am I anymore, really? The question remains unanswered.

Three days into my retreat, I awake to the monastery bells ringing at 4:45 a.m. I go quickly to the chapel for prayer with the monks. But after a few minutes I feel uncomfortable, then tensed up, and then like I just need to get out of there, like I don't belong here. When things conclude, I get up quickly and leave.

I take a walk around the grounds and reflect on the fact that I am but a pilgrim here. This is not my home. There is an atmosphere of calm here that doesn't connect with the reality of storm and stress in my life. I am a pilgrim with no place where I truly feel at home, a pilgrim dangling between worlds of experience that don't match up.

Later I spend some time in prayer reading from the gospel of Mark chapter 6. Jesus is in his hometown but he is clearly not at home. He says, "The birds have nests and the foxes their lairs, but the Son of Man has no place to lay his head." He is a pilgrim like me. I take some comfort in that. I am not alone on this journey. One of the songs the monks sang this morning goes something like, don't dwell on the past, don't be anxious about the future, just live in God's presence today. Those words bring me some peace, at least for now. I close my eyes and sit with the words of my mantra of late:

Let go…

Let be…

Be silent…

Be still in gentle peace.

23

UNFINISHED BUSINESS

January–February 1995

I had been debating it for some time. When I visited Mary Anne Perrone in Ann Arbor last August, I shared how I was grieving and feeling stuck between two worlds. She shared similar struggles that she had when she, her husband, and two children returned from their mission assignment in Bolivia. I had visited them while on break from language school in Cochabamba. She encouraged me to take the trip back to Peru, sharing how returning to Bolivia helped put more closure on that very intense time in her life. It had helped her move from a feeling of passionate involvement in the daily lives and events of the people there to a more healthy emotional distance. That clinched my decision to take some vacation time away from my work at Cristo Rey Church and go back to Peru.

～～～

Now it is Wednesday, January 25, the second morning of my three-week vacation in Peru. After a couple of nights of some good rest, I feel ready to begin processing how it feels to be back and see what it triggers in me. I hope it will help resolve some of my emotional struggles of this past year and a half since my return to the US.

I made it just fine to the Maryknoll Center House in Lima. It feels like there is a new calm in the air, something palpably different. The terrorism has diminished dramatically since the capture of Abimael Guzmán. For the first time I feel like I can breathe freely here. It feels good, sort of "at home" to be here in such familiar surroundings and with old friends at the Maryknoll Center House.

This morning at breakfast, Bob Hoffman, one of the Maryknoll priests, asked me about how things were going for me back in my home diocese in Michigan and whether I missed Peru. I talked about some of the ups and downs of making the transition and of how I have missed Peru a lot. At the same time I told him how I'm gradually feeling a bit more rooted again in Michigan.

But in talking I felt a great welling up of emotion, of some sadness and a kind of disorientation. I still grieve leaving Peru I guess. I also know I have left and this is not home. Perhaps some of the sense of disorientation is now the reverse. I have left, I am no longer "of this world," and yet there are so many feelings of "at home," such familiarity.

After three days in Lima, I'm at the airport waiting to board my flight which will take me to Arequipa. I look forward to spending some time with my *compadres* Segundo and Tina and my goddaughter Fatima. I treasure being their *compadre*, the family relationship we entered into when I became Fatima's godfather. They are staying with Tina's aunt while Tina takes summer classes at the university.

Check-in for my flight goes quickly and my plane is scheduled to leave on time, a nice surprise. As I sit here with some time to spare, my thoughts drift over the events of the past couple days. I saw Mike Briggs and met his mother. She had just flown in from the US for a visit and Mike had come down from the Altiplano to be with her. How fortunate it was to cross paths with him at the Center House. After three years of doing monthly spiritual direction with him while in the Altiplano, meeting up with him had a great feeling of friendship and familiarity, and even more so in the evening when we took a leisurely walk to get some gelato a few blocks from the Center House. In some ways it was almost like we were continuing our spiritual direction relationship. But there was an unspoken awareness between us that that was no longer our relationship and now we spoke as friends catching up on what has happened in our lives since we last met. As we talked, I felt calm compared to when I shared so many intense emotions with him during my sojourn in Peru.

As I continue waiting for the call to board my flight, I think about the walk I took from the Center House to the oceanfront. I walked, as I had many times before, the mile or so to the pathway along the high bluff overlooking the ocean. It felt calming and healing to watch the waves pounding on the beach and hear the water crashing in the distance below. I repeated my seaside mantra, *waves rolling over time*...and found myself asking, *What has it all meant?*...my experience in Peru...the hurts, the joys, and disappointments I took with me when I left...what emotions will I experience on my trip to the Altiplano? *Waves rolling over time*...words I repeated along the shores of Lake Titicaca, depressed over the conflicts that emerged in my work with Ricardo in Yunguyo.... The rhythm of the waves crashing below soothed me, drawing me into God's healing presence. *Waves rolling over time*...eternal energy of renewal and re-creation.

The surroundings of the airport come back into focus as I hear the announcement to board the plane. Only twenty minutes late. Not bad. I settle into my seat and the plane takes off without incident, heading to Arequipa where I will meet up with my *compadres*. The stewardess brings a cup of *mate de coca*, coca leaf tea. It is the first I've had since being back in the country. Its warmth and hint of bitterness bring a feeling of well-being, not so much for its gentle potency, but more so for the associations and memories it evokes. Ancient rituals...ancient remedies...conversations with friends over cups of tea...chewing coca leaf with Aymara families at funeral vigils and fiestas...climbing Mount Khapía to nearly sixteen thousand feet with the strength of coca leaf accompanying me.... The spirit of coca leaf dances on my tongue with each sip I take.

After we land in Arequipa, I step out of the plane and stand for a moment at the top of the steps leading down to the tarmac. It is a sunny day and Misti, Arequipa's gently sloping volcano, is clearly visible in the distance, keeping watch over the city. I see my *compadres* Segundo and Tina with *mi ahijada*, my goddaughter Fatima, smiling and waving to me from the open air balcony of the terminal just across the landing strip.

At the house we begin catching up on each other's lives. We talk and share with a sense of family confidence and openness. Segundo suddenly disappears into the street and quickly returns with two *Arequipeña grandes*, the large-size bottles of the beer named for the city. He also has in hand a bottle of Coca-Cola to mix with the beer, a common custom. Little Fatima, now three-and-a-half years old, amazes me. She is talking and running around so playfully. How does it happen that I hold her one moment as a defenseless one-year-old at her baptism, and now two-and-a-half years later she is walking, talking, and playing with so much independence? With filled glasses in hand, we lift them toward each other in unison saying, "Salud!" We all partake after Segundo makes the offering of a few drops to Pachamama.

"Fatima was sick a lot last year," Tina tells me. They go on to describe how, after many doctor visits and prescriptions for medicines during several illnesses, they finally consulted a *yatiri*, "one who knows" in Aymara, who divined through the reading of coca leaves that she was suffering from a *susto*, literally a "fright" or "scare." I remember people talking about *sustos* during my years in Peru. Something happens that causes a sudden fright in a person. It is understood that a malignant spirit from the underworld is acting against the person. The result is that some measure of the person's spirit or life force leaves the body, causing a sickness. That was the diagnosis for my goddaughter Fatima. The *yatiri* prescribed the ritual of calling back her spirit, combined with a *pago a la tierra*, a special offering to Pachamama. Segundo concludes the story with a smile, saying, "We engaged the *yatiri* to do this and she has been fine and healthy ever since."

Their telling of it takes me deep into the Aymara world of my time in Peru. With my return to the US, I am clearly distanced from that world physically, but not far from it in my heart and soul.

We spend the next day together having a picnic in the city park. I have a feeling of family closeness and well-being in spending time with them. That family feeling of being at home with each other is something I yearn to have more of in my life. My time in Arequipa has already made this trip back to Peru more than worth it. It is hard to leave them again.

After an emotional goodbye, I fly to Juliaca. From there I take a cab to the Puno Center House for my return to the shores of Lake Titicaca. The routine is familiar. I ask the seasoned taxi driver at the airport, "*¿Cuánto Cuesta?* How much to take me to the Maryknoll Center House in Puno?"

He knows the place from years of Maryknoll missionaries making the journey. The arrangements are quickly made and off we go.

I stay for an overnight in Puno, renewing old friendships as people come and go in that familiar rhythm of the house. Pat Ryan is there, still in charge of the Vicaría, having her usual large breakfast of eggs, pancakes, and sausage to fortify her for the day's human rights work. Abdón is in the office, working faithfully as administrator of the Center House. I see Jim, a priest from Jefferson City, Missouri, with whom I occasionally shared a bottle of Johnny Walker Red over an evening game of chess at the Center House.

Late in the afternoon on the first day of February, after a stopover in Juli, I arrive in Yunguyo. I get out of the passenger van on the outskirts of town with my bag and go first to the convent. I am just not quite ready to encounter Donald, the parish house, and the flood of emotions awaiting me there. Two of the sisters, Maria Gabriela and Anna Libia, welcome me and bring coffee and refreshments to the dining room table where we talk and laugh like old times. It feels like it was only yesterday that we were working together on the parish team. But as they talk about their current work in the parish that I'm no longer a part of, I find myself feeling detached, and with a certain sadness that what was my life here on the team with them, no longer is. Life and events have moved on without me.

The longer we sit and talk, the more I feel the ghosts of past tensions swirling in the space between the convent and the parish house. Being back in Yunguyo seems *too* familiar in some ways and I almost wonder why I'm here. Why *did* I come here, and what did I expect? Can I face the demons of unresolved conflicts from the life I lived here? Are the demons willing to be confronted?

I linger on at the convent and the sisters invite me to stay for supper. They call up to the parish house and announce that Donald, *Padre Donaldo* as they call him, will come down to join us for supper. Ready or not, I need to figure out how to confront the conflicting feelings I have toward him. What, eventually, will I say to him one-on-one? Perhaps I just need to acknowledge the hurts, angers, and frustrations I carried with me when I left—as well as the many good memories—and accept that we came together with very different personalities and had different expectations of what it meant to live and work together. Can I just leave it at that and let it go?

Well into the evening, I go up to the parish house with Donald. I make some small talk to break the silence as we walk. When we enter the house we say good night and he heads off to his room.

I walk my suitcase the short distance down the hall to the familiar sound of creaking floorboards and make a right turn into my old bedroom. It seems strange to be back. It is so empty. As I slowly look over the pieces of furniture that have not been moved, my eyes settle on some seashells and a little corn-husk doll I had left behind—the little German Frau on top of the empty bookshelf who's been standing there all this time in my absence. I make a slight bow to her with a little smile and say, "Thanks for watching over the room in my absence."

Later, in the quiet of the night, I remember the devil's mask I left behind when I packed to leave nearly two years ago. I had weighed the thought of taking it with me for quite a while as I held it in my hands. Somehow I just couldn't put it in my suitcase. But something prevented me from just throwing it away. It had so many associations with the violence and the evil of terrorism that had taken place during my four years in Peru. I had thought about turning it to ashes in the burn barrel. But in an odd way it also symbolized the joy of fiestas with the *diablada* dance and many other celebrations during my time in Peru. So at that time, without knowing exactly why, I placed it in the wooden cabinet that was built into the top of the bookcase that stood in the hallway just down from my bedroom. It had a pull-down door with an extending hinge. I remember how it creaked when I opened it and placed the mask inside, and then closed it up and tried to forget about it. *Would it still be there?*

With a click of the wall switch, I turn on the lightbulb hanging from the ceiling and step into the dark hallway. It takes a moment for my eyes to adjust to the dim light as I look around. The cabinet is still there, just as I remembered it. I face it squarely and hear the protest of the creaking hinge as I slowly pull the door down to open it. Yes, there it is. Waiting for me. Undisturbed all this time. Waiting, and now asking me, "Why did you leave me here?"

I respond, "Why should I have wanted to take you with me?"

"Because I am part of you."

"No," I say, "I reject the evil you represent, the terror, the violence."

"But it's not so easy is it? Just pick me up, go ahead. You're not going to go up in flames."

I gingerly pick it up. My thoughts are racing as I stare at it. *I remember you*, your likeness dancing in the fiestas of San Francisco de Borja and San Antonio de Padua. I remember the attraction and repulsion of seeing you represented with your grotesque features as you sat bigger than life on the shoulders of the one wearing your full devilish attire, spinning and weaving in and out of the synchronized phalanx of costumed dancers, you in your dervish dance of evil, evading St. Michael the Archangel pursuing you with his sword of goodness, the dance of good and evil, the dance emanating from the depths of the silver mines of Potosi, the dance of the underworld of darkness and death, the dance of terror unleashed upon this land.

I stand there, trancelike, weighing the mask first in my left hand, feeling the weight of the evil, terror, and painful conflicts from my time here. Then, shifting it to my right hand, it lightens under the memories of the joy and music of fiestas and the laughter of good times shared with so many of the people here.

Finally, I place it back in the cabinet, at least for now, and go back to my room to see if I can get some sleep.

I toss and turn in bed as the ghosts from the past swirl around me. Hurts, angers, disappointments, frustrations. Sleep eludes me as images and scenes keep playing in my head. I get up and decide to read to calm my mind. I pick up the book, *God's Passionate Desire*, that my spiritual director had given me before I left on this trip. I look over the table of contents and my eyes land on the chapter "Mysticism in Hell." I smile, thinking, well this definitely is the chapter for me tonight. *Mysticism in hell…*, the phrase seems to capture something about my time in Peru. So much pain, hurt and loneliness, and at the same time such deepening of prayer and self-knowledge that came with diving into the writings of St. Teresa of Avila. I open the chapter and slowly read it through, stopping to reflect on some of its pearls of wisdom as the night wears on. Eventually, some calm replaces my wrestling with all that came forth when I went face to face with the devil's mask. After finally getting a few hours of sleep, I awaken to a new day.

I have no particular plans so I spend some time visiting with people I worked with at the parish. Around midafternoon, I sit down in my bedroom and put some things in writing to Donald in the form of a letter. Writing things down helps me reflect and put things in a more balanced perspective.

We had breakfast together this morning, but as usual I got little response or acknowledgment from Donald when I tried to open up conversation about dealing with our past conflicts. Sensing his unwillingness to go there, and maybe just as much out of the fear and anxiety I have when dealing with conflict, I backed away. Maybe it's for the best. I hope he will be able to receive what I have written and digest it as he is ready. Or he may just dismiss it as something over and done with from the past as he tends to do. I likely will never know, at least not from him. I feel good that I have expressed my appreciation for how he mentored me in the beginning and mentioned many of the good memories along with some of my hurts and frustrations. I expressed the sadness I feel that we were never able to achieve a more adult-to-adult relationship beyond the kind of father-son dynamic we had at the beginning. I asked for forgiveness for any ways I may have hurt him. Now it is up to me to continue to work on letting go of the hurts and disappointments, to nurture the seeds of forgiveness and healing, and cultivate gratitude for the good experiences. That is what I can do from my side of the equation.

As I pack up my suitcase and get ready to leave Yunguyo, I weigh the idea of taking the mask with me. I take it back out of the cabinet and hold it in my hands. What registers this time is how small it is. Not much bigger than a softball. It is a devil's mask in miniature. Now that I had this chance to stand face-to-face with it and have it out, it no longer looms over me with the outsized presence it had taken on. It feels lighter in my hands now that I have confronted and "befriended" the demon of the hurt that was lingering in this house. I pack it up as I have seen shop owners do with breakable items for tourists, winding lots of course Peruvian toilet paper around it, binding it up for the journey. It seems appropriate.

Two weeks into my trip, I am on a three-hour bus ride from Juliaca to Ayaviri to see Ricardo. He is there for the summer working on a degree in education with a focus on youth. Riding this bus reminds me of the trip to the solidarity march nearly six years ago when I first arrived in Peru. The terrible condition of the road hasn't changed much. But the air feels lighter minus the tension of the terrorism and military atrocities that hung so heavily in the air back then. It's been quite a ride.

It is evening by the time I get to Ayaviri and Ricardo helps me get settled into a room. Then, as if we had prearranged it, we both sit down in my room and talk. I share a little bit about my visit to Yunguyo and ask how things went for him after I left. He relates how he and Donald arrived at a détente and were able to avoid any further disastrous arguments. Then he tells me, "I am looking seriously at getting married, possibly as soon as this April." I am not surprised. I knew the relationship that had begun in Yunguyo had continued.

He is obviously happy at the prospect, and I can't help but be supportive. The more we talk, the more complex the whole story behind his decision gets. The tensions between him and Donald took its toll. But there are other factors. He talks with me openly for the first time about when, while he was still in seminary, the police arrested and tortured him, accusing him of being involved with the terrorists. He tells me how that affected his need for intimacy and affection, and how for years after that he was unable to process and heal the effects of that horrible experience. This relationship leading to marriage is helping him to heal and feel whole again. "That is a good thing," I tell him, "And I'm really happy for you."

Two days later and back from my visit with Ricardo, a group of us are gathered at the monument where cousin Alberto died in the jeep crash. It was nine years ago today, February 9. The sun's rays are reflecting brightly off the white painted monument that stands just a few yards off the blacktop road. It has recently been repainted by the local community. As I look around, I am amazed that some thirty people have come. Yesterday as we were planning the event, I asked Narciso Valencia, a local and younger

Aymara priest to celebrate a memorial mass at the site. I watch as he opens an awayo on the ground, making Mother Earth the altar in Aymara fashion, then places the vessels of bread and wine upon the cloth. Someone else brings forth some flowers and a picture of Alberto. His presence is strong in our midst as we share memories of his life and ministry. At the conclusion, we stand around in a big circle to share a *brindis*, a toast in memory of Alberto. The gathering continues with an abundance of wine, cheese, crackers, Inca Kola, Pepsi, and cookies that combine with lively conversation, laughter, and more than a few tears shed in memory of a great man.

As we get into our vehicles to depart, I'm overflowing with emotion thinking about all the ways Alberto and all these people have touched my life. There are some fleeting thoughts of how good it might be to stay and pitch my tent here again. But in reality, I remind myself, it is one more stop on this journey of trying to bring more emotional closure to my years spent working here. Today has been more than a celebration of the anniversary of Alberto's death. It has been a remembrance of all the hopes, dreams, and struggles of faith and friendship that were part of my years here, and that I have continued to carry with me in my heart since I left. As I drive away, Alberto's monument slowly disappears from sight in the rearview mirror.

Five days later, I am in the Lima airport waiting to board my flight back to the US. The departure time has just been delayed by two hours. I settle into a seat in the waiting area. My three weeks in Peru have gone by quickly. In many ways I have felt "at home"... the familiar people and places, the local culture I could relate to so easily... and how I could so easily pick up on the threads of what's been happening in people's lives and tune in to social and political developments as if I'd only been away a few weeks. On the other hand, I always reached a point in conversations, especially when it came to talking about the pastoral work and problems, where I realized I wasn't feeling engaged, that I was no longer part of planning something or committing to do something here as part of a team.

I can't help but think fondly of the people who asked questions like, "When are you coming back?" or "Why don't you stay?" It was touching to feel wanted and missed, a sense of affection even. What could I say? Really, all I could say was what I did say to them in one version or another, which was that I am now committed to being the pastor of Cristo Rey Church in Lansing, and that for me it is a commitment of at least five years, just like it was when I made the commitment with Maryknoll to work in Peru. And then I would add that it is really important at this point in my life to be near my family and friends in Michigan again. They seemed, especially the Peruvians, to understand the family part more than anything else.

I could sense that it is hard for them to see people like me come and go so quickly, or at least what seems so quickly in their minds. Well, I did what I could to the best of my ability until I reached the emotional end of my rope. I couldn't hang on any longer. It was, and is, time to let go. And this trip has played an important role in the letting go part. In some ways I feel like the flying trapeze artists at the circuses I used to go to with my family as a child. They had to let go of one bar as they swung through the air in order to do a flying somersault and grab hold of the next one that would take them across the expanse to the platform on the other side. This feels like my somersault moment, still emotionally between two places, but in forward motion to the other side.

I remember my conversation about these things with Diego Irarrázaval, a Holy Cross priest from Chile, who has been working in the Altiplano for many years. We were talking in the Chucuito Plaza when, after we sat to drink some Inca Kola, he said, "I guess you always planned on being here for the five years," like he was trying to reconcile in his own mind some conflicting thoughts about why I had left or maybe just some sadness about it.

There is no announcement yet to board my flight. I decide to buy a bottle of beer from one of the airport vendors. After I sit down again, my eyes descend on the label, *Pilsen Callao*. The beer was named for the port city of Callao that is wrapped around by Lima. It is the preferred beer at the Lima Center House and has appeared at many a gathering. Peru does have good beer, thanks to those German immigrants way back when.

I'm grateful to have finally met up with Pat Ryan who has been in Lima on altitude leave. The emotions of my time with her are still very much with me, not only from our meeting last Monday, but from my years working with her on human rights issues at the Vicaría in Puno. She told me about the recent Music Festival for Peace and Life in Inchupalla. She shared what an emotional experience it was to gather in that remote mountain town north of Lake Titicaca that, like so many others, had been badly battered by the Sendero Luminoso terrorists. Music groups came from across the Altiplano for the competition. But far more than a competition, it was a celebration of a new moment in history. She described how the music groups dedicated newly composed songs to the people of the town who had suffered so much terror. They brought doves to release, symbolizing peace and the joy of being able to celebrate the festival in this town after all that has The doves circled above, then flew right to the church tower they had abandoned during the violence to take up residence again. It brought tears to my eyes listening to her account of it and thinking of all the violence, death, and suffering the people of that town have gone through, and indeed what the whole country has been through from both the terrorists and the counterviolence of government forces.

She concluded with the story of the winning music group driving back to Taraco five hours away in their rickety old truck badly leaking oil, waving the victory banners they had received for all to see in every town and community they passed. Tears are streaming down my cheeks even now as I picture it like a movie in my mind. They are waving the victory banners of life over death-dealing violence and terrorism. It is a display of the strength of family and community deeply rooted in ancient culture. It is resilience and healing. It is a victory I have yet to achieve over the post-traumatic stress the terrorism left me with, the PTS that is still awaiting healing as I fly away from this beloved land and its people so deeply embedded in my heart.

24

SHATTERED AND SCATTERED

March–August 1995

The vacation trip to Peru did help put some closure on that chapter of my life. Not in any final sense so much as a little more emotional distance from all the intensity of my life there as a Maryknoll missionary. Still, I frequently find myself in Peru in my thoughts. Even though it is nearly two years since my departure from the Altiplano, vivid images from my years in Peru roll through my mind in cinematic fashion every day.

I continue to wrestle with where and how and with whom I can feel at home. They say home is where the heart is, but where is my heart? I can't just return to some "before Peru" state of life. The missionary experience impacted me way too much for that. I still don't feel settled into the roles of being pastor of Cristo Rey Church and a "returned missionary" either. I am grateful for the recent letter I received from Sr. Cindy Meyer in Pennsylvania. We connected as kindred spirits during my first assignment at St. Casimir Church in Lansing where she was in charge of social outreach ministry. I wrote to her about some of my struggles in transition and she wrote back:

> *My missionary friends contend that you indeed never can come "home" again because in a way the global village has become home. What you don't ever come back to is the narrow interpretation of reality that most of us live. That must cause immense loneliness but also a real richness of experience and expansion of soul. May you learn to enjoy the ceaseless tension that has become your lot and that of every "returned" missionary. That's probably the only way to achieve peace.*

She has some understanding of what I am going through. Her letter is a gift that helps me describe it more clearly for myself. At the same time my struggles run deeper. The trauma from the terrorism and violence in Peru leaves me feeling like my former identity as been shattered and scattered. I no longer have a core identity I can trust will hold together through the storms and stresses of life. I was gifted with a solid core of stability by growing up in the same house until I went off to college, the stability of having feet planted on the same farmland through years of predictable seasons, and having parents who stayed together through all their difficulties. Now as I sit in my bedroom, I feel none of that. I am no more than fragments of the past scattered around the inner landscape of my life. Broken dreams, shattered hopes, lost idealism of being able to "change the world," overwhelmed by so much poverty, corruption, and violence. Trauma does that to you. In *Trauma and Recovery*, Judith Herman, MD, describes it on page 56: "Traumatized people suffer damage to the basic structures of the self.... The identity they have formed prior to the trauma is irrevocably destroyed." At least I know I am not the only one to feel this. I am not crazy. (I hope!) But where do I go from here?

Like so many things from "before Peru," even the farm life of my memories is fragmenting. I recently learned that the family farm operation is coming to an end. While my parents will continue to own the land and live in the farmhouse, the cattle and farm tools will all be sold off at a public auction. They are parts of the panorama of pictures in my memories that will be broken up and scattered around as the auctioneer awards them to the highest bidder. The tractors I drove, the implements and wagons our family used for generations.... It all adds to the fragmentation of my life. I grieve yet another loss of what was but no longer will be.

～～～

I have arrived for my next session with Catherine, my spiritual director. I'm sitting in the comfortable, cushiony chair facing her across the small, glass-top coffee table in the prayer room where we meet. I talk about my feeling of desolation, how I find the pieces of my broken life scattered across the dry and barren desert of my soul.

Then, as the candle on the table flickers, I tell her, "I feel like I am starting over again at the bottom when it comes to any sense of professional life. The people in ministry I know, especially the other priests of my diocese, have all continued on with their lives in my absence and I have not gotten much acknowledgement from them. I feel alone and isolated. I'm not sure how much most of them even care about what I have gone through. And they don't seem to have a clue about the Hispanic world I am ministering in now at Cristo Rey Church. Then there's the new guys who were ordained while I was gone; I don't even know their names. They seem like aliens dropped into our diocese from another planet."

Catherine takes this in and after a reflective pause says, "Jesus also felt desolate and abandoned in the Garden of Gethsemane. You might take that scene into prayer and let it speak to you. You are not alone." I take some comfort in that thought, and in feeling listened to by Catherine with her beautiful calm and empathy.

In my parish work at Cristo Rey, few if any would know what's going on inside of me. One of the "gifts" from my childhood family life, where we "did not do feelings," is that for the most part I can compartmentalize and separate my personal feelings from my work. From the perspective of my parishioners, I am doing the job and functioning just fine. Well, at least most people seem to see it that way. There is the small group that opposes me being their pastor because I am not Hispanic and am not letting them do whatever dysfunctional things they want to do.

The fact is I push myself, working very hard and long hours, taking responsibility for the welfare of the parish. Too much responsibility it seems, because every so often I "crash" and become unable to function for a day or two because of the stress. Is my workaholic style a way of avoiding the kind of self-care and personal time needed to process and heal from my PTS? I wonder how much my drive to be successful as a first-time pastor comes from some need to be able to control *something* in my life by putting order in the chaos of this parish, especially after things ended up feeling so out of my control in Peru. It feels like I am living out that old German phrase of my heritage, *alles in ordnung*, the need to put everything in order.

~~~

As May rolls around, I finally seek out a psychologist to help with my PTS, which was recommended at the end of my Return Program at Maryknoll almost two years ago. Why did I wait so long? Still scared of dealing with my deepest feelings? That's probably some of it. More so I think I just have not felt the energy to deal with it along with all the work I've taken on at the parish. But sometimes when it is time, it is just time, and maybe now is the right time.

~~~

My meetings with the psychologist have gotten off to a good start. I'm finding it helpful to explore my struggles with PTS, bouts of depression, and my struggle with relationships. "Good relationships," he tells me, "are key to rebuilding a life beyond trauma." We talk about my relationships of friendship, family, and my struggle with intimacy. All the levels of life that I have never been really good at or at ease with. I speak about my growing friendship with Kate and how that has become increasingly important to me during this time.

At one session he asks me, "Do you think you got into the wrong profession?," meaning one that asks for a commitment to celibacy. "It may be," he suggests, "that your chosen profession has delayed the exploration and development of the kinds of more deeply personal relationships we have been talking about."

I respond, "Well, what I know is that I have this deeply felt calling to be a priest. The requirement to not get married is something I always considered more like a rider attached to the commitment, but not something I have ever freely chosen. It is a part of the package I had to say yes to in order to pursue my calling."

The question stays with me, scares me really. But I have come to know that my healing and recovery and sense of well-being in life are somehow tied up with my ability to grow in my relationships. These days I find myself trying to pursue more contact with my family members. But communication and relationship building is an uphill battle given my family's history of dysfunction when it comes to relationships and dealing with emotions. Relationships at church are more professional and functional and as such can only go so far. I realize that my friendship with Kate is the most life-giving one I have and I make a mental leap in my mind that I would be a fool not to keep myself open to it. In addition to a deepening friendship, we share a passion for working on social justice in the world. It is a gift to find both in the same relationship.

Much time in our weekly counseling sessions is spent talking about the effects of my trauma and my trauma-related dreams. Today, I am recounting how in the dream on Margarita Island, I had the confrontation with Guzmán, founder of the Shining Path terrorist organization in Peru, and how the setting of the dream was in the family barn of my childhood where we each brandished weapons in a "dance with death," and I finally chased him off. As I describe the dream, I feel like I am being pulled into a black hole, like the hand of evil has a grip on me and won't let go. I go silent for a time, staring into oblivion. Then I will myself to resist it and pull myself out of the dark hole in order to be able to continue talking.

After a pause, he looks at me and says, "I think it might be helpful for you to take another journey through the dream in your imagination. But this time, instead of replaying it as it happened, try putting a different ending on it, one that will give expression to the anger you have at the violence and terrorism that still haunt you. Instead of holding back as you did in the original dream when you had the chance to stab him but let him run off, you might go for the kill, and thus symbolically kill the threat of terrorism, the experience of not feeling safe, and the presence of evil you feel in that dream."

"Ok," I say, still half staring into oblivion, "I will give that a try."

Eight days later I am at the Buersmeyer family cottage on Lake Huron where my priest support group is meeting. I am taking a long afternoon walk along the sandy beach to follow up on the suggestion made at my counseling session. As I walk, I bring to mind the scene of the "dance with death" in my dream about the confrontation with Guzmán. Then, I change the scene. Instead of my silence in the dream, I speak out loud to him in a steely and forceful voice:

"You will NOT be victorious. I am with the people and you are not. Death shall not prevail, get out of here! Out of the world, out of my life. Do not dare to think you can destroy me or overcome me!"

My pace quickens as I walk along the edge of the water. I speak an aside to myself, "And yet, I am afraid, fear eats away at my courage. Fear of death and fear of failure in my mission, fear, fear, fear." With that I cry out to the heavens, "It is too much!"

I stop at a small rise in the sand and sit, staring across the water. I continue the scene of the dream in my mind. I feel again the fear, the terror of the prospect of being physically attacked and stabbed by Guzmán. We are in the dance of terror around the inner wall of the barn. I begin to imagine a different ending as the scene unfolds. Instead of him running off with only a nick in his back from the point of my knife, I begin to stab him. I pick up a sharp stick from the sand where I am sitting on the beach and start stabbing into the sand over and over again, imagining it is Guzmán I am stabbing. As I stab the stick into the sand, I feel the resistance of his flesh as it is being torn open. The hissing sound of the sand is the knife boring into flesh and bone. Suddenly Guzmán melts away in the dream image, leaving only his clothes in a heap on the ground, just as the wicked witch in the *Wizard of Oz* does when she is struck by water.

I remember being terribly frightened by that movie as a little child, and how no one offered to hold me or hug me or say "it's alright." We watched it every year and I would curl up in a ball hiding under a blanket on the floor with my back against the couch, trying not to look at the scariest parts, but unable to totally resist. I'd peek out from time to time to see what was happening, feeling both the repulsion and attraction of the dark forces trying to overtake the good-hearted characters. When I was overwhelmed by fear, I didn't feel any power to change the scenario. I was alone with my childhood fright, just as I was alone in my dream with Guzmán.

The difference now on the beach is I am pushing back against the terror; I am not feeling helpless. I can choose to move forward into a new narrative.

The enactment of a new ending to the dream releases a tidal wave of primal energy. I can't sit still so I walk and walk a long distance up the beach and back. I swim out into the deep cresting waves carrying me up and down. I turn and float on my back, feeling the undulating waves below me and watching the billowing clouds above. I return to shore and at the cottage push out on a paddleboard and ride it like a kayak, paddling out into the vast open waters of Lake Huron. I paddle far out into the waters against the strong wind coming at me until the shoreline almost disappears behind me. I lose track of time as I continue riding the big waves up and down, feeling the surge of earth's energies with an awareness like never before of the raw elements of wind and water and pounding waves. I paddle and paddle until, nearly exhausted, I return to shore with the adrenaline still surging through me like a high voltage current.

Finally I sit down again on the sand to reflect on what just happened. Re-envisioning the dream brought me again to the edge of the "black hole" of terror and PTS that still seem all too ready to pull me into a kind of paralyzing emotional state. But now, after enacting a new ending to the dream, a new energy is surging up from deep within. It is energy for life and healing from the trauma. There is a resurgence of hope that the shattered shards of my inner self can be set into a new mosaic of life, however long that may take.

25

DEPRESSION

August 1995–August 2000

Work is like a drug providing escape from my post-traumatic stress. At work I can feel like I am in control, putting order in the chaos, whereas the trauma symptoms seem so out of my control. Trauma dreams haunt me through the night on an unpredictable timetable governed by unseen forces. Like with the terrorism in Peru, I never know when another trauma dream will strike.

Two weeks after my experience on the beach re-imagining my knife fight with Guzmán, I am awakened by a trauma dream at 4:30 a.m. It replays in my mind with total clarity. I'm in a jousting match: my opponent and I are on horseback covered head to toe in heavy medieval armor. The midday sun is shining across the wide, open field. Our long wooden spears are lowered in horizontal attack position as we charge at each other, horses at full gallop, hooves pounding the ground in a rapid drumbeat that matches the pounding of my heart. As we are about to collide, adrenaline is streaming through every centimeter of my body and my head is about to explode with fear that in the next second I could be sprawled out on the ground, mortally wounded. In the split second before we collide, I wake up.

As I lie on my bed, a chill runs through me as I consider its meaning. Neither of us backed off; each was determined to prevail over the other.

My opponent behind the armor represents the masked face of evil and terrorism charging at me, still trying to do me in.

Later on I re-imagine the scene, continuing the process I used successfully with the Guzmán dream. When I get to the point in my mind where the dream ended, just before we collided, the scene continues as if guided by the hand of an unseen film director. In this version the collision happens at full force. Our spears are crashing and splintering against our armor as we knock each other off our horses. I am lying on the ground, weak and injured … but alive. I have survived. Lying there I acknowledge my vulnerability and accept my fear in the face of death. With some reserve strength I didn't even know I had, I get up and carry on with my life.

I speak about these dreams in my next counseling session, and as I do, waves of anxiety and fear come crashing over me. As overwhelming as it is at times, talking about the trauma is helpful, and each time I talk about it and process what's going on, it gets a little less violently intense. Dealing with this deep-seated stuff that keeps surfacing is like body surfing on an ocean wave as it rolls into shore. I advance and crest and come forward, while at the same time the dark forces of the undertow are at work, trying to drag me into the abyss. I am finding that bit by bit, the trauma, like the pus in a deeply infected wound, works itself to the surface and slowly, over time, with professional help and self-care, healing takes place.

Balancing work and self-care has never been my forte. Currently, I am driven by the need for a larger church facility. When the community entered into a new goal-setting process during my first seven months at Cristo Rey, one of the goals was to assess our space needs and consider options for our growing community. As we investigated options, a much larger and nearby church facility became available for purchase that would meet our needs at a cost we could manage. But with that, a conflict erupted between those in favor and those against making a move. I have been taking blows from a small but determined opposition group. At one point I felt so depressed and discouraged by it that I questioned whether I should just give it up.

But by November 1998, with more support than opposition, we completed a fundraising campaign, purchased the former Baptist church complex, renovated it for our needs, and moved in. Then, with great enthusiasm and pride, and a packed church overflowing into the street, we celebrate the formal dedication of our new church on November 22. The big, open space with its massive wooden beams feels like a cathedral compared to our former cramped space. Like the story of *The Little Engine That Could*, we are the little Hispanic community that did. *¡Si se puede!*

I feel vindicated, even victorious, after my dogged pursuit of helping to make it happen. But it has taken a big toll. As December rolls around, I am feeling exhausted and searching for a way to renew my energies. New Year's 1999 does not bring with it that surge of new hope I usually experience at the start of a new year. My emotional energy drain continues in February as Mom has quadruple bypass open heart surgery. Then two members of our extended family commit suicide, one after the other. In April, Dad is diagnosed with heart problems. The stress keeps piling up. I need to get off the treadmill.

So I start looking seriously at taking a sabbatical. I pull out my daily planner and calculate that the fall of 2000 would be a good time. It is a year and a half away. It seems like a long time to wait. But in reality I am going to need the lead time to figure out what exactly I want to do so I can submit a plan and get approval from the diocese. After that I need to arrange for someone to fill in for me while I am gone. Setting out that timetable begins to lift my spirits. After the intensity of leading the parish in the purchase and renovation of our new church facility, I need some personal renovation. I have actually given myself permission to do it, not easy for a workaholic.

In the meantime, I can't help myself. Slowing down while on the job is not in my DNA. We are overdue to develop our next five-year parish plan and I feel the need to proceed. One of the criticisms from the opposition group during the last process was that I pushed ahead too fast without consulting them. According to them, I had already made the decisions and was just dragging everyone along. Untrue! I protested. Nevertheless, I still feel stung by that and am determined not to be the one leading the charge this time around. So I ask Hugo Romero, a young professional in the parish, to head up the Tomorrow's Parish planning process the diocese is promoting. I tell him, "Hugo, you are in charge. Here's the planning manual the diocese gave us and you can go to the training sessions. Consult with me when you need to, but you are in charge and you can take all the time you need." Am I being a little passive aggressive here? Maybe, but I think I earned the right to this one. There can be dialogue and consultation from now to eternity if necessary, but nobody is going to be able to legitimately complain they had not had the opportunity to be heard.

A few months later, when I go to my doctor for my annual physical, he notices I am in emotional trouble. With his white-haired wisdom and compassion he asks me, "Are you depressed?"

Tears well up in my eyes. It is hard for me admit it. It feels like weakness. But finally I say, "I have been under a lot of stress lately and feeling a lot of sadness. Maybe I am."

As we talk, he helps me acknowledge that I am exhausted and in a deep depression. He prescribes the antidepressant Prozac and gives me the name of a psychologist he holds in high esteem.

Two years ago I ended my sessions with the first psychologist I worked with. I felt we had reached the limit of what he could do for me. Then it became a question of getting the momentum going again to find a new psychologist. It was easier to just keep working, until depression overwhelmed me.

With my doctor's diagnosis, I reflect back on my life and realize I have gone through many cycles of depression. I just never called it that. This time is the worst of all. I'm having periodic moments of weeping over the loss of my former sense of self and purpose. After Peru, things that seemed so solid about my life have become like shifting sands. Especially now, with all the final details of the new church wrapped up, I am groping for something to latch on to, a new goal, something tangible to sink my teeth into. Some good friends, Ray and Mary, suggest the image of "postpartum depression" as a way to think about what I am experiencing after birthing the new church. It has a certain ring of truth to it, but this runs deeper than that.

So I probe deeper, asking, *What gives me comfort and a sense of well-being?* I make a list. Time spent at home with my parents where I grew up, time spent in prayer and walks in nature, and time spent in nurturing relationships.

I try the Prozac pills for the next four months and they do help lift my spirits some. But mostly they make me feel more zombie-like. I stop taking them. Now it is April 2000 and I finally set up my first appointment with Valerie Shebroe, the psychologist my doctor recommended back in December.

As I prepare for the appointment, I think back on how I found some respite on a retreat week in Florida in January. It seems when I actually step back from work mode, I feel some healing energy. Why did I wait four months to contact Ms. Shebroe? More of my old stuff of not dealing easily with emotions, relationships, and personal struggles. My default mode is to avoid talking openly about difficult and scary feelings. Some inner message says I should be strong enough to overcome these things on my own. Just tough it out and keep working harder. I am slowly realizing that that doesn't work over the long haul.

In my first counseling session with Valerie, there is an immediate rapport as she asks about my background and what issues I want to work on. My gut instincts tell me I have found the right person. A big relief.

In our next session, as I talk about what led up to my PTS, strong feelings around my experience of terrorism roll up from the depths and overwhelm me once again. At one point I stop talking and just sit there in stunned silence.

Valerie suggests that my post-traumatic stress and the feelings of loss and grief over what I left behind in Peru are connected to my depression. It is obvious I am doing a lot of grieving, she tells me, and assures me it is normal. I go on and share with her how in Peru I hit the wall of my inability to do much, in the end, to change the reality of so much poverty and injustice in people's lives, and how I feel so much sadness even now about all the suffering I saw in people's lives. It feels different at Cristo Rey, I tell her, where I have worked hard and have gotten concrete results; but that has been at the cost of not taking sufficient time for myself to heal the wounds from Peru and invest in personal relationships.

In June, I announce to the parish I will be taking a four-month sabbatical starting in August. The responses vary from encouraging words like, "Father, you deserve it," to, "Does that mean you are not coming back?" That night I dream that I am flying, and soaring around from place to place high above the ground. The meaning? I am more than ready to fly free from my parish responsibilities.

I literally fly away in August to San Diego, California. Phillip Sessions, my seminary classmate, meets me at the airport. I stay at his place overnight and bathe in his wonderful hospitality. The next day he drives me to the retreat house where I have arranged to spend the next month on a silent directed retreat. We walk up to the black wrought iron gate where I take a deep breath and ring the buzzer.

The retreat house is a double condominium with four sisters of the Sacred Heart living in community on one side and room for two retreatants in the unit on the other side. I found the place through an ad in the National Catholic Reporter that said retreat directors were available and made special note of the beautiful beach on the Pacific coast just a ten-minute walk away. It described how the unit where I will be staying has a common kitchen where I will do my own cooking, something I look forward to.

After I say goodbye to Phillip, Sr. Nancy Koke, who will be my spiritual director, gives me a tour of the place. As I unpack my suitcase, a great relief settles over me. I am really here and away from my parish responsibilities.

26

HEALING

August 22–September 2, 2000

I remember a person from my first parish assignment who came back from fighting in Vietnam and was never able to talk about it. He pretty clearly suffered from post-traumatic stress as evidenced by stories his wife told me of him frequently waking up nights with violent memories of his war experiences. He would not talk with her or anyone about his emotions and experiences connected to his time in Vietnam or get professional help. He seemed to be a rock of silence and his family life was suffering. That has been a cautionary story for me. I am determined to explore anything that will help me continue on the path of healing and wholeness. With all the effects of PTS still going on in my life seven years after I departed from Peru, someone hearing my story might think I'm quite a basket case of unresolved emotions and that I should think about checking myself into a psych ward some place. Yet, paradoxically, it might seem, in my public life I have functioned competently and accomplished a lot as pastor of Cristo Rey Church. I have provided good, solid leadership that has helped the parish thrive and come back from the brink of closing its doors before I arrived to take charge. I certainly have my flaws and have made my share of mistakes, but overall I have done well by the parish and I feel good about what I have been able to do in spite of suffering from PTS. I have come to understand that healing from PTS is a long-term affair. Its impact will never go away. It has and is shaping my life in ways I could never have imagined before embarking on the missionary journey with Maryknoll in Peru. A lot of healing and growth has taken place with the benefit of professional help and insights that have come my way even as some of the deeper effects of trauma continue to impact me. It just seems to be the nature of the beast of PTS. Aspects of it can linger on for years. Deep wounds don't always heal quickly. And in my case, taking this sabbatical time for healing, away from work, seems essential.

The day after my arrival at the retreat house, I have my first session with Sr. Nancy. She is a warm, wise, and experienced spiritual director. She invites me to share some of my history and my hopes for this retreat time. I talk about my exhaustion from my work at Cristo Rey, my PTS and how I want this to be a healing and renewing experience. She suggests that rather than something more structured, we can leave things open-ended to allow for the Spirit to guide the process. We will meet for an hour each day to talk about the spiritual journey. She concludes our session with a guided meditation. After inviting me to relax and close my eyes, she tells me, "Imagine you are walking out of town, away from the place where you lived in Peru.... Along the way, you meet a spiritual guide..."

My guide appears dressed in white, greets me, and offers to walk with me. And so my retreat begins.

Later in the afternoon, I take my first walk along the beach, listening to the rolling and crashing waves of the Pacific Ocean. I feel like I want to sit for hours in the coming days on the warm sand, staring out at the vast blue expanse. The sun's warmth is already beginning to soften the tightness in my neck and shoulders. I want the deeply lodged tensions, terrors, and exhaustion to slide out of my body and wash away into the deep blue sea. I know it won't be quick or easy. There is much pain and brokenness that still need to surface and be confronted on the path to healing. I start by recalling some of the positive experiences that have nourished and strengthened me over the years in difficult times.

The next day I pull out art supplies from the closet next to my room and draw a picture of the incredible experience of Pachamama I had after teaching the pre-seminary class in Peru. With that I ponder how I am a child of Mother Earth and how in my early childhood on the farm I helped my mom in the garden. She taught me how to plant butternut squash seeds, three seeds together in each little mound I carefully formed with my little hands. She gave me my own four-foot-square plot of land to plant whatever I chose. I delighted in how fast the radishes I planted grew and how later in the summer the snapdragons opened their mouths when I pinched them. They're still my favorite flower.

I bring these comforting images and memories to my afternoon conference with Nancy. But my serenity quickly pivots to anxiety. I recount the Guzmán dream which segues into speaking of the raw evil and suffering I encountered in Peru. That night I awaken at 1:30, feeling on edge. I make a long entry in my journal, recounting key moments in the buildup of fear in Peru and how that ultimately led to feeling terrorized by the time I left the country. It takes me back into the darkness of that moment on Margarita Island when, after the Guzmán dream, I was staring into a black cloud with the face of evil staring back at me.

The following morning, I decide to experiment some more with drawing as a way to process these experiences. I pull out the sketch pad and box of pastels I used yesterday. Twenty pastels are neatly arranged by shades of color in the white plastic container that has a separate cradle for each one. Unlike the crayons I drew with as a child, these are rectangular in shape and have no wrapping. They feel soft to the touch, and color slides off them easily when brushed across the medium-tooth paper. I select a slim stick of the blackest pastel and hold its smooth sides in my right hand between my thumb and next two fingers. I begin with quick circular strokes, drawing the large, dark eyes of the face of evil staring at me. This is followed by forming the ethereal shape of a face appearing out of a swirl of black clouds. I am drawn more and more into the two tunnels of blackness that are the eyes as I complete the image. Then, in a sudden shift, as I stare, semi-transfixed into the eyes, some part of me is *in* the eyes looking back at me. It is all part of me, I realize, the pain and fear and terror I experienced in Peru, it is all part of the long chain of experiences that have brought me to this day.

Later in the morning I have my conference with Nancy. I slowly read aloud the long entry I made in my journal last night, halting at times as tears of pain and sadness well up from within, choking my voice. I show Nancy the picture I drew of the face of evil and recount how I suddenly experienced a part of myself looking back at me through those big black eyes, and how the insight came that it is all part of who I am now. Then I say, "It's like I finally feel free to move on from that experience."

Nancy offers an insight, "The dream of your encounter with Guzmán is a gift, the gift of an awareness of the depth of the evil and the suffering of the people you encountered, and how you absorbed that into yourself. It is the gift of bringing it out into the open where you can face it. The journey of healing began there on Margarita Island."

"A gift," I say slowly. "That is a new way to look at it, and I guess it's true. It was a confirmation, in an odd sort of way, that I made the right decision to return home to the relationships and resources I needed to survive emotionally."

After a turkey sandwich with lettuce, tomato, and mayo for lunch, I go to my room and sleep for two hours. Then I put on my swimsuit, a T-shirt and flip-flops, and make my way to the beach where I walk aimlessly along the shoreline, listening to the waves. After a while, I venture out onto the long fishing pier that opens out horizontally at the end like a docked ship. A rustic restaurant advertising fish tacos is perched over the edge of the pier halfway out. Several people are casting fishing lines into the ocean. After walking the full length of it, I head back to the beach and dive into the warm ocean waters. The waves caress and roll me around. There is no hurry and nowhere to go. I sit on the beach to watch the sunset, and then return to my room where I sleep long and deeply through the night.

When I wake up in the morning I feel playful and newly alive. I do a spontaneous dance in my bedroom listening to a Donna Peña song I have on cassette, singing along with its refrain, "I say yes my Lord …" It's a new day.

In the retreat plan, there is a "free day" each week when I don't meet with Nancy. She suggested I do something fun. So I am at the San Diego Zoo, feeling like a kid again. I spend a half hour watching the polar bears waking up, yawning, and stretching, and then swimming in the water, massive, powerful, and yet playful. Then it's on to the aviaries, and the panda bears. I get in line at the food concession and buy an ice cream cone with two scoops of double chocolate. To my great delight and surprise, I come across a music group from Peru playing their panpipes, drums, and the *churango* that looks like a mini guitar. The music transports me back to Peru and all the emotions of my farewell party when I danced the night away.

As I walk further through the zoo, my thoughts turn to Kate, wondering how she is doing, wishing she were walking through the zoo with me, how she too would delight in this place, and how our friendship is such a gift in my life.

The joy I felt on my zoo day proves fickle. I am painfully reminded that the PTS is far from over as trauma dreams continue to assault me. There is no predicting which nights they will come or how intense they will be. I keep wondering, *Why was I so vulnerable to being traumatized in Peru?*

I am lying awake in bed, startled as I recall a terribly vivid traumatic dream. In the nightmare, I was driving a van with five friends sitting in the two seats behind me. The calm drive quickly turned dangerous as the road became slippery with snow and then was strewn with the debris of wrecked cars. I was swerving to avoid the large chunks of crashed cars that were appearing closer and closer to each other all over the road as I drove on. It became increasingly difficult to avoid hitting something. Suddenly, a lot of cars were coming at me head-on. A terrible crash was about to happen. In the split second before the deadly impact, I awoke with my heart racing and adrenaline pumping through me.

I sit up on the edge of my bed in silence, waiting for my pounding heart to slow down. I can feel it thumping against my chest like a drum beat. When my heartbeat slows below the threshold of panic, I pull out my notebook and write out the dream to process it and seek its meaning. Why this dream of a horrible crash about to take place? Why now? Why am I the driver of the vehicle? Suddenly, I flash back briefly to the train accident of my youth. The imagery of both the dream and the train crash stay with me as I wander through the rest of the day. It feels like the dream is pointing me to something I need to pay attention to.

Late that night in my room, I decide to draw a picture of the train bearing down on me. I pull out the darkest black pastel and draw a pretty fair rendition of the train heading toward me on the tracks. Not a bad drawing, I think to myself; it looks pretty realistic. I am feeling pretty calm about it until I pick up the bright yellow pastel and, with heavy strokes, draw the stream of the engine's headlight pouring down the tracks directly at me. I can see the engine, massive and heavy, emerging from the dark of the night. I continue drawing. Several times I think I am done, but return to it to fine-tune and develop it some more. Finally, there it is. I step back and stare at the light from the train engine. I turn off all the lights in the room, light a candle and set it at the back edge of the picture lying flat on the desk. The glow of the candle runs down the yellow beam of light coming from the locomotive. An eerie feeling creeps over me as I stand there working a few final modifications of the drawing. Suddenly, I step back again, holding the black pastel in my hand, unable to move. I drop the pastel and stare into the picture as the weight of the whole experience of the train accident, the high anxiety, and the trauma, hits me like a ton of bricks. I'm there, crossing the tracks, flashing back into the experience…

"Look out!" Johnny yells from the back seat of the car. In the same instant I turn to my left and see the big yellow headlight of the train engine bearing down the tracks at us, slicing the night like a laser-guided missile. The engineer, desperate to warn us, keeps blowing the whistle that sounds like a foghorn in the night. I'm faced with a split-second, life-and-death decision; hit the brakes or hit the accelerator. I instantaneously calculate that braking risks stopping the car dead on the tracks. The decision is made. I jam the accelerator to the floor, hoping the powerful V-8 engine of the Buick Wildcat will pull us across the tracks in time. The engine roars like a lion as the big boat of a car surges forward.

I was sixteen years old, driving the family car. Earlier that evening, some of my classmates and I had watched the Fowler Eagles varsity team win the Friday night basketball game on our home court. After the game, we were in a mood to celebrate. I was the only one who had both a driver's license and my parent's car for the evening. I was proud that my parents trusted me with the car and I could invite my friends to go for a ride. Five of us piled into the car and picked up a pizza and some cokes from Miller's Tavern before heading out to cruise the country roads. Someone brought up "the haunted house" not far from where we were headed and we dared ourselves to drive by and take a look. I stopped the car in front of it, half scared and half thrilled by the adventure of it.

"People have seen ghosts in there," Johnny said nervously from the back seat.

"That's why no one lives there anymore," his twin sister Joanie added. "I've heard that every owner has seen ghosts and moved out."

The wood siding on the two-story farm house was weather-beaten gray. The sagging wood and broken steps of the front porch sighed at us, beckoning us to come closer if we dared. "Should we go in?" I asked.

"I'm not going in there," Joanie responded. "Let's get out of here!"

We hastily drove off and continued cruising the country roads until we finished our pizza and cokes. Around midnight we arrived back in town. I dropped two of my classmates off at their homes on the north side. One had been in the front seat and the other in the back. I asked the twins, Joanie and Johnny, if one of them wanted to move up front. They said they would both just stay in the back seat since they would be dropped off in a few minutes.

If the answer had been yes, there would have been a delay. I would have pulled over and waited for one of them to open the back door, get out, walk around the car, open the front passenger door, and get in before I continued on. As it was, I just continued driving south on Main Street toward the only traffic light in town. I needed to make a right turn at the light on M-21, a block down from the tracks, and then head west for a mile to drop them off at their house. I was focusing my eyes on the red traffic light down the street, wondering if it would turn green by the time I got there. And just for good measure, rock and roll music was blaring from the radio. So the red flashing lights and bells clanging at the train crossing didn't register in my brain. There were no crossbars at the tracks and the big white Becker's Lumber Yard building on my left blocked the view down the tracks as I approached.

So now the engine is straining with all its might as the car surges forward onto the tracks. I almost think we are going to make it when I hear the sickening sound, the heavy *thud*, the strangely muffled yet unmistakable sound of the steel behemoth plowing into the left rear quarter panel of the car. The impact snaps our heads sideways and the car begins a circular movement on the ground. The back end is pivoting around the weight of the engine in the front while at the same time the car continues its forward glide on the momentum of my panicked acceleration. Time shifts into slow motion. As the car spins counter clockwise, I see the spare tire that had been popped out of the trunk by the impact floating through the air over the windshield and bouncing down the street. Becker's Furniture Store on the corner and the Main Street lights spin around us in a blur as the car turns a full 360 degrees before coming to a stop. Miraculously we are still sitting right side up. My first instinct is to turn to Joanie and Johnny in the back seat to see if they survived the crash that hit closer to them. "Are you ok?" I ask.

"Yes, I think so," Joanie responds.

We are all in shock. I feel around my body to make sure it is still in one piece. The sense of being awfully lucky to have survived slowly begins to register somewhere in my brain.

I get out and see townspeople walking toward us from the nearby bars and parked cars to see what happened. My neighbor Chuck Miller is the first one to approach and asks, "Were you drinking?"

"No," I respond.

"You're lucky you weren't or you would really be in trouble."

I can only nod some acknowledgement of his words, not yet sure how much trouble I really am in.

The black and white Clinton County cruiser pulls up and the officer ushers us into the back seat so he can make out a report. As I am answering his questions about what happened I am worrying more about what my dad will say when he finds out. Eventually I see my dad, who has pulled up in our old blue Chevy pickup, standing outside waiting. Even though he is short and of slight build, his red hair makes him stand out among the crowd gathered in the night. *What will he say? He'll be really mad,* I can't help thinking. When the police officer releases us from the car I walk over, shaken and fearing the worst from my father. My childhood memories flood me with the fear that he'll be explosively angry.

His first words *are* angry ones, but not out-of-control angry as first feared. "What were you doing!?" he asks, staring at me. Then after a pause he catches himself, does an emotional pivot and asks a little more gently, "How are you? Are you ok?"

At first my anger boils up and I think, *shouldn't that have been your first concern?* But I bottle up that feeling inside as I learned to do growing up. Then gratitude overtakes my flash of anger as his gentler question, *Are you ok?* sinks in. I am deeply moved that he is not yelling at me, that he really is concerned about me more than the car. I could almost hug him, except we don't do hugs. I look down at the ground and tell him, "I'm sorry about the car."

To which he says, "A car can be replaced."

After Dad makes arrangements for the car to be towed, we get into the pickup. It is a silent ride home. I continue to feel grateful for his words of genuine concern and worry over me. I can see in his face that he is badly shaken by how close I had come to being killed. A puff of unspoken love and gratitude hangs in the air between us. When we get home he sends me off to bed with no further ado.

That's the closest we came to sharing our feelings about the matter. It seems ironic it was in the face of a traumatic event that we shared that rare moment of tenderness in my adolescence. I'm blessed that as adults we have been able to gradually open up to sharing some of the emotional side of our lives, even sharing the occasional warm hug.

The day after the crash, other than having a sore and stiff neck, I went to school as if nothing had happened. During lunch hour at school, a few of us were shooting baskets in the gym and talking glibly about it. "Were you scared?" one friend asked me.

"Well, I think I left a bag of shit bricks in the car," I answered, as I forced a smile onto my face. I tried to make light of it and feigned calmness on the outside. Inside I was still deeply shaken by my brush with death. With no experience of talking about traumatic feelings, or much of any feelings for that matter, the trauma was left buried, raw and unprocessed.

I remember our neighbor down the road from our farm, Jim Goerge, who would always greet me that summer saying, "Hi lucky!" He reminded me how I did feel lucky and blessed to still be alive. He was the closest thing to giving any kind of adult acknowledgment to me of what had happened and what feelings I might have about it.

It is close to midnight, and I'm still in my retreat room staring at the picture I drew. I keep thinking about that **sound**, that strangely muffled yet loud *thud* of the massive weight of the locomotive collapsing the rear quarter panel of the car. Suddenly the realization comes. It is unnervingly similar to the sound I heard in Puno, Peru, when a terrorist bomb was set off not far from where I was. It was in the dark of night. I was in bed in the Maryknoll Center House, not quite asleep, when I heard the muffled *thud* of the explosion.

Was the fear I felt after the bomb went off in Puno intensified by the unconscious connection to the *thud* of the train crash that was buried in my memory all those years? Now, seven years after returning from Peru, it seems the full emotional impact of the train accident is finally hitting me.

I'm beginning to see that traumas got stacked up in my life like layers of ice on a glacier, each layer compacted further down by the ones above it. Each trauma not dealt with left me more vulnerable to the impact of the next ones. This proved especially true in Peru, which sent me into full blown PTS by the end of my time there. Healing has been happening as I've found the emotional safety and the help needed to make the connections, scrape back the layers, and process the feelings. I am seeing some light at the end of this tunnel called trauma, a light of healing and recovery and, thankfully, not the headlight of another train.

27

LOVE YOUR ENEMY

September 4–20, 2000

Three Wild West gunmen on horses are pursuing me at full gallop down an open road. I am frantically looking around for any possible avenue of escape. My desperate maneuvers to elude them go on and on for what seems like an eternity. They are getting closer and closer. Suddenly I wake up with a vague sense of having gotten away from them, but it is not clear. As I lie in bed mulling it over, I identify the elements of danger, vigilance, and adrenaline. Clearly another PTS dream. I've gotten pretty good at making these connections. But why this dream now? In the midst of my questioning, I feel a visceral connection between this dream and the one of my confrontation with Abimael Guzmán seven years ago. Apparently I'm not finished with him yet.

I talk about this in my next meeting with Nancy. She offers to lead me in a guided meditation to further explore the confrontation I had with Guzmán in the nightmare on Margarita Island.

I readily say yes. I trust her guidance and I'm keen on anything that might help the healing process.

In a soft voice she says, "Close your eyes, take some slow, deep breaths, and as you exhale, let any tensions drain out." After waiting for me to do this a couple of times, she continues, "Bring to mind the image of yourself in the dream with Guzmán. What do you see…?"

Now I am in the dream, seeing the images of how it began. I tell Nancy, "I am face-to-face with Guzmán, looking at him across the string of electric wire separating us at the wide opening to the barn on our family farm. I'm on the inside and he's on the outside. We are tense and on guard, staring at each other, not saying a word. I'm on high alert, my heart is pounding."

"What do you want to say to him...? What does he say to you...?"

In a kind of Gestalt therapy mode, I speak in a tense, audible voice, asking him, "Why are you here at my family farm? Why have you caused so much terror and destruction in Peru? What did you hope to accomplish?"

Then I assume Guzmán's part and give voice to his defensive response: "I wanted justice for the people and an end to the colonial oppression that the poor, the workers, and the outcasts have suffered for centuries. I was bringing hope for a new society of equality for all."

"It seems we both wanted some of the same things," I respond. And in a firmer voice, "But we are diametrically opposed in the means we would use to get there..." We continue along these lines, and then I say, "Some months before I left Peru you were captured and put in maximum security prison. So why is your spirit here, pursuing me?"

"My spirit lives on in my followers. The struggle, *la lucha*, continues..."

"It won't work," I say coldly, slowly, and deliberately. "They are too dependent on you for everything to carry on without you..."

Then, as he is about to leave, something totally unexpected wells up from within me, "One more thing," I say, "Let me clasp your hand." I take his hand as if I were giving him a handshake. Time stops as we both grip each other firmly and look into each other's eyes. It feels absolutely real— the touch of his flesh, the strength in the grasp of our hands.

With our right hands locked together, I say to Guzmán, "I will pray for you, that you have a change of heart." With that he vanishes into a fog.

～～～

Later in the day, I am walking on the beach reflecting on all this. The command in the Gospel of Matthew says, "Love your enemy." I have always wrestled with that one. Scholars say those words are so startling and original that there is no doubt it is an authentic saying of Jesus. For the first time in my life, I have an inkling of how this can be possible. The experience of the guided meditation brought me to a new moment of seeing

Abimael Guzmán as a fellow human and one I am called to love, even as an enemy in opposition to all I believe and stand for. There was grace in the encounter. I felt a release and a calm after the initial high energy anxiety of the "meeting" with Guzmán in the meditation. By transforming the script of the original dream into a dialogue, a personal encounter, it became a very different dynamic. I felt the Spirit of the Universe nudging me along, taking me a step further on the journey to healing and wholeness.

A week later in my spiritual direction session with Sr. Nancy, I talk about my friendship with Kate, how it has grown over the years and how important she is to me, how our relationship has helped me grow and heal and feel more whole as a person, especially in this time of dealing with PTS. I also talk about how during this retreat I have felt a deep affirmation of my call to priesthood. Both are part of who I am. What does it mean for my life going forward? When I finish, Nancy suggests I take time to reflect on the meaning of love and deep friendship in my life.

Late in the afternoon, I take a long rest stretched out on my beach towel in the warmth of the sun and soft sand on the beach. I still do not have a lot of reserve energy and I tire easily. Lots of rest has been helping me recover. Eventually I get up and go for a walk along the shoreline where I come across half of a small sand dollar that the waves have washed up. It would have been the size of a silver dollar before it broke apart. I hold it gently in my hand as I continue my walk. Then I see another half piece. I carefully pick it up and brush the sand off. The two halves fit perfectly together, forming a complete sand dollar. What are the odds of finding both halves on this random walk down the beach at this particular time in the late afternoon? Usually treasures washed up from the sea are picked up by early morning walkers.

Suddenly, I know with the certainty that only comes when you just know you know. It is a sign from the sea, from the Mystery of All Creation, confirming the goodness of my friendship with Kate and the blessing she is in my life. We are soulmates. We are these two halves that have found each other. A smile spreads across my face and a quiet, joyful laughter erupts from the depths of my being.

Back in my room, I pick up the little book of reflections by Anne Morrow Lindbergh that Nancy gave me a while back to read. It is called *Gift from the Sea*. She speaks from her experience of taking extended time at the sea for renewal. I open it again to the page where she writes, "Patience, patience, patience, is what the sea teaches. Patience and faith. One should be empty, open, choiceless as a beach—waiting for a gift from the sea."

Today I have received a great gift from the sea. I can only say with awe and reverence, *gracias*. As the great Mercedes Sosa from Argentina sings so passionately, "*Gracias a la vida que me ha dado tanto*." Thanks to life, which has given me so much.

I'm in my final days of retreat at Ocean Beach, California. I feel like Lazarus in the Gospel of John called forth from the tomb. I find myself reflecting a lot on the treasures I will take with me from this retreat on the coast, treasures that have washed up from the depths on the waves of time. Most precious of all are the gifts of healing and the affirmation of life-giving friendship.

It is September 20 and the sisters invite me to have mass with them and stay for a little breakfast celebration of my twentieth anniversary of ordination and my last day at the retreat house. They are so great. During the whole time, I'm welling up with gratitude for them and for my time here. Tears trickle down my cheeks as we say our final goodbyes with words of appreciation and hugs all around.

28

NOT A HELPLESS VICTIM

October 14–November 14, 2000

I'm at Catholic Theological Union in Chicago on the second leg of my four-month sabbatical. Three weeks ago, I began auditing two courses on faith and culture. When I arrived, I moved into the end room on the third floor of the old brownstone apartment building owned by the school. The walls and ornamental plaster in the living area have thick layers of off-white paint that is peeling in spots like fragments of the Dead Sea Scrolls. The old cast-iron steam radiators are covered in the same thick white paint. There is a rectangular space in the wall next to my freestanding single bed that used to hold a Murphy bed. Too bad it is not still there. It would add a little more of that old-time charm to my quarters and probably be more comfortable. The room has a ten-foot ceiling and large, wood-framed windows overlooking the graduate school's parking lot to the south. Next to my bed are a simple desk and a well-worn recliner chair with a floor lamp parked between them. A large wooden wardrobe stands against the opposite wall. On the southwest corner of the room, an open doorway leads into the efficiency kitchen that has a small stove, a little table, one creaky wooden chair, and an old stand-up refrigerator that sounds like it is protesting every time the compressor comes on. Everything paintable in the kitchen is coated in white except the floor which has black and white checkerboard tiles complete with cracks and missing corners. An added touch is the Metra train that rumbles by right next to my apartment, sending vibrations through the walls and delivering a free body massage every time.

I have gone from the quiet, slower rhythm of retreat in San Diego to the activity of coursework and class interaction here in Chicago. I'm enjoying my classes and the people I am meeting. The mental stimulation of exploring new ideas energizes me. From early on, doing well in school has always been a refuge, a space where I could excel and feel affirmed in the midst of whatever emotional struggles were going on. Even still, about midweek in each of my first two weeks here, I crashed in exhaustion as tensions built up and I just had to stop everything for a day to recover. Part of it has to do with my perfectionism that impels me to dive in and strive to do my best. I want to keep up with my fellow students working on their Doctor of Ministry programs. I completed my own Doctor of Ministry program just before starting with Maryknoll. So now I am just auditing. Theoretically, I shouldn't feel like I have to take on the full workload of these classes, but of course I do. It is hard to change a lifelong habit. Along with that, my struggles with PTS continue to take their toll at times and in ways I can seldom predict.

This past week has been better. While continuing to feel levels of tension and stress, I did not "crash." I'm getting a little better at pacing myself. My body is telling me to take time with the healing process and not lose sight of the fact that one of the main reasons I took this sabbatical was to slow down. I can't leapfrog over the process of recovery, much as I wish I could. One of the "homework assignments" I have given myself is to close my eyes from time to time and imagine I'm back sitting on the beach, letting the stress and anxiety drift away on the ocean currents.

I'm pressing the keys on my Blackberry cell phone to call Uncle Sy. I have been wondering how he is doing in the aftermath of the terrible car accident he had last summer. He inexplicably had a lapse of consciousness, as he describes it, and T-boned a car at a country intersection. The woman driving the other car is dead, her husband left widowed, her children motherless. Totally tragic. He could be facing lawsuits and even jail time. I feel more deeply drawn into his tragedy since I unearthed the emotions and trauma from my train accident.

He is my mother's brother and one of two uncles who are priests. His given name is Sylvester but, as long as I can remember, he has been called *Father* Sy in the family. His siblings, including my mother, began calling him Father Sy after his ordination as a priest. Such was the strong sense of respect for priests that my grandmother Elizabeth baked into their psyche along with the breads and pies she made for her eleven children. I just call him Uncle Sy. He has always struck me as a gentle, introverted workaholic. He is retired now, but he was known to be in his office late into the evening most nights, attending to the administration of the parishes he pastored.

He has been suffering from depression since the accident. According to occasional reports I hear from family members, he doesn't seem to be talking to anyone about it on any deeper level, keeping the feelings and traumatic stress mostly to himself. It has parallels to what happened to me after my train accident, how it never got talked about. Some part of me feels like I could be helpful, or at least supportive. More simply, I just feel an emotional connection and a gut impulse to reach out.

So, I make the call and wait for him to answer as it rings several times.

"Hello," comes Sy's tired, gravelly voice.

"Hello Sy, I'm calling from Chicago on my sabbatical at CTU. How are you doing?" After a moment of silence with no response, I continue, "How are you doing since the accident? I know it has been rough."

"Ok, I guess. My doctor has given me some pills for my depression, but they don't help much. I can't stop thinking about the poor lady who died and the awful pain that her family must be in. I have nightmares about it and I just can't figure out how it happened. I keep trying to remember, but it is just a blank in my mind."

"A terrible tragedy for the family and traumatic for you too. It must all seem pretty overwhelming."

"I just wish I could go back and change what happened..."

"You are a good person, Sy. You have spent your life serving others. It was an accident, and certainly not something you intended to do."

"There is just no end to it. The police investigation is continuing and there is nothing I can do about it. I don't know what's going to happen. I guess I just have to wait..."

"Ya.... Kind of a helpless feeling..."

As the conversation goes on I share with him how I have been working on healing from my own trauma, that it's been hard and is taking a long time. "God has been with me on the journey and God is there for you too," I try to assure him. The sound of my voice remains steady as I finish the phone call. But inside the trigger has been pulled. High anxiety is ripping through me like an exploding bullet. After hanging up the phone, I take some deep breaths, trying to slow the cascade of emotions. It doesn't work. The horror of Sy's accident and the trauma he's experiencing overtake me like a crashing train.

I pull out my journal, hoping that by writing it out I can get some control over my out-of-control feelings. The words come pouring out on the page in a scrawling stream of consciousness:

Trauma, does it ever stop? I don't have any stomach for it.... The anxiety, the anxiety, anxiety, horror, pain, sadness, tears. How I identify so closely with Sy's pain still from my accident when I was 16. I nearly killed, nearly killed two friends, the trauma of it all. Trauma so long buried in my soul. Buried, buried deep within, like a cancer affecting everything, so long in my unawares. Oh Lord, why such pain?.... Heal the pain ... so much pain in the world, so much trauma, sadness, depression. I need to hold on to someone. Hold me Lord. Heal me.

I set the journal aside and pull out a blank 8½″ × 11″ sheet of paper. In outsized letters, I continue the stream of words:

Terror,

Terror on every side

Terror,

Terror,

Terror...

Then I scrawl chaotic swirling lines through the words—it is the chaos of my feelings.

I begin to sob. I feel helpless in the face of this tsunami of feelings crashing over me. I get up from the desk and pull my Peruvian poncho off the bed that I have been using as a blanket. As I wrap it around me, I go down to the floor, curling up in a fetal position. I feel like a child knocked down and beaten up by bullies, trying to protect myself. Helpless, helpless, I'm feeling helpless to do anything. Will it ever end? Why this? Why now?

As I'm rocking back and forth on my side, something I read in the book *Trauma and Recovery* emerges through the fog—how therapists who empathize with their clients take on some of the same feelings. *That's it.* That's what just happened. I was empathizing with Sy, absorbing his feelings of deep sadness and helplessness to do anything to escape from his trauma, guilt, and pain. I could hear it and feel it in his voice. His trauma feelings were soaking deep down into my being, which, in turn, triggered my own trauma feelings. A double whammy.

With that insight a voice from deep within emerges and I cry out, "I am not helpless!" It is an awakening, a call to arms. I repeat it, shouting out to the universe, "I am *not* helpless!" And then more softly to myself, "I am not helpless."

Those words take hold of me and stand me up. I walk around the room as one awakened from a nightmare. Something deep within has changed. I know with conviction that I am not a helpless victim of what has occurred in my life. I am not without power to stand against the strong waves of post-traumatic stress when they crash over me. I can make choices for healing, love, and support. I can continue to learn and name the triggers of traumatic episodes and take action to minimize my exposure to them. I can set healthy limits to how much violence I expose myself to in books and films. I can choose more wisely than I did over the weekend when I watched two violent movies that caused high anxiety and probably helped set the stage for this episode. I could have stopped watching when I realized how they were affecting me. I can do better. Self-knowledge is power—power to act. I am *not* helpless.

~·~⌒

A few days later, I decide to call Dad and see how he's doing. I only have a limited number of minutes on my cell phone plan, but this, I have decided, is a priority, part of my resolution to be more in touch with family. Making calls like this are always a decision for me. I marvel at people who seem to spontaneously call friends and family and think nothing of spending an hour on the phone. So I punch in Dad's phone number on the tiny Blackberry keyboard. I have known it by heart ever since I was a kid on the farm.

When Dad answers, I hear his familiar low-toned, "Hello," and then the pause as he waits for me to speak.

"Hi Dad, how are you doing? I thought I'd call and see how things are going."

"Well, I'm doing fine, it's just your mom and me in the house."

"So how's Mom?"

"She's ok. She's been planning a surprise eightieth birthday party for me but she seems to forget I am sitting right here when she's talking to people on the phone about it. So I just play along. Sometimes I worry about her memory. How are things going in Chicago?"

"It's going good, it's great to have the time to rest and recharge my batteries. I felt so exhausted last year. I really needed this."

"I'm glad you got away. It reminds me of how I got so exhausted every spring when I was farming. It always seemed like I was never going to get everything done. There was so much to do along with the daily chores. I had to get the machinery greased and repaired before I could start plowing for the spring planting. You always prayed the weather would cooperate to get the seed in the ground on time. My back would scream at me a lot from that curvature of the spine."

"Wow, I never realized your back got so sore. I don't remember hearing you talk about that. I do remember you being pretty tired though. When I was growing up I guess we never talked much about our pains, we just kept on working. Well Dad, I'm going to sign off. I love you and I'm looking forward to being at your eightieth birthday party next month. Remember to look surprised."

"I'll do my best," he says. I can picture the twinkle in his eyes. He loves a bit of wry humor. Then he adds, "And we love you too."

It warms my heart every time to hear those words that I never heard growing up. *I love you*. Well, *we* love you. But close enough. Those words are healing balm for me. The hurts I felt from him in the past seem like just that at this point in my life—in the past. So much healing and growth has happened in our relationship. And I'm thankful for the technology that made this conversation possible, even though I cringe to think I went over my limit of cell phone minutes for the month and will have to pay extra. Gotta keep working on getting over my German frugalness when it comes to relationships.

~~~

In another week I will be done with my sabbatical time here in Chicago. After I go home for Thanksgiving, I have a trip planned out East to visit friends, and then it's back to work at the parish in mid-December. I'm feeling a lot of tension at the thought of going back to work. This morning my jaw was sore from clenching my teeth through the night. The clenching has been a problem for years, leading to cracks and then crowns on my teeth. It's one of the ways my body deals with stress.

Last night I had another PTS dream that seems to have been triggered by my anxiety around leaving here and heading back to Michigan. In the dream, I was driving a motorized luggage carrier down a road at high speed, trying to catch my train. I was frantically steering through a crowded area, barely avoiding hitting people. Suddenly, the steering malfunctioned at a curve and the carrier veered off the road down a steep embankment. Without warning, a steel-plated metal contraption popped up in my path, pointing razor-sharp knives straight at me. For a terrifying moment I didn't think I was going to get out of there alive. But then I glided through safely and the dream ended.

I write the dream out and realize it has a strong resonance with the final days and hours leading up to my exit from Peru when I felt terrorized, when I had overwhelming anxiety about whether I would make it to the airport and get out of the country alive before being killed by terrorists. Making the connection helps calm me.

I'll be going back to work at the parish for a while, and then I have a ten-day trip to Peru planned for February. I see it as the final leg of my sabbatical journey. Part of my reason for going is that I feel the need to keep connected to the land of Pachamama that has so deeply embedded itself in my life. Another part of me hopes the trip will bring more closure and healing.

29

RESHAPING SHARDS OF
THE SHATTERED POT

February–April 2001

I have been feeling a little crazy this week. I'm somewhere between the worlds of Peru and my life in Michigan. I got back a week ago from my trip to Peru and I'm at work again in the parish. I'm back physically, but my heart and my soul haven't made the return trip yet. I keep flashing back to images of places and people whose lives I was so strongly drawn into during my ten days in Peru. The trip took me back to another universe, the land of Pachamama and the Aymara people. It was a very emotional journey back to where I had a strong sense of identity as "missionary" and "courageous human rights worker."

But that identity got overwhelmed by the terrorism, the government oppression, and so much injustice and poverty. In the end, I imploded like the power-line towers in Peru that were bombed and toppled by terrorists, causing blackouts and chaos. I could not sustain my old sense of self in the face of it all.

So it seems odd that I felt so whole and at peace during this vacation trip to Peru. During meals and conversations, I reconnected with people, people with whom I had the common experience of working in Peru in a time of terrorism and civil war. There was a comradery like war veterans talk about having when they gather at VFW halls or platoon reunions. Many have come home with life- and relationship-shattering PTS. But the bonds of shared trial by fire can run deep. Anyone who wasn't there can't understand in the same way what you went through.

There is a connection that carries with it a feeling of support and affirmation of each other's existence just in being together.

In the end, two moments with people with whom I had not spent a lot of time during my Peru years proved the most important ones to help me on my journey to healing from PTS and understanding what made me so susceptible to it. The first was a conversation before supper with Barbara Fraser at the Lima Center House. I had gotten a bottle of Pilsen Callao from the beer-stocked refrigerator to sip on in the library before it was time to go into the dining room. Barb and her co-worker Marybeth were there waiting for a third person to join them for a meeting. We were sitting on the soft, well-worn chairs and couches around the coffee table strewn with Spanish-language newspapers. The familiar leather tabletop imprinted with Incan patterns and symbols was just as I remembered it. Barb is a journalist who writes about social justice issues in Peru and South America. She first came to Peru as a Maryknoll lay missionary and has launched out on her own.

As we sat around, Barb and I struck up a conversation. After the usual "how are things going for you" openings, I got to sharing about the trauma I took home with me after my years in Peru. Barb was in Peru during those same years of civil war that I lived through. She immediately connected with my experience of feeling threatened by terrorism and said, "I remember when Sendero Luminoso called the armed strike in June of '92 and I said to myself, 'if this national armed strike happens, I'm out of here.'" As she said this, her face muscles tightened with that same look of fear and worry that the terrorism had gripped me with. It was like a direct, hardwired communication link between us. I could see and feel in her expressions elements of the trauma that I experienced. Her face reflected back to me the memory of the buildup of fear and terror that got unleashed in me in full force during those final days when I was afraid I would not make it out of Peru alive.

As I recall from our conversation, Barb did leave for some time and later returned to Lima to continue her work. Seeing Barb and hearing her talk the same language of fear and terror was a kind of validation of my experience, an affirmation that I was not the only Maryknoll missionary to have reacted so strongly to the terrorism and needed to get out. I said to Barb, "I struggled to find people to talk to about this while I was working in the Altiplano. It seems like older Maryknoll priests tended to downplay the danger by not talking about it much and just kept plugging along with their work."

She immediately chimed in by saying, "Yes, that John Wayne cowboy culture of some of the older Maryknollers lives on!" We laughed at this as ones who have a shared knowledge garnered from living inside an organization. By this time Theresa, the third person for their meeting, had joined us, and was listening to our conversation. I reflected with Barb further about this style of coping. I said, "My own German upbringing made that style of coping my first inclination as well. My default style in the face of fear and danger was to bury the feelings and keep them at bay lest I 'lose control.'"

To which Theresa immediately added, "And because you are a man!"

"And that too!" I said, as we all enjoyed another bit of laughter together.

Just being with them and having that conversation made me feel somehow more normal and affirmed, and less alone in what I have been going through.

The other conversation that was so helpful was with a young Peruvian sociologist. I met him by chance at the Maryknoll Center House in Lima. But it now seems like much more than a coincidence.

We met when we happened to be sitting at the same table for lunch at the Lima Center House on the last full day of my trip. I had flown back from my time visiting people in the Altiplano and was set to fly back to the US the next day. He was a bright young man who wore the dark brown complexion and jet-black hair of indigenous Peruvians. We seemed to be talking the same language about the history and impact of terrorism and government violence in Peru. So I invited him to take a walk after supper.

The warm, humid evening air engulfed us when we stepped outside. We headed down the sidewalk of one of the main thoroughfares lined with small shops and places to buy ice cream. All seemed calm as we strolled along in the fading sunlight. After walking for a brief time in silence, I asked him about how he was dealing with the emotional aftermath of living through such a time of terrorism and military violence in Peru. He recounted matter-of-factly, "I was shot in the leg when the Peruvian military came to my village in the mountains and began opening fire in the name of fighting terrorism. We were in the town plaza where we had gathered for a community meeting. Suddenly, people were falling at my side as they tried to flee."

I marveled at how calm he was talking about it. He did not seem to be experiencing post-traumatic stress like I have. My radar would have picked it up if he were. He had recovered from being shot and was getting on with his life. He obviously had healed more than just physically from the horror of that day in the plaza.

So I reflected back to him, "You don't seem to be traumatized by that experience." He nodded slightly. I went on and shared with him some of what I was going through with my PTS. We had already talked over supper about my work in the Altiplano and the growing impact the terrorism had on me during my time there. Then I asked, "Why do you think you were able to recover so well compared to all the difficulty I am having?"

He responded with a sociologist's kind of analysis, "I grew up in that community. I had the strength of my family and community ties, and the resilience of being rooted in my culture. There is a long history of resistance in our culture. Through the centuries the people in their communities have exercised a communal resistance by withdrawing into themselves and not cooperating with oppressive forces. The ancient community structures have remained intact before, during, and after the time of the Incas. Over the centuries and even millennia, our people have been conquered on the outside, but never on the inside."

I pondered that for a moment and said, "And I really did not have that where I was working. I was isolated, far away from my family and the culture that I grew up with."

"Yes, I think that would make a big difference," he said.

As I look back on that conversation, I can't help but think about how during my time residing at the parish house in Yunguyo I often felt lonely and depressed. My network of emotionally supportive relationships and community life was weak in the living situation I had chosen. I did not find it easy to develop that kind of support and I was a long way away from any of those kinds of supports I might have had back home. That conversation on my last day in Peru added an important piece of insight to my question, *Why did I end up with PTS?* And it further convinced me that enmeshing myself in community life and relationships would be key to healing from my PTS.

In the book *Trauma and Recovery*, the author, Judith Herman, MD, speaks to this when she says, "The solidarity of a group provides the strongest protection against terror and despair, and the strongest antidote to traumatic experience." I think I need about a gallon-size shot of that antidote.

I felt connected and understood in my conversations with the young sociologist. His listening and sharing brought a level of comfort and insight. It meant a lot to me at the time, and still does.

It is the first day of Lent, the season of forty days of re-examining one's life before the Easter celebrations. I'm awake at 2:00 a.m. at the parish house with everything inside me bubbling up like a witch's brew in a hot cauldron. I have been tossing and turning for over an hour. I can't go on this way. Something has to give. I head down the steps from the second floor and make a detour to the garage to pick up a clay pot. Then I go down the stairs to the basement. The floor is a blank, open space bordered by cement block walls. The walls are coated with a dull green paint that is bubbling out in places from moisture seeping through. The gray-painted concrete floor is solid beneath my feet. I'm holding the large red-clay flower pot I brought down with me. Last summer it was on my patio filled with flowers. Now it is empty and its smooth surface feels cool and dry against the press of my hands. I slowly raise it above my head, suspending it for a moment like a weightlifter's barbell. Then, with full force, I throw it down. It crashes like a thunderbolt, scattering shards and chunks in a random array before me.

I stand staring at the holy mess, thinking about yesterday's spiritual direction session with Catherine when I poured myself out in slow desperation telling her, "I feel so shattered, *shattered, shattered!*" I voiced how the strong sense of purpose I initially had about working among the poor for peace and justice in Peru got shattered by the terrorism, the government violence, the poverty, and my helpless feeling in the end to do much about it.

So here's my life, scattered on the basement floor. Can I form a new mosaic from the shards of the old? The old, in the form that it was, no longer exists. The pieces can't just be glued back together. What could a new picture of my life look like? What are my deepest needs and values now? Where are my energies? Where is energy even to be found? I commit these forty days of Lent to a journey into grieving the loss of what has been shattered, with hope for what might emerge.

I light a candle and place it on the floor in the middle of the shards, then pull up a chair to sit with it all for a while. In the silence, a question comes to mind, the question God puts to the prophet Jeremiah as he is being called and commissioned into prophetic service. God asks him, "What do you see?" I hear the question now as one being asked of me.

"Shattered but not broken," is my response.

I reflect on how reaching a point of utter terror in Peru was the shattering of any sense I had that I could somehow live above the fray and emerge unscathed. I have had to acknowledge my weakness, my helplessness, my fragility, and my need for family, love, and security. It's only in retrospect that I have slowly been able to recognize what really happened in that moment of feeling totally terrorized at the end of my four years in Peru, and to acknowledge my life for what it is now; it is these shattered shards strewn across the landscape of my being.

What does God see in the shattered pieces? What is the invitation from the Mystery of All Creation? The journey into these forty days of Lent begins like no other. There is no going back to what my life was before Peru. I can only look forward with the hope of forging a new identity, a new integration out of the shards of the old.

The next day early in the morning, I sit silently before the shards scattered on the basement floor. Their blank surfaces stare at me like a journal page awaiting its script. I feel like Adam as God displays the birds and animals of creation before him to be named. But what names? I pull open the sketch book I brought back from my sabbatical time in California. In large letters I draw thirty words and phrases across five pages in a stream of consciousness, representing fragments of my identity. I etch sharp, jagged borders around each word or phrase to mimic the shards on the floor. Where do I start to recast this thing called *self*? In the stillness, one phrase comes to the fore, like a soldier stepping forward from his line of comrades to volunteer for a risky assignment. I pick up the largest piece of clay pot from the floor. Its broken edges rest tentatively against the palms of my hands. The large remnant is from the upper part of the pot. I brush my fingertips across its smooth surface to clear any dust away. Then, with a black felt tip marker, I write across the curved surface: *Need for family, friends, relationships—Web of Life.*

Web of Life.... In Peru, I suffered more than I ever imagined I would from being so far away from the web of life that had taken shape around me in Michigan. The physical distance, the snail-paced mail system, and the very limited possibilities of making phone calls were big obstacles to maintaining those connections. I often found myself emotionally shriveled into a shell of loneliness, loss, and depression, desperate for relief. Thankfully, I found respite in talks with Mike Briggs, my spiritual director, and in the social contact at the Puno Center House and with members of the commissions I served on. My supervisory work with Ricardo and time spent with the sisters at the convent in Yunguyo were good. It was all a meaningful network of relationships as I experienced again during the trip I just took back to Peru. But it could never be the same as what longer-term relationships of family, friendships, and a soulmate offer. As limited as the relationships in my web of life have been, I need to keep spinning the web, like the spiders I watched as a child, how even after a storm or the sweep of a broom they would weave their webs back again, larger and stronger than before. *Web of Life.* I place the newly named piece of clay pot back among the shards on the floor.

∼⌢∽

The next day, I pick up another shard and label it *Pax Christi*, then hold it gently in my hands. Pax Christi is the Catholic Peace movement I was so passionately involved with before going to Peru thirteen years ago. Why have I avoided getting back involved, even disdaining it at times since my return? Something of that too was shattered in Peru. Peace and justice, nonviolence, my sense of commitment to the cause, rattled by my disillusionment with what now seems like too-easy answers coming from a white liberal arrogance that doesn't perceive how limited and sheltered that white liberal world can be, especially if one hasn't entered into the world of another culture.

But really, this is more about how my view of things has changed. Viewing life now through the lens of my Peru experience among the Aymara people changes the picture dramatically. It is *my* white liberal world that has been shaken up. Any white liberal "answers" to injustice I took with me to Peru just didn't apply much. People have to find their own answers from within their own cultural world and values. The best I could do was to try to learn from the people and accompany them, try to enter their world, and pray that I wouldn't do more harm than good. It is more about recognizing the need to transform myself first as I try to help make the world a better place. I look again at the words I have written: *Pax Christi*, both nationally and locally, as well as internationally, promotes a spirituality of nonviolence and the need to deal with the violence in one's own heart in order to work effectively for peace and justice in the world. It has been an important part of my life journey.

After years of saying no to invitations to rejoin the Pax Christi Michigan State Council, I have agreed to come back on. I finally feel some new energy for reconnecting with that part of my web of life that is being respun. Last night, I sat in the living room with two longtime members, talking about Pax Christi's current work and sharing some laughter about things we have done together. It felt good to be in a circle of friendship recalling the memories. I place the shard named *Pax Christi* on the floor near the one called *Web of Life*. Together they suggest the beginning of a new mosaic.

∽〰〜

I continue over the days of Lent to name the shards. Some are core values that have held firm over time, at least in aspiration, like *Option for the Poor* and *Simple Lifestyle,* and the words *Peace* and *Justice.*

One day the words *Healing Ministry* come to the fore. I write the words on a piece of the shattered pot and reflect. Over the years, I have kept that one in the background, embarrassed at the thought of being associated with TV personalities who whip people into a frenzy, staging public healings and then asking for a lot of money. Yet I do feel the presence of a healing Spirit at work when I pray over people who are sick or troubled. Plus, I need a lot of healing in my own life. Often it is the emotional healing that is needed even more than the physical. Body, mind, and spirit. It all works together.

My mind drifts back to a healing that took place in Ann Arbor, that bastion of liberalism. Warren was a deacon at St. Thomas the Apostle Parish and taught creative writing at the University of Michigan. He was a serious-minded, soft-spoken ascetic. I was the associate pastor and Warren was part of our RCIA team, the program for initiating new members into the church. He asked if he could receive the sacrament of the anointing of the sick with all the program participants joining in the prayer. He had been diagnosed by his cardiologist at the University of Michigan hospital with a serious heart problem that was going to require surgery. He wasn't one to show a lot of emotion, but he was clearly shaken by this diagnosis. We gathered in a large circle that week after our RCIA program concluded for the evening. I invited everyone to extend their hands in the air over Warren as I laid hands on him to pray over him and anoint him.

A couple of weeks later, Warren came and told me with quiet excitement, "My cardiologist told me he didn't know how it was physically possible, but my heart problem has disappeared. He ran a series of tests again to confirm it and told me I clearly no longer needed the surgery." Then, with a slight smile that lit up his face, he said quietly, "It was the anointing."

The shard labeled *Healing Ministry* is still cradled in my hand. I am just an instrument. It is about personal healing, yes, but also the whole community needs to be about the healing of injustices in society. Both needed. I quietly place *Healing Ministry* among the emerging mosaic life spread across the basement floor.

I take a couple days off to go to a cottage for a gathering of some long-time peacemakers. I am tired and drained and grateful for this time for some relaxation with friends. It is also giving me time to take stock of where I am on my journey. Before going, I had finished the section, "Finding a Survivor Mission," too quickly in the book *Trauma and Recovery*, impatient for the "magic fix," when what I really needed was to sit longer with the shattered shards. I must sit, not do; contemplate, not plan; for now, with respect to my recovery. The author notes so well, "resolution of the trauma is never final, recovery is never complete." I must embrace the journey, not try to "resolve" it, or think that somehow it will be "over" one day. It is who I am, an integral piece of the pie, something that has shaped and continues to shape my life, for reasons I will perhaps never fully understand. Why has it all impacted me so strongly? It just is. My fragility, my human vulnerability—I'm not immune to any of it, just the opposite really.

Back from the gathering at the cottage, I'm looking at my original drawing of shards in my sketch book. *Peace and Justice Commission* steps forward from the page. I inscribe the words on one of the shards on the basement floor. It feels like sacred scripture. I think of how much energy and passion I put into forming the Diocesan Office of Peace and Justice Ministry in the early 1980s. I was the one who named it, like a parent naming his child. When we hired Myles McCabe as the first director, I converted the search committee into the Peace and Justice Commission and became its chair. After I returned from Peru in 1993, I accepted the invitation to come back on the commission. But after a short time I realized I just couldn't do it. It was overwhelming. I resigned. What happened? Why couldn't I reconnect with the people and work of the commission? In the book *Trauma*, the author tells us, "Traumatic events destroy the sustaining bonds between individual and community." I wasn't ready to re-engage on that level of the wider community. The PTS was still too unhealed. I did not have the emotional ability or the energy to do it, after so much got disconnected, isolated, and worn down in Peru.

I remember one day in Yunguyo when an Aymara man who was a leader of the local teachers' union came by, asking us as church leaders to support their strike. When we checked around, we got indications he might be connected to one of the terrorist movements. Was he trying to manipulate our concern for justice issues in order to provide some public appearance of support for him and his covert terrorist infiltration of the union? Or was he aboveboard and simply seeking support for the union cause? We never were able to sort that one out, except to keep our distance. That kind of thing, the infiltration by the terrorists, their threats and our suspicions, brought increasing mistrust and isolation from the wider social fabric of community organizations and public institutions. Some deep level of optimism about humanity was getting battered. Trust, especially trust of my instincts for how and where to take action for justice in the community, was unraveling. My pre-Peru ways of acting on social justice issues no longer seemed to apply in my missionary work. And then, when I got back home, what I learned and experienced in Peru didn't seem to connect with the work of the commission. It seemed like a total disconnect, a dissonance between two worlds. Yet, *Peace and Justice Commission* is such a part of my history that contributed to me even going to Peru. Now it feels like it is time to reconnect to that wider circle of my life and integrate what that represents into the new mosaic. The shard takes its place.

It is St. Patrick's Day, a good day to think about culture and identity while I sit again with the shards before me. The Irish in this country have exuberant public parades and celebrations. There isn't anything comparable on a national scale with German culture, even though people of German ancestry make up the largest percentage of the US population. I'm on a quest these days to search out my German roots, to understand how my cultural roots have influenced who I am today. I pick up one of the shards and label it *German Identity*. My third great grandfather on my mother's side, Adam Fedewa, came in 1848 to Westphalia, Michigan, a neighboring town from where I grew up. My mother's first language was German and her first years of elementary school were taught in German. I grew up aware that my father, who was born in 1920, never learned German because his German-speaking parents didn't want him to suffer the prejudice they feared would go with that as he grew up in the aftermath of World War I. Any celebration of German culture or the telling of ancestral stories was rare in our household. It was almost like a family secret or maybe an unspoken shame about it. During World War II, it was not uncommon in this country to have public bonfires burning books written in German.

Yet there were times when dignity and respect for our ancestors were communicated, as in the occasional stories about my great uncle Nick Bauer who farmed with German precision and made the best red wine in the area. I remember Mom and Grandma Fedewa peeling and canning peaches and pears every fall in our kitchen. They talked away happily in German as they peeled and sliced bushel baskets full of sweet-smelling fruit. I understood none of it except for the occasional "*ach ja!*" or a mention of one of our names. But the sheer sound of it communicated their mood and planted itself in my memory. It gave me the gift of an unarticulated awareness of my cultural roots that I would only begin to consciously explore years later, as when I chose German to fulfill a language requirement in college.

One time in the restaurant in my hometown of Fowler, I asked the waitress, a young woman of German ancestry, "Wouldn't it be good to have some German food on the menu, even something as simple as bratwurst and sauerkraut?" I was thinking how overwhelmingly the townspeople of the area are of German ancestry. I was dumbfounded when she said, "Oh, I don't think that would go over here."

German culture and identity were at best in tension between pride and shame when I was growing up. It all seems a little schizophrenic, the shame and the silence of untold stories vs. the rare but significant stories and experiences that communicated pride in our heritage. So much family history and cultural heritage was kept wrapped in a shroud of silence. But now there is an awakening, a growing hunger to explore that part of my life. I took a deep dive into the Spanish language and Aymara culture in Peru. Now it is time to get more in touch with my own cultural roots. I place the shard *German Identity* among the pieces of shattered clay on the floor.

Two weeks later on this daily journey, a cluster of smaller shards speak out the word *Trauma*. The shattering trauma that became PTS is embedded in my life now, like shards of glass from a bomb blast embedded so deeply in your body that they cannot be removed. You go on with life as your body heals around the damaged area, and whenever a wrong move gives you a sharp reminder that it is still there, you just go on, knowing that the healing at work is more powerful than the shards.

The shattered pieces strewn across the basement floor are my life now, with the potential of what is yet to take shape and what is yet to be discovered. What will continue to emerge from this, I am open to and welcome. I am finally feeling some new peace and wholeness, some new life and energy.

It's Palm Sunday and the beginning of Holy Week. Today after gathering in the parish hall, we will go forth in song and procession around the outside of the building and into the church with palm branches held high, recalling Jesus's triumphal entry into Jerusalem. On Friday we will enact the Stations of the Cross through the streets of Lansing, commemorating Jesus's journey to death on the cross. The final station, placing Jesus in the tomb, will anticipate his Easter resurrection. While readying these rituals, I think about how my own life is finally emerging from the tomb of trauma to the light of a new day.

Holy Week concludes the forty days of Lent. As it turns out, I am also reading the concluding chapter of the book *Trauma and Recovery*. The chapter title is "Commonality." The author, Judith Herman, MD, writes about how one of the key moments in recovery comes when the person begins "readmitting the fullness of the larger world from which (one) has been alienated." I remember how I felt so alienated from my fellow diocesan priests when I got back from Peru eight years ago. I had been in seminary with quite a few of them and I have cousins and uncles who are among the clergy. But now there was a big gap between my experience and theirs. Plus, a whole new group of young priests were ordained while

I was gone. I did not know them and their more conservative "retro" seminary training with little appreciation for social justice issues left me feeling very distant from their reality. And in general, the dominant reality of church in the US with its relative wealth compared to the reality of a much poorer church in Peru felt like two sides of the Grand Canyon with no bridge to connect them. I felt so alienated from the "fraternity" of priests of my diocese that I did not know if I even *wanted* to bridge the gap. The feeling was amplified at the three-day annual convocation of priests that took place that fall. At the opening assembly, the bishop was introducing a number of priests new or returned to the diocese. I kept waiting, but he did not call out my name and invite me to stand and receive a welcoming applause with the others. An innocent mistake? Yes, but it was a moment that crystalized all the alienation I was feeling after my return to life in the US.

Over the years since that event, those feelings have diminished and I have gradually been able to "readmit" myself into the reality and the relationships of my life here. In her final paragraph, Dr. Herman says, "Commonality with other people carries with it all the meanings of the word *common*. It means belonging to a society, having a public role." I think of the public role I have taken on as pastor of Cristo Rey Church and how I have striven to work with the people as one among them. The people I worked with in Peru are forever in my heart, but now my common, day-to-day life is here. My relationships with family, Mom and Dad, friends and parishioners, counselor, spiritual director, and soulmate continue to be re-spun into a web of new life.

I am at a time of closure in my life, and the new that is opening before me. Yesterday I met with my spiritual director and showed her the pictures I drew while on my sabbatical retreat last fall. They had remained in the travel tube unopened until two days ago. As I showed them to her, the image of staring into the face of evil felt close to overwhelming, but it was not. Others, of Pachamama, and me in the womb of ocean waves, reminded me of the gifts of beauty and blessings I have received on the journey. It brought me to tender tears, and the realization once again of how embedded in the fabric of my being these experiences are, and always will be.

Now I continue to weave the threads of the old and the new, of the torn and shredded and the new-spun fibers into a new image of my being, for the old image was long ago shattered—an image of clay too hard and brittle. An image woven of cloth is softer and more flexible and better suited for the journey ahead.

My task now is to live the rest of my life, and to live it as one more member of the human family. My story is unique, but so is the story of every person. I am one among so many who have experienced trauma in this world. I hope the story of my journey into trauma and healing can be helpful to others. At the very least, the telling of it has helped me bring together a new mosaic from the shattered shards of my life, and that is no small thing.

And while the image of a new mosaic of hard-edged pieces has served me well, the softer image of a tapestry being woven is a better fit going forward. There is comfort in knowing that hovering over it all is the Spirit of Pachamama and the Mystery of All Creation weaving the threads of our lives into the cloth of the universe, gently rolling off the loom, never quite finished.

ACKNOWLEDGMENTS

To all who read early drafts of my manuscript: Thank you for your invaluable feedback and encouragement.

To those who taught classes through the Iowa Summer Writing Festival and other venues: Thank you for nurturing the creative spirit and teaching the tools that were transformative.

To all at Mission Point Press who have provided professional services to bring this book to publication: My deep appreciation!

To counselors and spiritual directors who listened and offered words of wisdom: My gratitude for helping guide and sustain me on the journey.

To family, friends, coworkers, and soulmate: You are a web of relationships essential to recovery from trauma.

To the Aymara people, the Maryknoll organizations, and the people of Cristo Rey Church: Gracias for the privilege to serve across cultures among you.

To all who strive to create a more just and peaceful world: Blessings to you!

Made in United States
Orlando, FL
20 October 2024

52904763R00137